Introducing the HTML5 Web Speech API

Your Practical Introduction to Adding Browser-Based Speech Capabilities to your Websites and Online Applications

Alex Libby

Apress®

Introducing the HTML5 Web Speech API

Alex Libby
Rugby, UK

ISBN-13 (pbk): 978-1-4842-5734-0   ISBN-13 (electronic): 978-1-4842-5735-7
https://doi.org/10.1007/978-1-4842-5735-7

Managing Director, Apress media LLC: Welmoed Spahr
Acquisitions Editor: Louise Corrigan
Development Editor: James Markham
Coordinating Editor: Nancy Chen

Cover designed by eStudioCalamar

Cover image designed by Freepik (www.freepik.com)

Distributed to the book trade worldwide by Springer Science+Business Media New York, 1 New York Plaza, New York, NY 10004. Phone 1-800-SPRINGER, fax (201) 348-4505, e-mail orders-ny@springer-sbm.com, or visit www.springeronline.com. Apress Media, LLC is a California LLC and the sole member (owner) is Springer Science + Business Media Finance Inc (SSBM Finance Inc). SSBM Finance Inc is a **Delaware** corporation.

For information on translations, please e-mail rights@apress.com, or visit http://www.apress.com/rights-permissions.

Apress titles may be purchased in bulk for academic, corporate, or promotional use. eBook versions and licenses are also available for most titles. For more information, reference our Print and eBook Bulk Sales web page at http://www.apress.com/bulk-sales.

Any source code or other supplementary material referenced by the author in this book is available to readers on GitHub via the book's product page, located at www.apress.com/9781484257340. For more detailed information, please visit http://www.apress.com/source-code.

Printed on acid-free paper

This is dedicated to my family, with thanks for their love and support while writing this book.

Table of Contents

About the Author

Alex Libby is a front-end engineer and seasoned computer book author who hails from England. His passion for all things open source dates back to the days of his degree studies, where he first came across web development, and he has been hooked ever since. His daily work involves extensive use of JavaScript, HTML, and CSS to manipulate existing web site content. Alex enjoys tinkering with different open source libraries to see how they work. He has spent a stint maintaining the jQuery Tools library and enjoys writing about open source technologies, principally for front-end UI development.

About the Technical Reviewer

Kenneth Fukizi is a software engineer, architect, and consultant with experience in coding on different platforms internationally. Prior to dedicated software development, he worked as a lecturer for a year and was then head of IT in different organizations. He has domain experience working with technology for companies in a wide variety of sectors. When he's not working, he likes reading up on emerging technologies and strives to be an active member of the software community.

Acknowledgments

Writing a book can be a long but rewarding process; it is not possible to complete it without the help of other people. I would like to offer a huge thanks to my editors – in particular, Nancy Chen and Louise Corrigan. My thanks also to Kenneth Fukizi as my technical reviewer and James Markham for his help during the process. All four have made writing this book a painless and enjoyable process, even with the edits!

My thanks also to my family for being understanding and supporting me while writing – I frequently spent lots of late nights writing alone, so their words of encouragement have been a real help in getting past those bumps in the road and producing the finished book that you now hold in your hands.

Introduction

Introducing the HTML5 Web Speech API is for people who want to quickly add speech capabilities natively in the browser, without the need for extra libraries or costly subscription to speech service providers.

First introduced by the W3C in 2012, the HTML5 Web Speech API consists of two APIs for speech recognition and synthesis. It is designed to add speech capabilities natively in the browser, using a clean, consistent API that allows us developers to focus on providing a next-level interface and superior user experience, without having to worry about the mechanics of how the API operates.

Over the course of this book, I'll take you on a journey through using the API, showing you how easy it is to quickly add speech capabilities to your projects, with the minimum of fuss. We'll focus on topics such as making our browsers recite anything from a simple phrase to performing actions based on verbal commands, with lots of simple exercises to help develop your skills with this API.

Introducing the HTML5 Web Speech API is for the web site developer who is keen to learn how to quickly add in speech capabilities to any project, without the need for extra libraries or costly services. It's perfect for those who work in Agile development, where time is of the essence and developers can produce reusable code that makes use of the API within their chosen framework or development process.

CHAPTER 1

Getting Started

Introducing the APIs

"Hey Alexa, what time is it...?"

In an age of smart assistant (SA) devices, I'll bet that those words will be uttered dozens of times a day worldwide – it does not matter where; smart assistants have become immensely popular. Indeed, Juniper Research has forecasted that the number of smart assistants will triple from 2.5 billion in use at the end of 2018 to 8 billion by 2023. Just imagine – changing TV channels by voice (**already possible**, and which alone is expected to increase 120% over the next five years) or simply doing mundane tasks like reordering goods from the likes of Amazon.

But I digress. Smart assistants are great, but what if we could use them to control functionality in our online web site or application? "How?" I hear you ask. Well, let me introduce the HTML5 Speech API; it uses the same principle as smart assistants, to turn speech into text and vice versa. It's available now for use in the browser, albeit still somewhat experimental.

Initially created back in 2012, but only really coming into full use now, this experimental API can be used to perform all manner of different tasks by the power of voice. How about using it to add products to a shopping cart and pay for them – all done remotely by voice? Adding in speech capabilities opens up some real possibilities for us. Over the course of this

© Alex Libby 2020
A. Libby, *Introducing the HTML5 Web Speech API*,
https://doi.org/10.1007/978-1-4842-5735-7_1

book, we'll explore a handful of these in detail, to show you how we can put this API to good use. Before we do so, there is a little housekeeping we must take care of first. Let's cover this off now, before we continue our journey through this API.

If you would like to get into the detail of how this API has been constructed and the standards that browser vendors must follow, then take a look at the W3C guidelines for this API at `https://wicg.github.io/speech-api/`. Beware – it makes for very dry reading!

Setting up our development environment

I'm pretty sure that no one likes admin, but in this instance, there are a couple of tasks we have to perform before we can use the API.

Don't worry – they are straightforward. This is what we need to do:

- The API only works in a secure HTTPS environment (yes, don't even try running it under HTTP – it doesn't work) – this means we need to have some secure web space we can use for the purposes of our demos. There are several ways to achieve this:

  - The simplest is to use CodePen (`https://www.codepen.io`) – you will need to create an account to save work, but it is free to sign up if you don't already have an account you can use.

  - Do you have any web space available for another project, which could be used temporarily? As long as it can be secured under HTTPS, then this will work for our demos.

- If you happen to be a developer who uses an MS tech stack, you can create an ASP.Net Core web application, with "Configure for HTTPS" selected, and click OK when prompted to trust the self-signed certificate, upon running the application. This will work fine for the demos throughout this book.

- You can always try running a local web server – there are dozens available online. My personal favorite is MAMP PRO, available from `https://www.mamp.info`. It's a paid-for option that runs on Windows and Mac; it makes generating the SSL certificates we need to use a cinch. Alternatively, if you have the likes of Node.js installed, then you can use one such as local web server (`https://github.com/lwsjs/local-web-server`), or create your own if you prefer. You will need to create a certificate for it and add it to your certificate store – a handy method for creating the certificate is outlined at `https://bit.ly/3ORjADo`.

- The next important task is to avail yourself of a suitable microphone – after all, we clearly won't get very far without one! You may already have one; if not, pretty much any microphone will work fine. My personal preference is to use a microphone/headset combo, as you might for talking over Skype. You should be able to pick up a relatively inexpensive one via Amazon or your local audio store.

A word of note   If you are a laptop user, then you can use any microphone that is built-in to your laptop. The drawback is that reception won't be so good – you might find yourself having to lean forward an awful lot for the best reception!

- For all of our demos, we'll use a central project folder – for the purposes of this book, I'll assume you've created one called speech and that it is stored at the root of your C: drive. The exact location is not critical; if you've chosen a different location, then you will need to adjust the location accordingly when we come to complete the demos.

Excellent! With that admin now out of the way, we can focus on the interesting stuff! The HTML5 Speech API (or "the API") comes in two parts: The first part is the **SpeechSynthesis API**, which takes care of reciting back any given text as speech. Second, in comparison – and to coin a phrase – the **SpeechRecognition API** does pretty much what it says in the name. We can say a phrase, and provided it matches preconfigured text it can recognize, it will perform any number of tasks that we assign on receipt of that phrase.

We could dive into how they work, but I know you're itching to get stuck in, right? Absolutely. So without further ado, let's run through two quick demos, so you get a flavor for how the API works before we use it in projects later in this book.

Don't worry though about what it all means – we will absolutely explore the code in detail after each exercise! We'll look at both in turn, starting first with the SpeechSynthesis API.

Implementing our first examples

Although both APIs require a bit of configuration to make them work, they are relatively easy to set up; neither requires the use of any specific frameworks or external libraries for basic operation.

To see what I mean, I've put together two quick demos using CodePen – they demonstrate the basics of what is needed to get started and will form code that we will use in projects later in this book. Let's take a look at each, in turn, starting with reading back text as speech, using the SpeechSynthesis API.

Reading back text as speech

Our first exercise will keep things simple and make use of CodePen to host our code; for this, you will need to create an account if you want to save your work for future reference. If you've not used CodePen before, then don't worry – it's free to sign up! It's a great way to get started with the API. We will move to using something more local in subsequent demos.

All of the code used in examples throughout this book is available in the code download that accompanies this book. We will use a mix of ECMAScript 2015 and vanilla JavaScript in most demos; you may need to adjust if you want to use a newer version of ECMAScript.

READING BACK TEXT

Assuming you've signed up and now have a CodePen account you can use, let's make a start on creating our first example:

1. First, go ahead and fire up your browser, then navigate to `https://codepen.io`, and sign in with your account details. Once done, click Pen on the left to create our demo.

2. We need to add in the markup for this demo – for this, go ahead and add the following code into the HTML window:

```
<link href="https://fonts.googleapis.com/css?family=Open+
Sans&display=swap" rel="stylesheet">

<div id="page-wrapper">
  <h2>Introducing HTML5 Speech API: Reading Text back as
  Speech</h2>
  <p id="msg"></p>
  <input type="text" name="speech-msg" id="speech-msg">
  <div class="option">
    <label for="voice">Voice</label>
    <select name="voice" id="voice"></select>
    <button id="speak">Speak</button>
  </div>
</div>
```

3. Our demo will look very ordinary if we run it now – let alone the fact that it won't actually work as expected! We can easily fix this. Let's first add in some rudimentary styles to make our demo more presentable. There are a few styles to add in, so we will do it block by block. Leave a line between each block, when you add it into the demo:

```
*, *:before, *:after { box-sizing: border-box; }
```

```
html { font-family: 'Open Sans', sans-serif; font-size:
100%; }
```

```
#page-wrapper { width: 640px; background: #ffffff;
padding: 16px; margin: 32px auto; border-top: 5px solid
#9d9d9d; box-shadow: 0 2px 10px rgba(0,0,0,0.8); }
```

```
h2 { margin-top: 0; }
```

4. We need to add in some styles to indicate whether our browser
    supports the API:

```
#msg { font-size: 14px; line-height: 22px; }
#msg.not-supported strong { color: #cc0000; }
#msg > span { font-size: 24px; vertical-align: bottom; }
#msg > span.ok { color: #00ff00; }
#msg > span.notok { color: #ff0000; }
```

5. Next up are the styles for the voice drop-down:

```
#voice { margin: 0 70px 0 -70px; vertical-align: super; }
```

6. For the API to have something it can convert to speech, we
    need to have a way to enter text. For this, add in the following
    style rules:

```
input[type="text"] { width: 100%; padding: 8px;
font-size: 19px;
border-radius: 3px; border: 1px solid #d9d9d9;
box-shadow: 0 2px 3px rgba(0,0,0,0.1) inset; }
```

```
label { display: inline-block; float: left; width: 150px; }
```

```
.option { margin: 16px 0; }
```

7. The last element to style is the Speak button at the bottom-right
    corner of our demo:

```css
button { display: inline-block; border-radius: 3px;
border: none; font-size: 14px; padding: 8px 12px;
background: #dcdcdc;
border-bottom: 2px solid #9d9d9d; color: #000000;
-webkit-font-smoothing: antialiased; font-weight: bold;
margin: 0; width: 20%; text-align: center; }

button:hover, button:focus { opacity: 0.75; cursor:
pointer; }
button:active { opacity: 1; box-shadow: 0 -3px 10px
rgba(0, 0, 0, 0.1) inset; }
```

8. With the styles in place, we can now turn our attention to adding the glue to make this work. I don't mean that literally, but in a figurative sense! All of the code we need to add goes in the JS window of our CodePen; we start with a check to see if our browser supports the API:

```javascript
var supportMsg = document.getElementById('msg');

if ('speechSynthesis' in window) {
  supportMsg.innerHTML = '<span class="ok">&#x2611;
  </span> Your browser <strong>supports</strong> speech
  synthesis.';
} else {
  supportMsg.innerHTML = '<span class="notok">&#x2612;</
  span> Sorry your browser <strong>does not support</
  strong> speech synthesis.';
  supportMsg.classList.add('not-supported');
}
```

9. Next up, we define three variables to store references to elements in our demo:

```javascript
var button = document.getElementById('speak');
var speechMsgInput = document.getElementById('speech-msg');
var voiceSelect = document.getElementById('voice');
```

10. When using the API, we can relay speech back using a variety of different voices – we need to load these into our demo before we can use them. For this, go ahead and drop in the following lines:

```
function loadVoices() {
  var voices = speechSynthesis.getVoices();

  voices.forEach(function(voice, i) {
    var option = document.createElement('option');
    option.value = voice.name;
    option.innerHTML = voice.name;
    voiceSelect.appendChild(option);
  });
}

loadVoices();

window.speechSynthesis.onvoiceschanged = function(e) {
  loadVoices();
};
```

11. We come to the real meat of our demo – this is where we see the text we add be turned into speech! For this, leave a line after the previous block, and add in the following code:

```
function speak(text) {
  var msg = new SpeechSynthesisUtterance();
  msg.text = text;

  if (voiceSelect.value) {
    msg.voice = speechSynthesis.getVoices()
.filter(function(voice) {
      return voice.name == voiceSelect.value;
    })[0];
  }

  window.speechSynthesis.speak(msg);
}
```

12.   We're almost there. The last step is to add in an event handler
       that fires off the conversion from text to speech when we hit
       the Speak button:

```
button.addEventListener('click', function(e) {
  if (speechMsgInput.value.length > 0) {
    speak(speechMsgInput.value);
  }
});
```

13.   Go ahead and save your work. If all is well, we should see
       something akin to the screenshot shown in Figure 1-1.

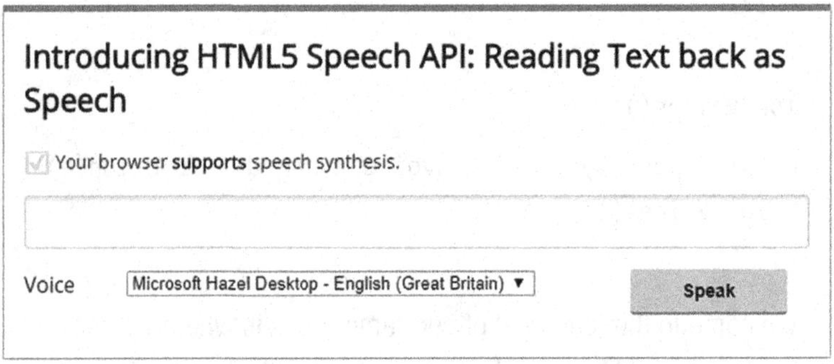

Introducing HTML5 Speech API: Reading Text back as Speech

☑ Your browser **supports** speech synthesis.

Voice | Microsoft Hazel Desktop - English (Great Britain) ▼ | **Speak**

Figure 1-1. *Our completed text-to-speech demo*

Try then typing in some text and hit the Speech button. If all is working as
expected, then you will hear your words recited back to you. If you choose
a voice from the drop-down, you will hear your words spoken back with
an accent; depending on what you type, you will get some very interesting
results!

A completed version of this demo can be found in the code download that accompanies this book – it's in the `readingback` folder.

At this stage, we now have the basic setup in place to allow our browser to read back any text we desire – granted it might still sound a little robotic. However, this is to be expected when working with an API that is still somewhat experimental!

This aside, I'll bet there are two questions on your mind: How does this API function? And – more to the point – is it still safe to use, even though it is still technically an unofficial API? Don't worry – the answers to these questions and more will be revealed later in this chapter. Let us first start with exploring how our demo works in more detail.

Understanding what happened

If we take a closer look at our code, you might be forgiven for thinking it looks a little complex – in reality though, it is very straightforward.

We start with some simple HTML markup and styling, to display an input box on the screen for the content to be replayed. We also have a drop-down which we will use to list the available voices. The real magic happens in the script that we've used – this starts by performing a check to see if our browser supports the API and displays a suitable message.

Assuming your browser does support the API (and most browsers from the last 3–4 years will), we then define a number of placeholder variables for various elements on the page. We then (through the `loadVoices()` function) iterate through the available voices before populating the drop-down with the results. Of particular note is the second call to `loadVoices()`; this is necessary as Chrome loads them asynchronously.

It's important to note that the extra voices (which start with
"Chrome…") are added as part of the API interacting with Google and
so only appear in Chrome.

If we then jump to the end of the demo for a moment, we can see an
event handler for the button element; this calls the `speak()` function that
creates a new utterance of the `SpeechSynthesisUtterance()` object that
acts as a request to speak. It then checks to make sure we've selected a
voice, which we do using the `speechSynthesis.getVoices()` function. If a
voice is selected, then the API queues the utterance and renders it as audio
via your PC's speakers.

Okay, let's move on. We've explored the basics of how to render text as
speech. This is only half of the story though. What about converting verbal
content into text? This we can do by using the SpeechRecognition API – it
requires a little more effort, so let's dive into the second of our two demos
to see what's involved in making our laptops talk.

Converting speech to text

The ability to vocalize content through our PC's speakers (or even
headphones) is certainly useful, but a little limiting. What if we can ask
the browser to perform something using the power of our voice? Well, we
can do that using the second of the two Speech APIs. Let me introduce the
SpeechRecognition API!

This sister API allows us to speak into any microphone connected to
our PC, for our browser to perform any manner of preconfigured tasks,
from something as simple as transcribing tasks to searching for the nearest
restaurant to your given location. We'll explore some examples of how to
use this API in projects later in this book, but for now, let's implement a
simple demo so you can see how the API works in action.

I would not recommend using Firefox when working with demos that use the Speech Recognition API; although documentation on the Mozilla Developer Network (MDN) site suggests it is supported, this isn't the case, and you will likely end up with a "SpeechRecognition is not a constructor" error in your console log.

"WHAT DID I SAY?"

Let's crack on with our next exercise:

1. We'll start by browsing to `https://www.codepen.io` and then clicking Pen. Make sure you've logged in with the account you created back in the first exercise.

2. Our demo makes use of Font Awesome for the microphone icon that you will see in use shortly – for this, we need to add in references for two CSS libraries. Go ahead and click Settings ➤ CSS. Then add in the following links into the spare slots at the bottom of the dialog box:

   ```
   https://use.fontawesome.com/releases/v5.0.8/css/
   fontawesome.css
   https://use.fontawesome.com/releases/v5.0.8/css/solid.css
   ```

3. Next, switch to the HTML pane and add the following markup which will form the basis for our demo:

   ```
   <link href="https://fonts.googleapis.com/css?family=Open+
   Sans&display=swap" rel="stylesheet">

   <div id="page-wrapper">
     <h2>Introducing HTML5 Speech API: Converting Speech to
     Text</h2>
   ```

13

```
<button>
  <i class="fa fa-microphone"></i> Click and talk to me!
</button>
<div class="response">
  <span class="output_log"></span>
</div>

<p class="output">You said: <strong class="output_
result"></strong></p>
<span class="voice">Spoken voice: US English</span>
</div>
```

4. On its own, our markup certainly won't win any awards for style! To fix this, we need to add in a few styles to make our demo look presentable. For this, add the following rules into the CSS pane, starting with some basic rules to style the container for our demo:

```
*, *:before, *:after { box-sizing: border-box; }
html { font-family: 'Open Sans', sans-serif; font-size:
100%; }

#page-wrapper { width: 640px; background: #ffffff;
padding: 16px; margin: 32px auto; border-top: 5px solid
#9d9d9d; box-shadow: 0 2px 10px rgba(0,0,0,0.8); }

h2 { margin-top: 0; }
```

5. Next come the rules we need to style our talk button:

```
button { color: #0000000; background: #dcdcdc; border-
radius: 6px; text-shadow: 0 1px 1px rgba(0, 0, 0, 0.2);
font-size: 19px; padding: 8px 16px; margin-right: 15px; }
button:focus { outline: 0; }

input[type=text] { border-radius: 6px; font-size: 19px;
padding: 8px; box-shadow: inset 0 0 5px #666; width:
300px; margin-bottom: 8px; }
```

6. Our next rule makes use of Font Awesome to display a suitable microphone icon on the talk button:

```
.fa-microphone:before { content: "\f130"; }
```

7. This next set of rules will style the output once it has been transcribed, along with the confidence level and the voice characterization used:

```
.output_log { font-family: monospace; font-size: 24px;
color: #999; display: inline-block; }
.output { height: 50px; font-size: 19px; color: #000000;
margin-top: 30px; }

.response { padding-left: 260px; margin-top: -35px;
height: 50px}
.voice { float: right; margin-top: -20px; }
```

8. Okay, so we have our markup in place, and it looks reasonably OK. What's missing? Ah yes, the script to make it all work! For this, go ahead and add in the following code to the JS pane. We have a good chunk of code, so let's break it down block by block, starting with some variable declarations:

```
'use strict';

const log = document.querySelector('.output_log');
const output = document.querySelector('.output_result');

const SpeechRecognition = window.SpeechRecognition ||
window.webkitSpeechRecognition;
const recognition = new SpeechRecognition();

recognition.interimResults = true;
recognition.maxAlternatives = 1;
```

9. Next up is an event handler that triggers the microphone. Leave a blank line and then add the following code:

```
document.querySelector('button').
addEventListener('click', () => {
    let recogLang = 'en-US';
    recognition.lang = recogLang.value;
    recognition.start();
});
```

10. When using the Speech Recognition API, we trigger a number of events to which we must respond; the first one recognizes when we start talking. Go ahead and add the following lines into the JS pane of our CodePen demo:

```
recognition.addEventListener('speechstart', () => {
    log.textContent = 'Speech has been detected.';
});
```

11. Leave a blank line and then add in these lines – this event handler takes care of recognizing and transcribing anything we say into the microphone, as well as calculating a confidence level for accuracy:

```
recognition.addEventListener('result', (e) => {
    log.textContent = 'Result has been detected.';

    let last = e.results.length - 1;
    let text = e.results[last][0].transcript;

    output.textContent = text;

    log.textContent = 'Confidence: ' + (e.results[0][0].
    confidence * 100).toFixed(2) + "%";
});
```

12. We're almost done, but have two more event handlers to add in – these take care of switching off the Recognition API when we're done and also displaying any errors on screen if any should appear. Leave a line and then drop in the following code:

```
recognition.addEventListener('speechend', () => {
  recognition.stop();
});
```

```
recognition.addEventListener('error', (e) => {
  output.textContent = 'Error: ' + e.error;
});
```

13. At this point, we're done with editing code. Go ahead and hit the Save button to save our work.

A completed version of this demo can be found in the code download that accompanies this book – it's in the whatdidIsay folder.

At this point, we should be good to run our demo, but if you were to do so, it's likely that you won't get any response. How come? The simple reason is that we have to grant permission to use our PC's microphone from within the browser. It is possible to activate it via the Settings entry in the site's certificate details, but it's not the cleanest method. There is a better way to prompt for access, which I will demonstrate in the next exercise.

Allowing access to the microphone

When using the Speech API, there is one thing we must bear in mind – access to the microphone will by default be disabled for security reasons; we must explicitly enable it before we can put it to use.

This is easy to do, although the exact steps will vary between browsers – it involves adding a couple of lines of code to our demo to request access to the microphone and changing a setting once prompted. We'll see how to do this in our next exercise, which assumes you are using Chrome as your browser.

ADJUSTING PERMISSIONS

Let's make a start on setting up permissions:

1. First, go ahead and browse to the microphone settings in Chrome, which you can get to via `chrome://settings/content/microphone`. Make sure the slider against "Ask before accessing…" is over to the right.

2. In a separate tab, switch back to the SpeechRecognition API demo in CodePen that you created in the previous exercise; look for this line:

   ```
   const output = document.querySelector('.output_result');
   ```

3. Leave a line blank below it and then add in this code:

   ```
   navigator.mediaDevices.getUserMedia({ audio: true
   }).then(function(stream) {
   ```

4. Scroll down your code until you get to the end. Then add in this small block of code:

   ```
   })
   .catch(function(err) {
     console.log(err);
   });
   ```

5. Next, go ahead and click the drop-down arrow to the far right of the JS pane. When it pops up, you will see an entry for Tidy JS. Click it to reformat the code correctly.

6. Save the update and then refresh the page. If all is well, you will see an icon appear at the end of the address bar (Figure 1-2).

Figure 1-2. *Microphone support has been added, but is disabled...*

7. Click it. Make sure the "Always allow `https://codepen. io...`" option is selected. Then click Done.

8. Refresh the window. The icon will change to a solid black one, without the forbidden cross symbol showing.

Try clicking the "Click and talk to me!" button and then talking into your microphone. If all is well, we should see something akin to the screenshot shown in Figure 1-3, where it displays the result of a spoken test phrase, along with the confidence level.

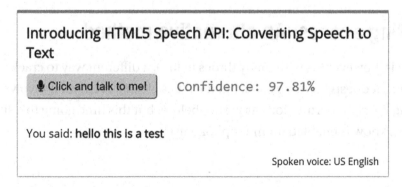

Figure 1-3. *The results of talking into our microphone...*

19

When talking, did you notice how the red dot/circle appears in the browser window tab (as illustrated in Figure 1-4, overleaf)? This indicates that the microphone is active and will record any spoken words.

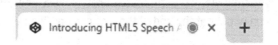

Figure 1-4. *The red dot signifies an active microphone*

If we hit the "Click and talk to me!" button again, this red circular icon will disappear, to signify that the microphone has been turned off. In our previous demo, we made use of `navigator.mediaDevices.getUserMedia()` to achieve this – this is something we will likely have to do for any site where we implement speech, as we can't be sure that users will have enabled their microphone!

If you would like to know more about using `navigator.mediaDevices.getUserMedia()`, there is a useful article on the Mozilla Developer Network site at `https://developer.mozilla.org/en-US/docs/Web/API/MediaDevices/getUserMedia`.

Setting access: An alternative method

There is, however (as with many things in life), a different way to crack this nut; it doesn't require code, but it isn't as clean a method. It involves setting the right permissions as we did before, but this time going to a site that we know is enabled for microphone use.

ENABLING THE MICROPHONE: AN ALTERNATIVE METHOD

This method assumes the use of Chrome, although it is likely a similar method will be available for Firefox and other browsers:

1. In a separate tab, browse to `chrome://settings/content/`
    `siteDetails?site=https%3A%2F%2Fcodepen.io` and
    then make sure that the entry for the microphone is set to Ask.

2. Revert back to the tab where your CodePen demo is running,
    and refresh the window. You should see a prompt appear, as
    indicated in Figure 1-5, overleaf.

Figure 1-5. *Requesting access to the microphone from the browser*

Over the course of the last few pages, we worked through three exercises. It's important to note though that when working with this API, there will be a little extra effort required. In addition to initiating the request for the API, we've also had to add in code to enable access to the microphone. We'll revisit the subject (and security implications) of using it a little later on, but for now, let us review the code we used in the last two exercises, in more detail.

Breaking apart our code

As in the previous text-to-speech demo, we start with some basic markup and styling to give us a button we can use to activate recording our voice and two placeholder slots for the converted text and confidence level.

The magic, however, happens in the JavaScript code that we've added in. We start by defining references to the `.output_` elements within our markup. Next, we define `window.SpeechRecognition as a reference to the API`; note that we have it set as an OR statement, to ensure we cover those browsers that still require vendor prefix support. As part of this, we also set two attributes: `recognition.interimResults` is set to true to enable the display of text as it is being converted from speech. The other, `recognition.maxAlternatives`, is set to 1 to display a maximum of one alternative word, when it has been recognized by the speech recognition service.

It's important to note that the bulk of our JavaScript code will be wrapped inside a `navigator.mediaDevices.getUserMedia()` block, so it runs once we've enabled access to the microphone.

Our code then contains a set of event handlers, to recognize different events: The first is fired by clicking the "Click and talk to me!" button. This sets the language to be used (US English) and starts the recognition service. The second event handler, `speechstart`, takes care of recognizing when we start talking and transcribing any spoken content. The final two (`result` and `error`) are fired when we stop talking or if an error is thrown, such as access to the microphone that has been blocked. In the final part of this extended demo, we then explore a couple of options for enabling the microphone; we discuss how the code route will be preferable for users.

Okay, let's move on. Now that we've been introduced to both of the APIs, it's time we delved into a little of the theory, to see how these APIs operate! We'll examine each API in more detail in the next chapter, but for now, let's answer two critical questions: How well are these APIs supported (and can I provide fallback support)? How do I manage the security implications of accessing someone's microphone remotely?

Allowing for browser support

Cast your mind back to the start of this chapter – remember how I mentioned the words "experimental API"? Yes, it has to be said that these APIs are yet to reach official status. However, before you run to the hills thinking "What have I let myself in for?", it's not as bad as it sounds! Let me explain what I mean.

It is true that the API is still experimental – we can make allowances for this with careful research and by working on the basis that we only enhance an existing service, not replace it. As a start, our first port of call should be a web site such as CanIUse.com; a quick check shows that the SpeechSynthesis API has excellent support, at least on desktop (Figure 1-6).

IE	Edge	Firefox	Chrome	Safari	Opera	iOS Safari	Opera Mini	Android Browser
		2-30	4-32					
	12-13	31-48	33-54	3.1-6.1	10-26	3.2-6.1		
6-10	14-17	49-67	55-75	7-12	27-60	7-12.1		2.1-4.4.4
11	18	68	76	12.1	62	12.3	all	67
	76	69-70	77-79	13-TP		13		

Figure 1-6. *Browser support for the Speech Synthesis API*

In contrast, though, support for the Speech Recognition API is not so advanced, as indicated in Figure 1-7.

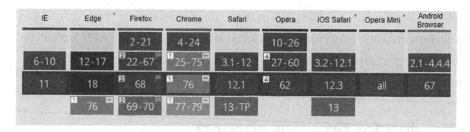

IE	Edge	Firefox	Chrome	Safari	Opera	iOS Safari	Opera Mini	Android Browser
		2-21	4-24		10-26			
6-10	12-17	22-67	25-75	3.1-12	27-60	3.2-12.1		2.1-4.4.4
11	18	68	76	12.1	62	12.3	all	67
	76	69-70	77-79	13-TP		13		

Figure 1-7. *Browser support for the Speech Recognition API*
Source: `https://caniuse.com/#search=speech`

We can clearly see that support isn't so advanced as for the Speech Synthesis API, yet the chart is hiding a secret: Safari does indeed support both APIs! Although a site such as CanIUse.com is a good starting point, it is only ever as accurate as the information it is based on. It does indeed pay to check support with each browser vendor as much as possible; otherwise, we may base a future financial information on inaccurate information.

Now, I hear you ask, "What about mobile?" Well, support for both APIs is still being developed; although it has yet to extend to all platforms, it nevertheless covers the key platforms of Android (for both Chrome and Firefox) and Samsung.

Now that we're aware of the level of support each browser provides, what about those browsers which don't support either API? Is there a fallback option or some other alternative we can use…?

Providing fallback support

Well, the answers to both questions at the end of that discussion aren't as straightforward as we might like. Let me explain what I mean.

At the heart of this question lies one important point – the Speech Synthesis API relies on using Google's neural AI capabilities to decode and return text as speech in the chosen style. So what does this mean for us?

The reliance on Google for the Synthesis API means that support will be limited to newer browsers only; this covers all recent desktop browsers, except Internet Explorer (IE). For those of you supporting mobile devices, it is only available for Chrome or Firefox for Android, Samsung Internet, and two smaller specialist browsers.

At the moment, there isn't really a suitable fallback in the strictest sense. While for some this may be disappointing, there is an argument that says we should be looking forward and not backward when it comes to browser support. That IE doesn't offer support for the Speech Synthesis API will come as no surprise to many; those mobile platforms that don't support the API (such as Android Browser) add up to around 5% of total usage, so this can be safely discounted. There is equally an argument that says we should not rely on either API for core functionality in our site or application; speech provision should enhance the basic service and not replace it.

If we switch to the Speech Recognition API though, support is a different story – support is still very much in its early stages. It's limited to recent versions of Edge, Firefox, and Chrome which are supported for desktop; the bulk of support in the mobile world falls to Chrome for Android. The same arguments vis-à-vis looking forward apply here too; APIs such as Speech should be considered as a tool for progressively enhancing the experience.

Talking of progressive enhancement, there are a couple of options we can consider. These are

- ResponsiveVoice – this is a commercial service available from `https://responsivevoice.com`; it provides extra support such as better accessibility for navigation, but this comes at a price of USD39 a month, which will need to be factored into any operational costs.

- Annyang is a free library by Tal Ater, which is designed to make the Speech Recognition API easier to use; this is available under the MIT license from `https://www.talater.com/annyang/`.

The downside of these though is that they will only progressively enhance service provided by a browser that already supports the API; this lends extra weight to the argument that we should encourage people to use newer browsers where possible!

Understanding security concerns

Over the course of this chapter, we've been introduced to the Speech API for the first time and seen the basics of how it works. Yet, I'm sure (as with any new technology) there is one burning question we have yet to ask: what about security and privacy? With the presence of the European-wide GDPR legislation now in effect, the question of privacy has come to the fore; this is no more important a consideration than when using the Speech API.

The main consideration is getting permission to use the microphone when working with the Speech API; this used to be every time a request is made in a nonsecure HTTP environment. There was a time when this wasn't necessary, but dubious web sites began to exploit this with advertising and scams. As a result, Google (and now others) enforces the need to use the API in an HTTPS-secured environment and that permission to use the microphone has to be given explicitly by the user.

If you want to read up on the technical reasons for this, details are given in the official bug report on this vulnerability, which is listed at `https://bugs.chromium.org/p/chromium/issues/detail?id=812767`

As a user, you may only get asked once for permission on a fully secured site, before audio can be captured; subsequent uses in the same session will utilize the same permission until the page has been refreshed. For some, this might be seen as a vulnerability, as a secure web page can effectively record any content, once it has been authorized. This is compounded by the fact that the Chrome API interacts with Google, so will not stay within the confines of your browser!

So can we do anything to help maintain security and our privacy? There are a few things we can bear in mind when working with the APIs:

- Although any page using the Speech Recognition API in Chrome will interact with Google, the only information that is sent to Google is an audio recording, the domain of your web site, your default browser language, and current language settings of your web site (no cookies are sent). If the Speech Recognition API is used in a different browser, this does not interact with Google.

- If you are using the Speech Recognition API, make sure you do not create any event handlers that contain sensitive information, which could potentially be sent to Google. Ideally this information should be stored locally, and any command sent is effectively a key to unlock access.

- The entire page will have access to the output of the audio capture, so if your page or site is compromised, the data from the audio instance can be read. It makes it incumbent on us to ensure that we are securing access (which has become the default for many sites now), but also that we are using good-quality certificates on a properly secured and updated server.

- The API (and particularly the Speech Recognition API) is still very much in a state of flux; it is possible that Google's role could change or be discontinued at some point in the future. Nothing can be considered official until the W3C has granted official recognition to using the APIs in browsers.

- At this time, I would recommend carefully checking through your site's analytics, to explore which browsers are being used that support the API. If there is sufficient demand, then you can consider starting to add functionality, but as mentioned earlier, I would strongly recommend taking a careful and measured approach, so that you maintain a good experience for customers.

Okay, certainly some food for thought there! Hopefully this won't have put you off; as with any new technology, it's important to embrace it, but to take a measured approach, rather than jumping in blindly! Throughout the course of this book, we will dig into the API in more detail and use it in a number of example projects, so you get a feel for how it can be used in a practical context. Just imagine: how about using the API to add products to a shopping cart and pay for them, all with the power of your voice?

Summary

In an age of modern smart assistants (such as Amazon's Alexa), the ability to create web applications that can be controlled using the power of voice opens up some really interesting possibilities. We must equally consider how best to make use of the API, particularly with privacy being at the forefront of users' minds! Over the course of this chapter, we've started to take a look at the Speech API in detail; let's take a moment to review what we have learned in more detail.

We kicked off by introducing both the Speech Synthesis and Recognition APIs, before taking a quick look at what is required to start developing with these APIs.

We then moved onto implementing our first examples - we started with reading back text as speech, before switching to creating an example using the Speech Recognition API. We then talked briefly about how to enable access to the microphone for the second of these two APIs, before exploring some of the concerns about providing support and allowing for privacy and security when using the APIs.

Phew! We've only just gotten started, folks. Hope you're ready to really get stuck in to the detail! Up next, we'll take a look at the API in more detail while creating a more practical example and exploring how we can provide more support for different languages. As one might say in Dutch, *Laten we doorgaan,* or let's crack on...!

CHAPTER 2

Exploring the APIs in More Detail

Understanding the API terminology

"Great! My PC can now talk and recognize my voice. But what's the SpeechSynthesisUtterance keyword that I see in the code mean...?"

It's a good question. Now that you've seen the API in operation, I'll bet you're eager to understand how it hangs together, right? We've only touched on the basics of making our PC speak or recognize our voice. There is much more we can do!

Over the course of this chapter, we're going to dive into some of the theory behind the API, before using it (or them – depending on how you see it), to create something a little more practical. At the same time, we'll also give our code a little international flavor – yes, we are not limited to speaking just English! All will become clearer later in the chapter, but for now, let's start by breaking down the Speech Recognition API into its constituent parts.

© Alex Libby 2020
A. Libby, *Introducing the HTML5 Web Speech API*,
https://doi.org/10.1007/978-1-4842-5735-7_2

Exploring the Speech Synthesis API

Take a look back at the code we created for our first demo, where our PC replayed some sample text as speech. At first glance, it looks like we need a fair chunk of code to achieve this, right? What if I said you could do this in as little as one line of code…?

Yes, you heard me correctly. The crux of that demo centers around this line of code:

```
window.speechSynthesis.speak(msg);
```

where we invoke a call to speechSynthesis and ask it to speak the value of msg. By itself, this won't work, but if we alter it a little, to this:

```
speechSynthesis.speak(new SpeechSynthesisUtterance('Hello, my
name is [insert your name here]'))
```

it will work fine when executed in a browser console (you may need to allow pasting in the console, if you're using Firefox). Go on, put your name in as indicated, and give it a try! However, there is more we can do with the API than this simple one-liner. What about this SpeechSynthesisUtterance() I see in the code or the call to getVoices()? Well, one is an object and the other a method. Let's dive in and see how this API works in more detail.

Breaking apart the API

At the core of the Speech Recognition API is the SpeechSynthesis interface; this is our interface into the speech service. We can use a host of methods to control activity, but before we do so, we must first define the SpeechSynthesisUtterance object. This object represents a speech request, into which we pass a string that the browser should read aloud:

```
const utterance = new SpeechSynthesisUtterance('Hey')
```

Once this has been defined, we can use it to tweak individual speech properties, such as those listed in Table 2-1, with a more complete list in the Appendix at the back of this book.

Table 2-1. *Properties of the SpeechSynthesisUtterance object*

Property	Purpose
utterance.rate	Sets the speed, accepts between [0.1 and 10], defaults to 1.
utterance.pitch	Sets the pitch, accepts between [0 and 2], defaults to 1.
utterance.volume	Sets the volume, accepts between [0 and 1], defaults to 1.
utterance.lang	Sets the language (values use a Best Current Practice 47 [BCP47] language tag, like en-US or it-IT).
utterance.text	Instead of setting it in the constructor, you can pass it as a property. Text can be a maximum of 32767 characters.
utterance.voice:	Sets the voice (more on this in the following).

If we put this together into a simple example that we can run in a console session (not forgetting to add our name as indicated!), it would look something like this:

```
const utterance = new SpeechSynthesisUtterance('Hey, my name is
[insert your name here]')
utterance.pitch = 1.5
utterance.volume = 0.5
utterance.rate = 8
speechSynthesis.speak(utterance)
```

We can then use the speak(), pause(), resume(), or cancel() method to control the SpeechSynthesis object.

In our next exercise, we'll put this additional functionality to good use and expand our original demo from Chapter 1, to include options that provide finer control over the speech returned, as our next demo. When we're done, our demo will look like the screenshot shown in Figure 2-1.

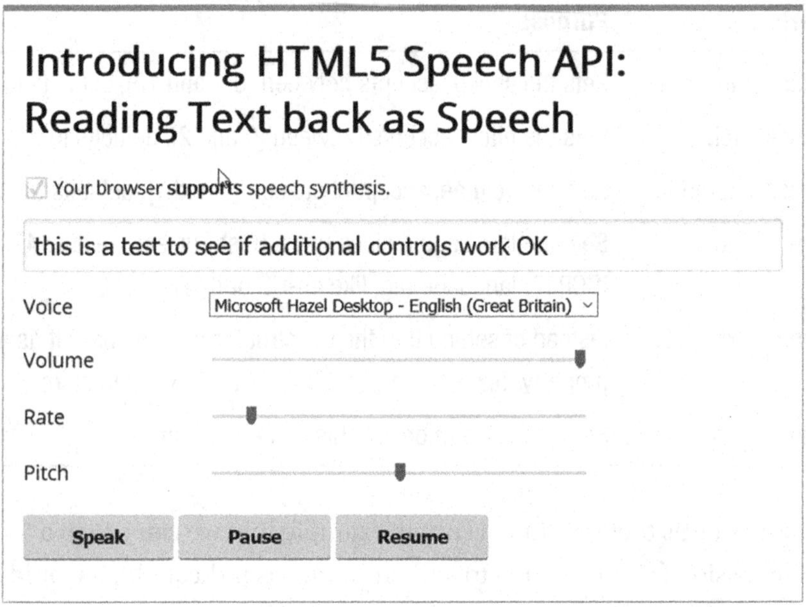

Figure 2-1. *Our updated SpeechSynthesis demo, with added controls*

The changes we will make will be relatively straightforward, but a good indication of how we can start to develop our original. Let's jump in and take a look at what's needed, in more detail.

Improving our SpeechSynthesis demo

In our next exercise, we will add in three sliders to control levels such as volume, pitch, and rate, along with buttons to pause and resume spoken content.

ADDING FUNCTIONALITY

Let's make a start on adding the extra markup needed for our demo:

All of the code you need for this demo is in the updating speechsynthesis folder, in the code download that accompanies this book.

---

1. We'll begin by browsing back to the demo you created in CodePen, back in Chapter 1 – when there, make sure you log in, so we can save changes to the demo.

2. First, look for this block of code:

```
<div class="option">
  <label for="voice">Voice</label>
  <select name="voice" id="voice"></select>
  <button id="speak">Speak</button>
</div>
```

3. Immediately below this block (and before the closing page-wrapper <div>), insert the following code – this adds in sliders for volume, rate, and pitch levels:

```
<div class="option">
  <label for="volume">Volume</label>
  <input type="range" min="0" max="1" step="0.1"
  name="volume" id="volume" value="1">
</div>
<div class="option">
  <label for="rate">Rate</label>
  <input type="range" min="0.1" max="10" step="0.1"
  name="rate" id="rate" value="1">
</div>
```

```
<div class="option">
  <label for="pitch">Pitch</label>
  <input type="range" min="0" max="2" step="0.1"
  name="pitch" id="pitch" value="1">
</div>
```

4. Next, look for this line of code, and remove it from its current location in the markup:

```
<button id="speak">Speak</button>
```

5. Scroll down to the end of the markup, and add in the following three lines immediately before the closing `</div>`, as highlighted:

```
<button id="speak">Speak</button>
<button id="pause">Pause</button>
<button id="resume">Resume</button>
</div>
```

6. With the markup in place, we need to make a couple of adjustments to our styling; otherwise, elements will not appear properly on the page. For this, go ahead and comment out or remove the highlighted line of code from the #voice style rule:

```
#voice { /*margin-left: -70px;*/ margin-right: 70px;
vertical-align: super; }
```

7. The range sliders we've added also need adjusting. Go ahead and add this in below the input[type="text"] rule, leaving a blank line after that rule:

```
input[type="range"] { width: 300px; }
```

8. It's time to add in the JavaScript code to bring life to our new buttons and range controls. Look for the button variable declaration and then add in the following code as highlighted:

```
var button = document.getElementById('speak');
var pause = document.getElementById('pause');
var resume = document.getElementById('resume');
```

9. Next up, leave a blank line and then add in the following declarations – these are cache references to each of the range sliders we are using to adjust volume, rate, and pitch:

```
// Get the attribute controls.
var volumeInput = document.getElementById('volume');
var rateInput = document.getElementById('rate');
var pitchInput = document.getElementById('pitch');
```

10. Scroll down until you see the onvoiceschanged event handler. Then leave a blank line just below it and add in this new error handler:

```
window.speechSynthesis.onerror = function(event) {
  console.log('Speech recognition error detected: ' +
  event.error);
  console.log('Additional information: ' + event.
  message);
}
```

11. The next block is the speak() function – inside it, look for msg.text = text, then leave a blank line, and add in these assignments:

```
// Set the attributes.
msg.volume = parseFloat(volumeInput.value);
msg.rate = parseFloat(rateInput.value);
msg.pitch = parseFloat(pitchInput.value);
```

12. We're almost done. Scroll to the end of the JS code section,
     then leave a blank line, and add in these two event handlers.
     The first takes care of pausing spoken content:

```
// Set up an event listener for when the 'pause' button
is clicked.
pause.addEventListener('click', function(e) {
  if (speechMsgInput.value.length > 0 && speechSynthesis.
  speaking) {
    speechSynthesis.pause();
  }
});
```

13. The second event handler is fired when clicking the resume
     button – for this, leave a blank line after the previous handler,
     and add in the following code:

```
// Set up an event listener for when the 'resume' button
is clicked.
resume.addEventListener('click', function(e) {
  if (speechSynthesis.paused) {
    speechSynthesis.resume();
  }
});
```

14. We're done with adding code. Make sure you save your work. If
     all is working, we should see something akin to the screenshot
     shown at the start of this exercise.

Try running the demo and adding something into the text box and
then altering the controls. With a little practice, we can produce some
interesting effects! Our code is now beginning to take shape and give us
something more complete we can use. Let's quickly review the changes we
made to the code, in more detail.

Dissecting our code

We kicked off by adding in some markup to create suitable range sliders for controlling volume, pitch, and rate settings – in all cases, we're using standard input elements and marking them as HTML5 range types. We then followed this by adding in two new buttons – these are used to pause and resume spoken content.

The real magic came when we added in our script. We started by adding in references to the two new buttons we created; these are assigned the IDs of pause and resume, respectively.

Next up, we then created references to the three range sliders; these were declared as volumeInput, rateInput, and pitchInput, respectively. We then added in declarations within the speak() function, to capture the values set for these range sliders, before assigning them to the SpeechSynthesisUtterance object, as appropriate. We then finished off the demo by adding in three new event handlers – the first to render any errors generated to the console, the second to pause content when our computer is talking, and the third to resume it when a user clicks the resume button.

That was pretty straightforward, right? This is only part of the changes we can make though. What about the sister API, Speech Recognition? As we will soon see, this one requires a different mind-set when it comes to making changes. Let's take a look in more detail at some of the changes we can make to augment the overall experience.

Exploring the Speech Recognition API

We've explored how we can make our browsers talk, but what about recognizing what we say? In the demo we created back in Chapter 1, we came across terms such as navigator.mediaDevices.getUserMedia(), the speechstart event handler, and recognition.interimResults. What do they all do?

Well, the first isn't strictly part of the SpeechRecognition API; we use this to control access to a microphone from within the browser. However, the other two are indeed part of the API; unlike the SpeechSynthesis API, this is not one we can run as a one-liner in console. Instead, we need to specify a few settings when working with this API – the key one being to allow access to the microphone before we do anything!

Breaking apart the API

At the heart of the SpeechRecognition API is the SpeechRecognition interface; this controls access to the speech recognition interface within the browser. We first have to define a reference to this; once in place, we can create an instance of the API interface using this line of code:

```
const recognition = new SpeechRecognition();
```

It's important to note that within Chrome, this API makes use of a remote server-based recognition engine, to process all requests. This means it will not work offline – for that, we must use a different browser, such as Firefox.

We can then specify suitable values for settings such as `interimResults` or `maxAlternatives`, along with appropriate event handlers to stop or start the speech service. Let's take a look at some of these settings in more detail; these are listed in Table 2-2.

Table 2-2. *Properties of SpeechRecognition API*

Property	Purpose of property
SpeechRecognition. grammars	Returns and sets a collection of SpeechGrammar objects that represent the grammars that will be understood by the current instance of the SpeechRecognition API.
SpeechRecognition. lang	Returns and sets the language of the current SpeechRecognition. If not specified, this defaults to the HTML lang attribute value, or the user agent's language setting if that isn't set either.
SpeechRecognition. continuous	Controls whether continuous results are returned for each recognition, or only a single result. Defaults to single (or false).
SpeechRecognition. interimResults	Controls whether interim results should be returned (true) or not (false). Interim results are results that are not yet final (e.g., the SpeechRecognitionResult.isFinal property is false).
SpeechRecognition. maxAlternatives	Sets the maximum number of alternatives provided per result. The default value is 1.
SpeechRecognition. serviceURI	Specifies the location of the speech recognition service used by the current SpeechRecognition to handle the actual recognition. The default is the user agent's default speech service.

Once we've defined our chosen settings for the SpeechRecognition object, we can then control it using three methods. We can start() the service, stop() it, or abort() a reference to a current SpeechRecognition object, in much the same way as we did for the Speech Synthesis demo earlier in this chapter.

There is a full list of API commands available in the Appendix, at the end of this book.

However, unlike the Speech Synthesis API, there are not so many options available for customizing the experience in quite the same way; nevertheless, we can still implement a few changes to improve the experience. With this in mind, let's take a look at what we can to augment our original demo.

Updating our SpeechRecognition demo

When working with the SpeechSynthesis API demo, we were able to add in some additional properties from the API to help fine-tune the experience for our users; this is not the case with the SpeechRecognition API. Instead, we will take a different tack; we'll add in some additional error management features and better controls for automatically shutting off the microphone using `navigator.mediaDevices.getUserMedia()`.

EXPANDING THE OPTIONS

For the purposes of this exercise, we will go through each change in smaller blocks; a screenshot of any visual changes will be displayed as appropriate.

Code for this demo is available in the code download that accompanies this book – look in the `updating speechrecognition` folder.

Let's make a start:

1. First, go ahead and browse to the Speech Recognition you created back in Chapter 1, on the CodePen web site – make sure you are also logged in, so you can save your changes.

2. Next, look for this line of code, and add the following (highlighted) below it, leaving a line after the new code:

```
recognition.interimResults = true;
recognition.maxAlternatives = 1;
recognition.continuous = true;
```

3. The first change we're going to implement is to begin to improve the error handling – at present, we're piping out the error message verbatim, which doesn't look great. With a few changes, we can make it more friendly, so go ahead and alter the error event handler, as indicated:

```
recognition.addEventListener("error", e => {
  if (e.error == "no-speech") {
    output.textContent = "Error: no speech detected";
  } else { output.textContent = "Error: " + e.error;  }
});
```

It's worth noting that we can expand this with other error codes, later if so desired.

---

4. The second change will be an auto turn-off for the speech recognition engine – after all, we don't necessarily want our microphone to stay enabled if we're not using it for a period of time, right? For this change, look for the speechend event handler, then leave a blank line, and add in this function:

```
recognition.onspeechend = function() {
  log.textContent = 'You were quiet for a while so voice
recognition turned itself off.';
  stream.getTracks().forEach(function(track) { track.stop() });
  console.log("off");
}
```

We can see the result of this change in Figure 2-2.

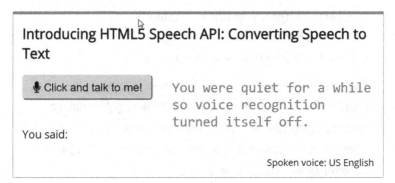

Introducing HTML5 Speech API: Converting Speech to Text

🎤 Click and talk to me!   You were quiet for a while
                             so voice recognition
You said: turned itself off.

Spoken voice: US English

Figure 2-2. *The addition of an auto shut-off feature*

5. The third and final change is to exert more control over the shutting off of our microphone – there will be occasions where we may want to control when it is switched off, rather than it appear to have a mind of its own! Fortunately, the changes for this are very straightforward – the first is to add in an element in our HTML markup as indicated:

    ```
    <p class="output">You said: <strong class="output_
    result"> </strong></p>
    <button id="micoff">Turn off</button>
    ```

6. The second change requires us to add in a new event handler – rather than rely on the Speech Recognition API automatically shutting off, or trying to transcribe speech it hears that isn't intended, we can control when to turn off the microphone. To do this, look for this line of code:

    ```
    recognition.continuous = true
    ```

    then leave a blank line and drop in the following code:

    ```
    document.getElementById("micoff").
    addEventListener("click", () => {
      stream.getTracks().forEach(function(track)
      { track.stop() });
      console.log("off");
    });
    ```

7. We've made all of the changes needed. Go ahead and save the results of your work. If all is well, we should see something akin to the screenshot shown in Figure 2-3, where we can see our improved error handling in action.

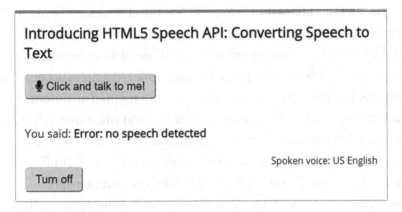

Figure 2-3. *Our updated Speech Recognition demo*

If you try clicking the Turn off button to deactivate the microphone, be patient – it can take a few seconds for the red indicator to disappear!

When researching code for this demo, I was struck by the amount of apparent crossover that there seems to be with the event that can be triggered when using the Speech Recognition API.

It's for this reason that although we don't have as many configuration options to tweak as the Speech Synthesis API, the different event handlers in the Speech Recognition API can still trip us up! With this in mind, let's take a look at the code from the demo we've just completed in more detail.

Understanding the code

Over the course of the last few pages, we've taken a different approach to developing our original demo – this time around, we've expanded it by adding to or improving the overall experience, rather than simply adding more options. Let's take a moment to review the changes we've made to our original demo in more detail.

We kicked off by updating the error event handler, where we did a check for the no-speech error property and rendered a more acceptable message back to the user. Our next change implemented an automatic shut-off option – one thing we have to bear in mind when using the Speech Recognition API (we don't want it running without some control!)

The final change we made was to alter the automatic shut-off function – an automatic turn-off is a useful feature, but there are occasions where we might want control over when this happens. This is particularly useful to help prevent our microphone from recording things automatically, which should not be shared!

Okay, time for us to move on. We've explored the basics of how to implement both the Speech Recognition and Synthesis APIs; it's time we put them to a more practical use! To show how we can combine them together, we're going to create a simple video player that is controllable by voice; it will confirm any action we ask of it, vocally, rather than displaying a message on the screen. This will use principles from both of the demos we've created. Let's dive in and take a look at how this might work in action.

Creating a more practical example

For this next exercise, we're going to add basic speech capabilities to a video player that uses the HTML5 <video> element.

We'll focus on adding the play and pause commands for now, but we can easily add extra commands such as increasing volume or muting sounds at a later date. When finished, it will look like the screenshot shown in Figure 2-4.

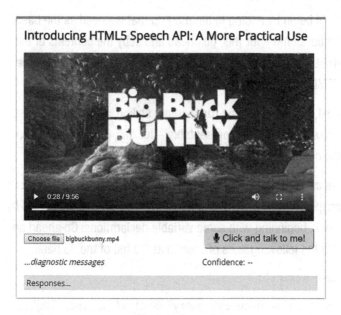

Figure 2-4. *Our voice-controlled video player*

As you set up the demo, take a look at some of the functions and handlers in close detail – hopefully you should recognize a few elements from previous demos! With that in mind, let's crack on and make a start on our demo.

ADDING SPEECH CAPABILITIES TO VIDEO

This next demo has a couple of requirements: You need to make sure you have a suitable video available (MP4 format is fine; there is an example video in the code download if you don't have something suitable). We'll be building in a CodePen session, so make sure you've browsed to the site at https://codepen.io and have logged in, before continuing:

1. We'll begin by adding in the markup that we need as the basis for our demo – for this, go ahead and copy the contents of the HTML.txt file from the practical example folder into the HTML pane on the right.

2. Next, let's add in some rudimentary styling, so we can at least make our demo look presentable – for this, go ahead and add the contents of the CSS.txt file into the CSS pane.

3. We can now turn our attention to the really important part – our script! There is a good chunk to add in, so we'll do this block by block, beginning with some variable declarations. Go ahead and add the following lines of code in at the top of the JS pane:

    ```
    "use strict";

    const log = document.querySelector(".output_log");
    const output = document.querySelector(".output");
    const confidence = document.querySelector(".confidence em");

    // Simple function that checks existence of s in str
    var userSaid = function(str, s) {
      return str.indexOf(s) > -1;
    };
    ```

4. The next block of code takes care of loading our video player with our choice of video – this is so we can have it ready to play when we give the command. Leave a blank line and then add in the following code:

    ```
    video_file.onchange = function() {
      var files = this.files;
      var file = URL.createObjectURL(files[0]);
      video_player.src = file;
    };
    ```

5. This next part gets a little trickier – we need to allow users
    to request access to their microphone. For this, we use
    `navigator.mediaDevices.getUserMedia`; we'll begin by
    adding in the construct for this first. Leave a blank line and then
    add in this method call:

```
navigator.mediaDevices
    .getUserMedia({ audio: true })
    .then(function(stream) {

...add in code here...

}).catch(function(err) {
  console.log(err);
});
```

6. With this in place, we can now start to add in the various
    components needed to operate the Speech Recognition API; we
    first need to define an instance of the API. Go ahead and add
    this in, replacing the text `...add in code here...`:

```
const SpeechRecognition = window.SpeechRecognition ||
window.webkitSpeechRecognition;
const recognition = new SpeechRecognition();
```

7. Next comes our first event handler, which we will use to invoke
    access to the microphone. For this, leave a line after the
    SpeechRecognition API declarations and then add in this code:

```
document.querySelector("button").addEventListener
("click", () => {
  let recoglang = "en-US";
  recognition.lang = recoglang;
  recognition.continuous = true;
  recognition.start();
});
```

8. We now need to add in event handlers that take care of switching on the API when we begin to talk, or turning it off at the appropriate moment; leave a line blank after the previous handler and then add in this code:

```
recognition.addEventListener("speechstart", e => {
  log.textContent = "Speech has been detected.";
});

recognition.addEventListener("speechend", e => {
  recognition.stop();
});

recognition.onspeechend = function() {
  log.textContent =
    "You were quiet for a while so voice recognition
    turned itself off.";
    stream.getTracks().forEach(function(track) {
      track.stop();
    });
  console.log("off");
};
```

9. This next block is where the real magic happens – this controls our video player by converting our spoken commands into something it recognizes and translating it into the appropriate command. Leave a line after the previous event handler and then drop in this code:

```
// Process the results when they are returned from the
    recogniser
recognition.onresult = function(e) {
// Check each result starting from the last one
for (var i = e.resultIndex; i < e.results.length; ++i) {
var str = e.results[i][0].transcript;
```

```
console.log("Recognised: " + str);
// If the user said 'video' then parse it further
if (request(str, "video")) {
// Play the video
if (request(str, "play")) {
video_player.play();
log.innerHTML = "playing video...";
} else if (request(str, "pause")) {
// Stop the video
video_player.pause();
log.innerHTML = "video paused...";
}
}
}

confidence.textContent =
(e.results[0][0].confidence * 100).toFixed(2) + "%";
};
```

10. We're almost done. The last event handler to add in will take care of some basic error trapping. Go ahead and add in this event handler, leaving a line blank after the previous block:

```
recognition.addEventListener("error", e => {
  if (e.error == "no-speech") {
    log.textContent = "Error: no speech detected";
  } else {
    log.textContent = "Error: " + e.error;
  }
});
```

11. Save your work. If all is well, we should see something akin to the screenshot shown at the start of this exercise.

Try choosing a video using the Choose file button and then saying "video play" to kick it off – yes, it's a little gimmicky, but it does serve a valid point. Who says you always have to press buttons to start something? Yes, I would absolutely consider myself to be a fan of old-school methods, but there comes a time when one must adapt…!

If you take a closer look at the code in this demo, you will see that it uses terms which we've already met from earlier demos; in the main, most of it should start to look familiar now! There is one exception though – I don't see an event handler for result; what's this .onresult handler I see…?

Exploring the code in detail

Aha! That is an important change to how we're tracking the final output of the API! It does work in a similar fashion to the result event handler we've used before, but with one difference: that event handler is only called once. I will explain what I mean shortly, but first, let's go through our code in more detail. I'll focus on the JavaScript, as the CSS and HTML used are very standard and should be self-explanatory.

We began with declaring a number of variables for storing references to elements in our markup, and to help with finding text in our spoken input (more in a moment). We then moved on to creating a basic function to load our video player with our chosen video, ready to play it on command.

The next block up is the start of the real crux of our demo – we initialize a call to navigator.getUserMedia() to allow access to our microphone, before declaring instances of the API (depending on the browser we use).

We then added in an event handler that initializes our API instance with various properties – lang being set to US English and continuous to prevent the API shutting down too quickly, before switching it on. Next up came three event handlers to respond to speech – speechstart kicks in when the API detects spoken content, speechend will terminate it, and onspeechend will recognize if the API has been quiet and switch itself off.

The real focus of our demo comes next – here we made use of onresult. This differs from the result event handler we've used before in that this doesn't fire once (which result does), but fires each time we've spoken and the API detects that we've stopped speaking. I should point out that this is **not** stopped speaking completely, but more a pause between each command that we give! This function parses through the result using a for loop, to assign each in turn to str, before performing the appropriate video command based on what it hears. So, if we had said "play video," it would search for each word individually. Based on what it hears, it will detect that we've said video, so it checks to see if we've said play or pause. If we said play (as we've done here), it would then pause the video and display confirmation on screen.

Okay, let's crack on! Although many of the demos we've done so far will likely be in English, there is one thing we should bear in mind: what about support for different languages? In an age of global connectivity, we can't assume that people will just speak English (or indeed just one language, for that matter!). We should absolutely consider adding support for different languages; thankfully we can do this without too much difficulty using the Speech APIs. Let's dive in and take a look at what we need to do to add multilingual support in more detail.

Going multilingual

In an ideal world, it would be great if we all spoke the same language – after all, we'd be able to communicate with others in a different country, and there'd be no misunderstandings...but that would be so boring!

There is something to be said for speaking to someone in a different tongue; embracing a different culture and language adds an extra element to a holiday or trip. The same applies to reading texts such as those found in a museum; of course, you might not understand much or any of it, but you will still get a feel for what things must have been like in that country's past history.

But I digress. Bringing things back to reality, we've talked about how to turn speech into text or vice versa. What about other languages though? We don't all speak English (or indeed the same language), so how does that work within either API?

Exploring support for languages

One of the benefits of using either the Speech Recognition or Speech Synthesis API is its support for other languages – there are a host of different options available for us to use. The exact number, as we will shortly see, will depend on which browser we use; this might be as many as 21 or as few as just three!

We've already touched on including language support as part of the Speech Synthesis demo we created back in Chapter 1 – remember the rather intriguing list of names displayed in that demo? We can see an extract of it in Figure 2-5.

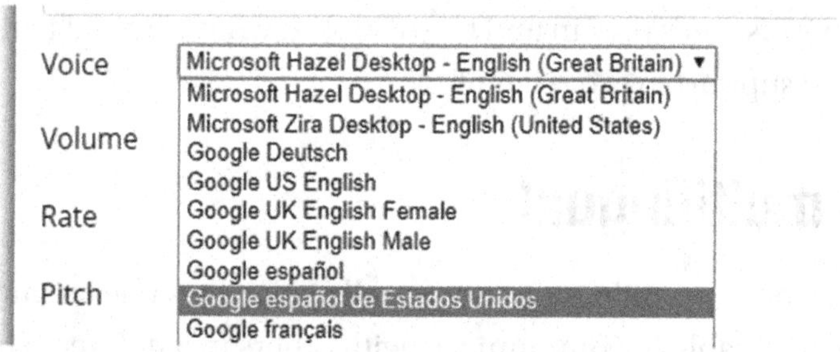

Figure 2-5. *(An extract of) Languages available for the SpeechSynthesis API*

To implement this, we created a loadVoices() function to iterate through each language option, before adding it into a drop-down. We then used the getVoices() method to select our chosen language, before applying the change to the SpeechRecognition object.

If you want a reminder of how we did this, try running this simple example in your browser console – I would recommend running it in the console log for one of your CodePen demos, so that you can trigger access to the microphone:

```
console.log(`Voices #: {speechSynthesis.getVoices().length}`);
speechSynthesis.getVoices().forEach(voice => {
  console.log(voice.name, voice.lang)
});
```

At this point, it's worth noting that this should work in most modern browsers. You *may* find though you come across a cross-browser issue when using this code with the SpeechSynthesis API – in some older versions of Chrome, the original code we used won't operate.

It works fine in Firefox and Edge (and possibly Safari, for those of you who are Mac users); instead, you may find you have to use a callback to get the list to display, before using .getVoices to display the list:

```
const voiceschanged = () => {
  console.log(`Voices #: ${speechSynthesis.getVoices().length}`);
  speechSynthesis.getVoices().forEach(voice => {
    console.log(voice.name, voice.lang)
  })
}
speechSynthesis.onvoiceschanged = voiceschanged
```

You may find though that the number of languages returned differs when using Chrome – the extra ones that start with "Google..." will only be available if there is a valid network connection available. A copy of the list is displayed in full, in Figure 2-6.

Voices #: 21	VM47:1
Microsoft Hazel Desktop - English (Great Britain) en-GB	VM47:3
Microsoft Zira Desktop - English (United States) en-US	VM47:3
Google Deutsch de-DE	VM47:3
Google US English en-US	VM47:3
Google UK English Female en-GB	VM47:3
Google UK English Male en-GB	VM47:3
Google español es-ES	VM47:3
Google español de Estados Unidos es-US	VM47:3
Google français fr-FR	VM47:3
Google हिन्दी hi-IN	VM47:3
Google Bahasa Indonesia id-ID	VM47:3
Google italiano it-IT	VM47:3
Google 日本語 ja-JP	VM47:3
Google 한국의 ko-KR	VM47:3
Google Nederlands nl-NL	VM47:3
Google polski pl-PL	VM47:3
Google português do Brasil pt-BR	VM47:3
Google русский ru-RU	VM47:3
Google 普通话（中国大陆） zh-CN	VM47:3
Google 粤語（香港） zh-HK	VM47:3
Google 國語（臺灣） zh-TW	VM47:3

Figure 2-6. *A list of languages supported in the API*

Otherwise, it will be reduced; Edge currently displays three, while Firefox shows two. Suffice to say, it's just another point to consider when using the Speech APIs!

In contrast, adding lingual support into the Speech Synthesis API gets more interesting – not only can we choose a language but we can even set a dialect too! This does require some more work though to implement. We'll see how to achieve this shortly, in our next exercise.

Setting a custom language

If we have a need to set language support when using the Speech Recognition API, we have to take a different tack – instead of simply calling the list from the API, we *provide* it with a list. This takes the form of what is effectively a double array. This is a little complicated to explain, so bear with me on this; I will use the following extract taken from our next exercise.

We start with the array – notice how not all entries are equal? Okay, before you say anything, I'm referring to the number, not the text within! In most cases, we have just the language and the BCP47 code (such as af-ZA), but in the last one we have three values:

```
var langs =
    [['Afrikaans',        ['af-ZA']],
     ['Bahasa Indonesia',['id-ID']],
     ['Bahasa Melayu',    ['ms-MY']],
     ['Català',           ['ca-ES']],
     ['Čeština',          ['cs-CZ']],
     ['Deutsch',          ['de-DE']],
     ['English',          ['en-AU', 'Australia'],
...
```
(abridged for brevity)

BCP47, or Best Current Practice 47, is an IEFT international standard used to identify human languages, such as de-DE for German. If you would like to learn more, then head over to the Wikipedia article for a good introduction, at `https://en.wikipedia.org/wiki/IETF_language_tag`.

We then iterate through the array using a construct such as this:

```
for (var i = 0; i < langs.length; i++) {
  select_language.options[i] = new Option(langs[i][0], i);
}
```

which puts it into an object from which we can pick the item that should be displayed by default (in this case English):

```
select_language.selectedIndex = 6;
```

By itself, this won't have any effect on the API; to make it work, we need to add in one more function. At a high level, we iterate through the array again, but this time pick out the dialect value (in this case, values from the second column), before adding these to a `<select>` drop-down box. We then need to set the visibility such that if we pick a language that has multiple dialects, the dialect drop-down is displayed or hidden accordingly. Hopefully this will begin to make some sense; to see how this works in practice, let's swiftly move to our next exercise, where we will see how this code fits into our demo.

ALLOWING FOR LANGUAGES IN SPEECH RECOGNITION

For this next exercise, we'll need to revert to the Speech Synthesis demo we created back in Chapter 1 – to keep a copy of your previous code, I would recommend logging in to CodePen and hitting the Fork button. Our demo will start with you ready to edit the HTML code, so make sure you're at this point before continuing with the steps in this demo.

Although some of the changes we're about to make are simple, others are more involved. I would recommend making sure you avail yourself of a copy of the code download for this book; everything will be in the `language support` folder.

Assuming you're there, let's get started with updating our demo:

1. The first change is in indeed in our HTML markup, so look for this line and comment it out:

    ```
    <span class="voice">Spoken voice: US English</span>
    ```

2. Next, go ahead and insert this block immediately below it:

    ```
    <span class="voice">
      Spoken voice and dialect:
        <div id="div_language">
    ```

```
      <select id="select_language"
       onchange="updateCountry()">
  </select>
      <select id="select_dialect"></select>
    </div>
  </span>
```

3. We now need to adjust where the new drop-downs sit – for this, go ahead and add in the following CSS style at the bottom of the CSS pane:

```
.voice { float: right;   margin-top: -20px; }
```

4. The real changes though are in our JavaScript code (naturally!) – for this, go ahead and open a copy of the JS.txt file from the code download and then look for this line of code: var langs = (it will be around line 7).

5. Copy it, and the following lines, down as far as (and including) the closing bracket after this line:

```
    select_dialect.style.visibility = list[1].length == 1 ?
    'hidden' : 'visible';
  }
```

6. Paste the contents of the JavaScript from the code download, immediately after this line, leaving a line between it and your new block:

```
const output = document.querySelector(".output_result");
```

7. Okay, next change: Scroll down until you see the start of this event handler:

```
document.querySelector("button").addEventListener("click", ()
```

8. Comment out let recoglang = "en-US" inside this function, and replace it with this:

```
recognition.lang = select_dialect.value;
```

9. Scroll down until you see this line: `output.textContent = text;`

10. Next, add a blank line and then drop in this line of code, before the closing bracket and parenthesis:

```
log.textContent = "Confidence: " + (e.results[0][0].
confidence * 100).toFixed(2) + "%";
```

11. At this point, we should have all of our code changes in place; go ahead and save your work.

12. Try running the demo. If all is well, we should have something akin to the screenshot shown in Figure 2-7. Try changing the voice to a different language and then saying something – hopefully you or a friend might know enough words to say something that makes sense!

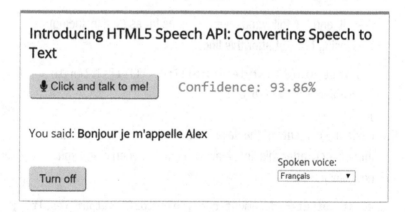

Figure 2-7. *The results of speaking French to our demo*

As we can see from the demo, it shows that I do know some French; I can also get by with Spanish, although it's nowhere near at the same level! This aside, we've added a critical feature to this demo that is worth exploring in more detail – let's take a moment to explore how it works in more detail.

Breaking apart our code

If we take a closer look at the code we've just written, you might just spot an oddity – don't worry if you don't though, as it isn't immediately obvious! I'll give you a clue to get you started: it has something to do with the value we assign as our language – it's not what you might at first expect...

Okay, I digress. Back to our demo, we kicked off by commenting out the original text that indicated which language was being used; we replaced this with two drop-downs, one for language and the other for the dialect. We then brought in a substantial chunk of code, which first sets up an array langs that stores both the language and dialect values. This we followed with a for loop to iterate through the first set of values and insert each into the select_language drop-down. We then set a couple of default values – in this case English – for both the language and dialect properties.

Next up came the updateCountry() function – it looks a little complex, but isn't too hard to get our heads around it. We simply cleared out the dialect drop-down (select_dialect) before populating it with values from the second column of data (in this case, where we have the BCP47 values that we talked about earlier).

The remaining changes are small ones – we reassigned the output value from the select_dialect drop-down to recognition.lang and added in a confidence statement which is rendered in the output_log span element. Makes sense? Well, it would, if only for one nagging problem. Why on earth does it look like we're setting the dialect value, rather than the language value...?

The difference between language and dialect

If I were to ask you the subject of this section as a question, hopefully you would say that language is something we would speak and that a dialect is effectively a regional variation of that language...or something to that effect! However, you'd be really confused if I said that, at least within the context of this API, the two were actually two halves of the same thing, and in some cases were the same! What gives…?

Well, the answer to that lies in five characters – BCP47. This is the international standard that I alluded to earlier, where we see codes such as pt-BR, or the Brazilian dialect of Portuguese. But the real trick though is in *how* we make use of this in our code – although we select both the language and dialect (where the latter is available), it's not until we select that *dialect* value that we get the real value used.

If, for example, we were to select that dialect of Portuguese, we would get pt-BR; this is the value that the lang property needs for Speech Recognition. In effect, we're using the language drop-down to filter our choices, before selecting the real language via the dialect drop-down for use in our demo.

Okay, let's move on. There is one more feature we need to explore, before we get into the practical fun stuff of building projects! As I hope you've seen from the demos, speech recognition is developing well, but it's not perfect. There may be occasions where we might want to give it a helping hand. Let me introduce you to `SpeechRecognition.Grammars`.

Making use of grammar objects

Over the course of this chapter, we've explored the Speech APIs in more detail, covering features such as adding multi-language support, providing better control over when the microphone can be used, and refining what is returned if we should encounter an error when using the APIs.

However, there may be instances where we need that helping hand – this is where the grammars part of the SpeechRecognition API can play its role. However, this feature is something of an oddity and comes with a potential sting in its tail. Why?

Many have found it to be confusing at best, or actually not do what they were otherwise expecting it to do. A part of this is likely due to when the original specification was written; it was done at a time when the word recognition rate wasn't as good as it is now, and so it needed something to give what could be described as a boost.

Consequently, support for the `SpeechGrammarList` interface is poor – it's currently only supported in Chrome. It also makes use of the JSpeech Grammar Format (or JSGF) which has been removed from most browsers. Therefore, I would not recommend using this feature unless absolutely necessary, and be aware that it should be used at your own risk and that it is likely to be removed in the future.

If you want to see the technical detail and discussion around the proposed removal, please refer to the W3C GitHub site at `https://github.com/w3c/speech-api/pull/57` and `https://github.com/w3c/speech-api/pull/58`.

Summary

When working with the Speech APIs, there are a host of options we can use; we covered some of them when we were first introduced to the APIs back in Chapter 1. Over the course of this chapter, we've built on what we learned there with additional options. Let's take a moment to review what we have learned.

We kicked off by creating demos to explore both the Speech Synthesis and Speech Recognition APIs in greater detail; we first covered more of the options available within each API, before adding functionality to each demo.

Moving on, we then took a look at how we can add multi-language support when using the APIs. We explored the basic principles behind each API and how to set a custom language. This was swiftly followed by a demo, before exploring the differences between setting language and dialect properties and how both interact with each other to give us our desired language setting.

We then rounded out the chapter with a look at the SpeechGrammar interface. We covered how this could be used, but that there are plans to drop support for it in the future; we covered some of the reasons why this might be the case and how it may or may not affect your code in practice.

Phew! Covered a lot, huh? Well, the pace isn't going to slow down – things will start to get really interesting! Over the course of the next few chapters, we're going to implement some sample projects that illustrate how we might make of the APIs in a practical context. This will cover anything from leaving verbal review feedback to automating part or all of a purchase process; we're really only limited by our imagination! To kick us off, we're going to start with a relatively new addition for some sites. How about using the API to develop a chatbot, for example? Turn the page to find out how we can start to have a proper conversation with your web site...

CHAPTER 3

Supporting Mobile Devices

> *"Juniper Research has forecasted that the number of smart assistants will triple from 2.5 billion in use at the end of 2018 to 8 billion by 2023."*

Remember that shocker from the start of Chapter 1? Given that mobile usage has now overtaken desktop, this makes for a powerful combination! But – I hear you: "What is the significance of those two facts?" Well, let me reveal all.

In previous chapters thus far, you may have noticed a focus on using the desktop as our environment. There's nothing wrong with this per se, but it misses out one crucial point: what about using mobile devices? Given that more and more people use smart devices to purchase products, then it makes absolute sense to consider mobile devices when using the Web Speech APIs.

Over the course of this chapter, we'll take a look at some of the demos we've created in earlier chapters and explore using them on mobile devices. Based on what you've seen so far, you might think this shouldn't be a problem, as most recent browsers support the APIs on the desktop, right? Well, things are not all they may seem – be prepared to make some decisions.

© Alex Libby 2020
A. Libby, *Introducing the HTML5 Web Speech API*,
https://doi.org/10.1007/978-1-4842-5735-7_3

Supporting the Speech Synthesis API

Yes, that last comment might seem a little intriguing, but we will have some decisions to make about how we might use the APIs within a mobile environment! Let me explain what I mean by first illustrating the level of support for the APIs on more popular mobile platforms, beginning with Speech Synthesis (Figure 3-1).

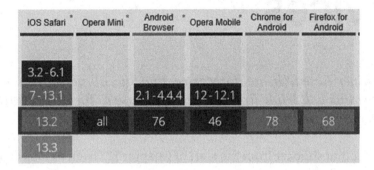

Figure 3-1. *Support for the Speech Synthesis API Source: CanIUse.com*

Ouch! That doesn't seem quite as good as desktop, right? Granted coverage isn't as extensive as standard desktop users, but then with the plethora of different platforms available, it's not surprising that support isn't so uniform! However, it's not as bad as it might seem – to understand why relies on us making a conscious decision about one key question: how much do we want to support Google Chrome?

Breaking down the numbers

To understand the answer to that last question, we should first see just who supports the API and the current usage of that browser. Table 3-1 shows a more detailed version of the information presented from Figure 3-1, where we can see just which of the more popular browsers support the API.

Table 3-1. *Support for the Speech Synthesis API on mobile devices*

Mobile browser	Supported?	% usage, as of December 2019
iOS Safari	Yes	2.89
Opera Mini	No	1.17
Android Browser	No	0
Opera Mobile	No	0.01
Chrome for Android	Yes	35.16
Firefox for Android	Yes	0.23
UC Browser for Android	No	2.88
Samsung Internet	Yes	2.73
QQ Browser	Yes	0.2
Baidu Browser	No	0
KaiOS Browser	Yes	0.2

It's easy to see that usage of Google Chrome far outstrips all of the other browsers combined, by a factor of almost 3 to 1! It therefore raises the question about whom we should support, particularly for any minimum viable product (or MVP).

As either all other browser manufacturers don't support the API on mobile devices or usage of that browser is well below 5%, it would make sense to focus on Chrome. To really ram the point home (as if it is needed!), we can see just how much Chrome is used in Figure 3-2.

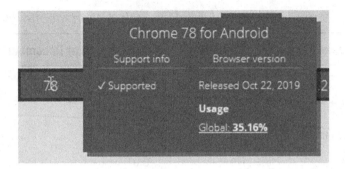

Figure 3-2. *Chrome usage as of December 2019 Source:*
CanIUse.com

This might seem a little drastic to cut out support for that number of
browsers, but in today's world we need to be pragmatic: do we have the
resources or time to develop for all of the different browsers? Support for
Chrome is far outstripping others, so it makes commercial sense to focus
on this browser and only include others if the revenue is sufficiently large
enough to warrant deploying resources (such as for very large customers).

Supporting the Speech Recognition API

We've explored what the support is like for the Speech Synthesis API. How
does it compare with its sister, the Speech Recognition API?

Well, at first glance, support is not as good – in some respects, this isn't
a real shock, as this API is more complex than the Speech Synthesis API, so
support isn't as far advanced as that API. We can see an outline summary
for popular mobile platforms in Figure 3-3, shown overleaf.

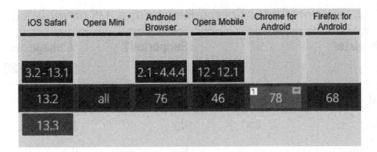

iOS Safari *	Opera Mini *	Android * Browser	Opera Mobile *	Chrome for Android	Firefox for Android
3.2-13.1		2.1-4.4.4	12-12.1		
13.2	all	76	46	▣ 78 ◻	68
13.3					

Figure 3-3. *Support for the Speech Recognition API on mobile devices Source: CanIUse.com*

At first glance, the main difference is that any support for this API has yet to reach fully ratified status (whereas the other API already has); it just means that we need to use the -webkit prefix when working with this API. As we'll see shortly, this is no big deal; the real question though is in the numbers of those who use the browser! To see what I mean, let's dive in and take a look at those numbers in more detail, just as we did for the Speech Synthesis API.

Understanding the numbers

If we were to look at the detail of who supports the Speech Recognition API, we see the same numbers of people using each browser as before. This time around though, support for the API within each browser is just under 25% less than those that support the Speech Synthesis API (allowing for the use of a vendor prefix and that one browser requires it to be enabled manually). We can see the results listed in Table 3-2.

Table 3-2. *Support for the Speech Recognition API on mobile devices*

Mobile browser	Supported?	% usage, as of December 2019
iOS Safari	No	2.89
Opera Mini	No	1.17
Android Browser	No	0
Opera Mobile	No	0.01
Chrome for Android *(uses webkit prefix)*	Yes – partial	35.16
Firefox for Android	No	0.23
UC Browser for Android	No	2.88
Samsung Internet *(uses webkit prefix)*	Yes – partial	2.73
QQ Browser *(uses webkit prefix)*	Yes – partial	0.2
Baidu Browser *(uses webkit prefix)*	Yes – partial	0
KaiOS Browser *(uses webkit prefix)*	Can be enabled	0.2

It will be no surprise then that Chrome is the standout of this table, just as it was for the Speech Synthesis API. If we were to hover over the figure from the CanIUse.com web site, we would see the same result shown as before!

A check of the numbers shown in Table 3-2 shows that it would make perfect sense to focus efforts on developing for Google Chrome; any time spent on other browsers should only be for large clients where revenue opportunities can justify the effort required! Now that we've seen the numbers for both APIs, it's worth taking a few moments to summarize why we should consider only developing for Chrome:

- Chrome is the most popular, so we will get the biggest exposure by focusing on this browser, where we can reuse the same core functionality in both mobile and desktop environments.

- If (heaven forbid) we come across any problems, we should see them appear quickly and can then decide to deactivate or pause the speech option sooner. It will be harder to find issues on browsers where the usage levels are much lower and with which we might not know of any issue as quickly as with Chrome.

Okay, we've outlined the case for focusing on Chrome, given its popularity and level of support; it's time to get practical! Before we do so, there are a couple of points we need to cover off with respect to the demos in this chapter; this is to ensure you get the best effect when testing the results of each exercise.

A couple of prerequisites

Over the course of this chapter, we will revisit some of the exercises we created in CodePen from earlier chapters, with a view to adapting them for display on a mobile device such as your cell phone.

We could of course create new demos – there's nothing wrong with this approach, but a more beneficial approach would be to see how easy it is to adapt existing demos to work on a mobile platform. With this in mind, there are a couple of points to note:

- The code can be edited from within the Pen that we create on a desktop, but to get the best effect when testing our demo, it should be displayed from a cell phone.

- For the purposes of each demo and to prove our earlier discussion, we will be using Chrome only – given the level of usage stands head and shoulders above all other browsers, it makes sense to use the most popular one!

- We will make use of the code download for this book as before – make sure you have a copy to hand, before you commence with the demos in this chapter.

With this in mind, let's get stuck into developing some code, beginning with checking support for the APIs from within our browser.

Checking support for the APIs

Our first demo will be to help establish if a chosen browser supports the APIs – it's worth pointing out that if we had decided to solely work with Chrome (as outlined previously), then this test might seem a little superfluous!

However, it's still worth running; not only are we checking support but we will also use a different method to achieve the same result. There is no overriding reason for either method to work better than the other; each will work fine, and you can choose which you prefer to use in your own projects.

ESTABLISHING SUPPORT FOR SPEECH APIS

We'll start with checking for the Speech Synthesis API, but the code will also work with the Speech Recognition API (just replace all instances of the word "Synthesis" with "Recognition" in your code, then save it, and run it).

To establish if a browser supports the APIs, go ahead with these steps:

1. We'll begin by extracting a copy of the checksupport folder from the code download and saving it to our project area.

2. Next, go ahead and browse to CodePen at https://codepen.io. Then log in with the same account details you used back in Chapter 1.

3. On the left, choose Create ➤ Pen. Then copy and paste the contents of JS.txt into the JS pane of our Pen – make sure you save the Pen! If all is well, we should have something akin to the screenshot shown in Figure 3-4.

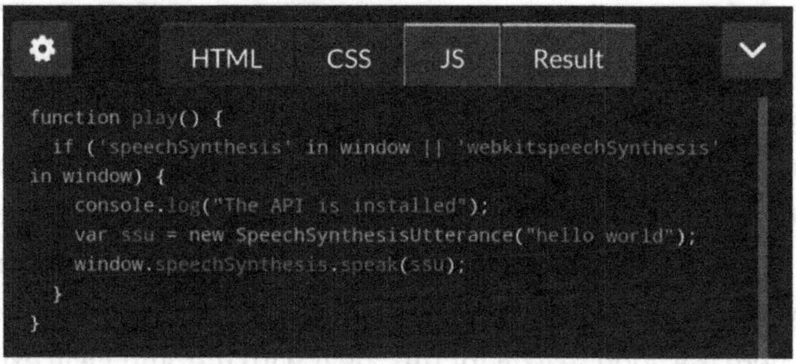

***Figure 3-4.** The code entered into the JS pane of CodePen*

4. Next, open a copy of the code from HTML.txt and paste the contents into the HTML pane of our Pen.

5. Once saved, we can test the results – for this, go ahead and browse to your CodePen from your cell phone, then make sure you have Editor View displayed, and hit the Console button. We don't need to do anything. If your browser supports either API, then we will see confirmation of this in the CodePen console, as shown in Figure 3-5.

Figure 3-5. *Proving that our cell phone supports the APIs*

Excellent! We've confirmed that our mobile browser can support the API (and yes, I am assuming you've used Chrome!).

This means we can now move on and start to adapt our previous exercises to display on mobile devices. Before we do so, there is one little tip I want to quickly run through: working out the available viewport area. Yes, I know you might well be asking what this has to do with the Speech APIs, but there is a good reason for this; bear with me, and I will explain all.

Determining space available

Anyone who spends time designing for mobile will no doubt be aware of the constraints in space available on pages – it's that age-old question of what to offer when the viewport area is so small.

This is particularly important when using the Speech APIs – we have to be mindful of how much space is needed to display elements such as the input field needed for the Speech Synthesis API, or the space needed to display transcribed text when using the Speech Recognition API.

This is where working out the viewport area using code could be of help – not just to establish how much space we have in code, but to also set Chrome's responsive view to fit your cell phone's available space. Let's see what this means in reality and how they both can help the Speech APIs, in more detail.

Setting available space using code

As space will be of a premium, we need to work out just how much space we can afford to use. Rather than try to guess values or work out by trial and error, we can get the values automatically using JavaScript.

This is great for testing on multiple devices, so we can get a feel for how much space we will have to play with, when it comes to laying out the elements for the Speech APIs. To do this, you can use the function I've set up in a CodePen at https://codepen.io/alexlibby/pen/MWYVBGJ, for this purpose.

As an aside, don't forget to add in the right meta tags too – you will need something like this: `<meta name="viewport" content="width=device-width, initial-scale=1.0">`

Configuring Chrome's Responsive Mode

In addition, we can use these values to help set up Chrome's Responsive Mode (or Mobile Emulation mode, as it is officially called). It goes without saying that no two cellphones will have the same space or viewport, so to help with this, we can set up our own custom areas. Let's take a look at how in our next exercise.

SETTING UP VIEWPORTS IN CHROME

This next exercise can be done either in Chrome for mobile or desktop if you want to practice the steps; ultimately you will need to set it in Chrome to get the best effect during testing. We can set up a viewport using these steps:

1. Fire up Chrome, and browse to a site – I'll assume we'll use CodePen, which is great for testing responsive views.

2. Next, we need to enable Responsive Mode, which we can do using Ctrl+Shift+I (Windows and Linux) or Cmd+Shift+I (Mac).

3. At the top of the resized page will be an option to choose a different viewport; it will look something akin to the screenshot shown in Figure 3-6.

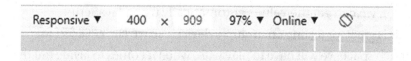

Figure 3-6. *Chrome's Responsive Mode option*

4. Click the drop-down on the left, and select Edit ➤ Add custom device...

5. In the Device Name field, enter the make and model of your cell phone or chosen mobile device.

6. Below this are three fields – enter the width in the left and height in the middle, and leave the right field unchanged. Make sure Usage agent string is set to Mobile.

7. Hit Add. You will now be able to set this as your chosen viewport area when testing the Speech APIs.

This is just one small area to consider when working with the Speech APIs - we've only touched on two methods here and not explored some of the quirks around the values returned. However, it should give you a nice heads-up in terms of what space you will likely have, so that you can set up a simple way to allocate space and test features, without having to work entirely on a mobile device or use an external service such as BrowserStack.

This isn't to say we should ignore services such as BrowserStack, which perform a useful function – it's intended that this little trick would work during development, prior to completing proper testing!

Okay, let's get back on track with the APIs. Now that we have a quick and dirty way to work out available viewport areas, it's time we got stuck into the APIs and see how they work on mobile devices! I suspect you might be thinking that we have to make lots of changes, right? If not to the APIs themselves, at least to the styling, surely...?

Well, I hate to disappoint, but the answer is no – if we're careful about our styling, then we shouldn't need more than just a handful of tweaks. Let's put this theory to the test and see how it works by adapting two CodePen demos from earlier in the book.

Implementing the Speech Synthesis API

Remember this demo (displayed in Figure 3-7) from way back in Chapter 1?

Figure 3-7. *Our original Speech Synthesis API demo from Chapter 1*

This was a simple demo to show off how we can implement the Speech Synthesis – it allowed us to enter any text we wish into the input field and then adjust settings such as the voice and pitch, before asking the computer to render the text as speech.

Hopefully you will still have a version saved as a Pen from Chapter 1 – do you? If not, I would recommend you go set it up again using the code from the readingback demo; you will need it for later demos too!

Assuming you have either set it up again or have the link from the version you created earlier, try running it in Chrome for mobile on your cell phone. If you enter something into the input field, then tap on Speak; you should find Chrome will render it back as speech.

Trouble is the UI doesn't look that great, does it? It's the same code as before, but this time we need to scroll back and forth – a sure-fire way of putting people off! Ironically this whole setup is one of the reasons why I would advocate working solely with Chrome, at least for the immediate future. We don't need to touch any of the JavaScript required for the Speech Synthesis API, but can instead focus on tweaking our markup and styling to better fit the available space. To see what I mean, let's put this to the test and adapt that demo to better fit your cell phone, as part of the next exercise.

Adapting design for mobile

For this next exercise, we will reuse a demo from way back in Chapter 1 (I know, it wasn't that long ago, although it may seem otherwise!). We'll implement some tweaks to ensure it better fits the limited space available while making sure that the functionality still operates as expected. Ready to dive in and take a look?

SPEAKING ON A MOBILE

Let's go ahead and update our demo, using these steps:

1. We'll begin by browsing to CodePen at `https://codepen.io` and then logging in with the same account details you used back in Chapter 1.

2. Switch to the HTML pane. Then change the `<h1>` tags around the page title to `<h3>`.

3. Next, change to the CSS pane, and add in the following CSS alterations at the bottom of that pane:

    ```
    /* ADAPTATIONS FOR MOBILE */
    h3 { margin: 0; }
    #page-wrapper { width: 350px; margin: 13px auto;
    padding: 5px 16px; }
    #voice { vertical-align: super; width: 320px;
    margin-left: -3px; }
    button { width: 28%; }
    input[type="text"] { padding: 2px 5px; font-size:
    16px; }
    ```

4. Save the Pen. If all is well, we should see our demo's styling has been updated; we can see evidence of this in the screenshot in Figure 3-8.

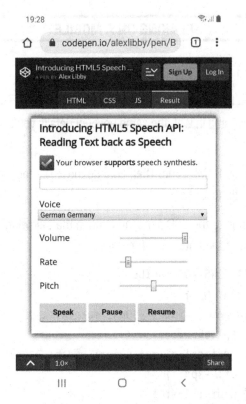

Figure 3-8. *Our updated Speech Synthesis API, running on a cell phone*

Although this is something of a simplistic demo, it shows that if we're brave enough to work solely on Chrome, then there should be no need to change the core functionality that pertains to the Speech Synthesis API! All we had to do was tweak some of the styles to allow the visual UI to better fit the available space, while the core JavaScript code remained unchanged from the original demo.

There is one small thing though – is that...*Germany* I see selected as our default voice? It is indeed; a quirk of using Speech Synthesis API in a mobile device means that you may find you get a different voice selected as the default, in comparison to what you might see on a standard desktop. If we tap on the drop-down, we can see that Germany is indeed the default, as indicated in Figure 3-9.

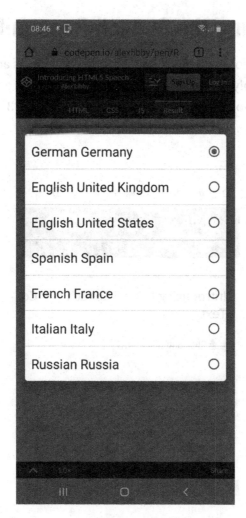

Figure 3-9. *The default voice is different on a mobile...*

At this point, I'll bet some of you may be asking, "What about the Speech Recognition API?" Assuming we chose to work with just Chrome, what kind of changes would we need to do here? These are good questions, and I'm happy to report that we can apply the same principles here, when it comes to updating our code. To see what I mean, let's dive in and take a look at those changes, in more detail.

Implementing the Speech Recognition API

Although support for the Speech Recognition API isn't as advanced, we can absolutely apply the same changes. If we were to run a version of the original demo in Google Chrome on a cell phone, Figure 3-10 shows what this would look like.

Figure 3-10. *Our original Speech Recognition demo on a cell phone*

Not great, huh? Try tapping on the Click and talk to me! button, and say something into the phone's microphone. It will render something on screen, but it's not easy to read, right? The great thing though is that we only need to make minimal changes to our styling, in order for this demo to work better. Our next exercise will explore what these changes are, in more detail.

Adapting for mobile use

In the previous exercise we've just completed, we saw how to adapt our design to allow the Speech Synthesis API to better fit the available space and that we didn't have to change any of the JavaScript code used to create the feature. The great thing is that we can use the same principles for the Speech Recognition API too. Let's explore what this means in the form of our next exercise.

RECOGNIZING SPEECH ON A MOBILE

Okay, let's crack on by following these steps:

1. We'll begin by browsing to CodePen at `https://codepen.io` and then logging in with the same account details you used back in Chapter 1.

2. Switch to the HTML pane and then change the `<h1>` tags around the page title to `<h3>`.

3. Next, change to the CSS pane, and add in the following CSS alterations at the bottom of that pane:

```
/* ADAPTATIONS FOR MOBILE */
h3 { margin: 0 0 20px 0; }

#page-wrapper { width: 350px; }

.voice { float: right; margin-top: 5px; }

.response { padding-left: 0px; margin-top: 0px;
height: inherit; }

.output_log { font-size: 20px; margin-top: 5px; }
```

4. Save the Pen. If all is well, we should see our demo's styling has been updated; we can see evidence of this in Figure 3-11 overleaf, where spoken words have already been rendered and the API turned off due to inactivity.

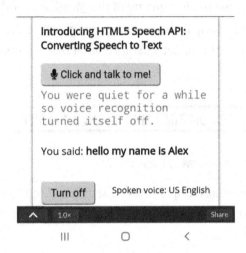

Figure 3-11. *Recognizing speech on a mobile, with the API*

Hold on a moment. Some of those selectors look familiar, right? Yes, that is indeed correct, although if you look closely at the properties defined within, there are some differences.

I'm not sure if this was by pure chance or design (the desktop versions came first, honest!), but it shows that even though support for both APIs is not at parity across browsers, the basic JavaScript code has remained untouched in both instances.

It does make the assumption though that we work solely with Chrome – while some of you may be concerned that this appears to limit our options, it's worth bearing in mind that the APIs (at the time of writing) are still in something of a state of flux, even though they do operate fairly well at this stage. It's perfectly acceptable to limit features at this stage, on the basis that we're offering a new feature and that we can more easily monitor take-up of our new feature.

Okay, let's move on. We've covered both APIs in isolation, but what about putting them together? No problem, this is something we'll do more of in the projects later in this book, but for now, let's take a look at how this might work when coding for a mobile environment.

Putting it together: A practical example

Throughout this chapter, we've seen how the APIs work on mobile devices, and that if we're happy to work just with Chrome, this can reduce the amount of JavaScript changes we need to make!

It's time to bring both APIs together for one more demo in this chapter – for this, we're going to set up a little app that will tell us the time in one of my favorite cities, Copenhagen. For this demo, we'll make use of both APIs – the Speech Recognition API to ask it to tell us the time and the Speech Synthesis API to give us the response. Let's get stuck in and take a look at setting up our demo in more detail.

If you want to use a different city, then you will need to change the time zone – Wikipedia has an extensive list of suitable time zones, at `https://en.wikipedia.org/wiki/List_of_tz_database_time_zones`.

GETTING TIME

To create our demo, follow these steps:

1. We'll begin by extracting a copy of the `practicalexample` folder from the code download and saving it to our project area.

2. Next, go ahead and browse to CodePen at `https://codepen.io` and then log in with the same account details you used back in Chapter 1.

3. On the left, choose Create ➤ Pen.

4. We need to add in a couple of external libraries to help with the demo – for this, click Settings ➤ CSS and then add in these two links in the slots at the bottom of the dialog box:

    ```
    https://use.fontawesome.com/releases/v5.0.8/
    css/fontawesome.css
    ```

    ```
    https://use.fontawesome.com/releases/v5.0.8/
    css/solid.css
    ```

5. Next, click JavaScript in the same dialog box – this time, add in this link, which will help with getting the right time in our chosen city:

    ```
    https://cdn.jsdelivr.net/npm/luxon@1.21.3/
    build/global/luxon.min.js
    ```

6. Hit Save and Close. Then copy and paste the contents of JS.txt into the JS pane of our Pen.

7. Next, open a copy of the code from HTML.txt and paste the contents into the HTML pane of our Pen.

8. Go ahead and do the same thing for the CSS.txt file, pasting it into the CSS pane.

Make sure you hit the Save button or press Ctrl+S (or Cmd+S) to save your work!

---

9. Once saved, we can test the results – for this, go ahead and browse to your CodePen demo from your cell phone, then make sure you have Editor View displayed, and hit the Console button.

10. We don't need to do anything. If your browser supports either API, then we will see confirmation of this in the CodePen console, as shown in Figure 3-12.

**Introducing HTML5 Speech API:
Reading Text back as Speech**

☑ Your browser **supports** speech synthesis.

Voice

Microsoft Hazel Desktop - English (Great Britain) ▼

🎤 Click and talk to me!

You were quiet for a while
so voice recognition turned
itself off.

The time in Copenhagen is 09:37

You said:
what's the time in Copenhagen

Spoken voice: US English

Figure 3-12. *Our practical example in action*

In this last exercise, we've brought together the code from two earlier demos and adapted the UI to allow us to get and display the time. Although the code should by now begin to be more familiar, it's worth taking a moment to go through the code in more detail, to see how the APIs can work together in a mobile environment.

Dissecting the code in detail

Take another look at the JavaScript we've used in this demo – granted there is a fair chunk involved, but most of it is not new. It was lifted from two previous demos we created earlier in the book. The same applies to the CSS and markup used; although we've removed some of the elements that were not needed (such as the input field), the rest is standard HTML, which came straight from the same two demos.

The real magic though is in the JavaScript we've used – we kick off by defining a number of variables to cache elements, before checking our browser does indeed support the Synthesis API. Ideally, we would have included a check here for the Recognition API too, but given that we're using Chrome, we would get the same positive response here too.

Next up comes the same `loadVoices()` function that we've used before; this gets the available voices from the browser and loads them into the drop-down box. We then have the `onerror` event to trap for any issues; this will display anything in the console log area. We then round out the first part of this demo with the `speak()` function, which we created in an earlier demo and reused in our practical example.

The second half of this code block is for the Speech Recognition API; the first function is a new one that uses the Luxon time library to get the current time in our chosen city (in this instance, Copenhagen). We set the initial time value using `luxon.DateTime.local()`, before switching the time zone to Copenhagen and reformatting the time accordingly.

We then move onto defining an instance of the Speech Recognition API as an object, before assigning a number of properties such as whether to display `interimResults`, have more than one alternative, or set the API to run `continuously`.

Next up comes the click event handler – although our code will automatically fire off the microphone, we still need this to start the Recognition API, as well as set the language (here it is set to `en-GB`, but we could set it to any appropriate value if needed). We then have the same event handlers as before, for `speechstart`, `speechend`, `onspeechend`, and `error`. The only changed handler is `result` – most of it stays the same, but we've added a block to split the transcribed text, before determining if we've spoken the word "Copenhagen" and responding accordingly if this is the case.

Working with mobile: An epilog

The demos we've built throughout this chapter are very straightforward – one might be forgiven for thinking that life is easy, and that implementing the APIs is a doddle! But things are not always as they seem; before we move onto the next chapter, I want to leave you with a thought.

When researching for this book, my original intention was to create a voice-controlled video player that worked on mobile – after all, we did one for desktop, so it should be just a matter of tweaking styles, right? Well, the answer is yes – and perhaps no.

Assembling the demo was very easy – most of it had been done earlier, so I reused the code for this and turned off some of the options around shutting down the service. However, it seems there may be differences in how Speech Recognition works on the mobile – yes, Chrome is indeed supported, but I suspect that not every browser (that supports the APIs) offers the same *consistent level* of support! I could play the video demo on my cell phone, but it would stop the recognition service very quickly or potentially throw a network error.

I think this might be down to how CodePen works and that it frequently refreshes – the demo works fine on desktop, so pointing to a potential issue somewhere in the environment! It's something to bear in mind – you will need to test your solutions thoroughly to ensure they work as expected for customers.

You can see the video demo I created in CodePen, at `https://codepen.io/alexlibby/pen/xxbpOBN`; if you need a sample video, try downloading one from `https://file-examples.com/index.php/sample-video-files/sample-mp4-files/`.

Summary

Mention the words "working with mobile," and you are likely to send a shudder down the spine of any developer – it's hard enough working across desktop as it is, without the added extra of a mobile platform! The Speech APIs though are one area where functionality is less of a problem. Over the course of this chapter, we've explored how we can adapt existing code to work on mobile devices, assuming we are happy to limit the exposure based on the type of browser used. We've covered some important topics throughout this chapter, so let's take a breather and review what we've learned.

We kicked off by examining the current level of support for both the Speech Synthesis and Recognition APIs, before understanding how limiting exposure to Chrome might make sense in the short term. We then covered how to determine if your chosen mobile browser does indeed support the APIs, before exploring a quick tip to work out the available on-screen space and how this is important for the APIs.

Next up, we took two original demos (one for each API) and converted them to work on the mobile platform, before understanding what changes we had to make to get them operational. We then rounded out the chapter with a look at updating a more practical example, before finishing with some final thoughts on using mobile devices with the API.

Phew! Theory is now over. Time for some fun! It's at this point where we get to start playing with some example projects. How about using your voice to find a nearby restaurant, ask for the time, or even pay for products? These are just three of the tricks we will cover as part of the upcoming projects; we'll kick off with that all-important task of giving feedback and just how we can put a new spin on an age-old problem... Intrigued? Stay with me, as I feed back just how we can use the APIs (yes, pun most definitely intended!) in the next chapter.

CHAPTER 4

Combining the APIs: Building a Chatbot

Over the course of the last few chapters, we've explored the Speech API in detail and used it to set up some basic examples of speech capabilities. This is only the start though – there is so much more we can do! Making use of the APIs opens up a host of innovative ideas for us to explore, and that's before we even personalize the functionality we offer to customers.

Over the course of the remainder of this book, we're going to put the APIs to good use to build various projects that showcase how we might add speech capabilities. This will range from features such as leaving vocal feedback through to automating parts of the checkout process. For now though, we're going to combine both APIs together to build a simple chatbot that will respond to some basic phrases and display the results on screen. As I am sure someone once said, we have to start somewhere, so there's no better place than to set the scene and explore how using chatbots can be beneficial to us.

Why use a chatbot?

So why would we want to use a chatbot? What makes them so special?

Traditionally companies have customer service teams who might deal with all manner of different requests – this could be from arranging refunds to helping with diagnosing issues on your Internet access.

© Alex Libby 2020
A. Libby, *Introducing the HTML5 Web Speech API*,
https://doi.org/10.1007/978-1-4842-5735-7_4

This becomes an expensive use of resources, particularly when customers can frequently ask the same type of question! With care, we can create a chatbot to handle some of these questions for us, which helps free up staff for more complex queries that require human intervention.

Is this a good thing? Well, yes – and no. Chatbots can be set up in such a way as to allow contextual-based conversation for certain tasks; while this frees up staff for more complex requests, it can equally cause problems if the chatbot hasn't been configured for the optimal experience! In a sense, we should place greater emphasis on making the customer feel special, if we decide to use bots – they can perform mundane tasks well, but we will be seen as being cheap and put customers off, if they feel that our use of bots is anything less than perfect. This is particularly important with heavyweights such as Gartner predicting that 30% of browsing will be done by users using screenless devices by 2020. It means that the use of chatbots will increase, particularly in the social media arena – after all, where is it most likely to find people, particularly if they need to complain about poor service?

Things to consider when building a chatbot

Okay, so we've decided we have a need to build something, but what should it be and whom should it serve?

These are good questions; building a bot shouldn't be seen as an excuse to save money, but something that can help augment existing human staff and allow them to take on more demanding or complex queries. It doesn't matter which niche we are considering though. There are a handful of best practices we should consider as some of the first steps to building a bot:

- Would your customers or users want to be served only by real humans?

- Is your use case better served by an alternate channel – for example, a web site or a native application?

- How will you let the end user know they're chatting with a bot or a live agent? The conversation may start with the former, but there could be occasions where they need to be handed off to a live agent.

- How many tasks does the bot need to handle? Your bot might collect a variety of information but ideally should be responsible for handling one or two items per flow – it is a case of quality over quantity!

- How much of an impact would bots make for your environment – are the tasks such that automating just a handful provides a real benefit for your company, or could it be a case of the return doesn't justify the effort?

At this point, you might be right for thinking that we've diverged a little from our main topic of using the Speech API, but there is a good reason for this: there is little point in adding speech capabilities if the basic dialog is less than optimal! It's important to consider not just topics such as the voice to use and whether they can choose which to use, but also that the conversation seems natural and includes the right phrases and that our responses match the kind of phrases customers would use when interacting with our chatbot.

Downsides to bots

Creating a bot, and particularly one that can speak, is good, but they can suffer from one potential drawback – they can only simulate human interaction. A bot is only as good as its configuration; functionally it may be perfect, but if the phrases and terms used are badly chosen, then this will only serve to put off humans!

It doesn't matter if they can speak – indeed, adding speech capabilities will only serve to frustrate customers even more if their conversation isn't natural. This will be particularly felt by anyone who relies on vocal interaction to complete tasks online. It means that as part of creating something using the Speech APIs we're exploring in this book, we absolutely need to give thought to topics such as the right voice to use, plus the correct terminology or phrasing when configuring our bot.

This is one area where it pays to perform lots of research – the more you can undertake, the better! As part of this, it's important to appreciate the types of bots that are available, as this will have an impact not only on how we build them but also when setting up their speech capabilities. Bots come in all manner of guises, but can be broadly separated into two different types. Let's take a look at each in turn and how they stack up against each other in more detail.

Different types of chatbots

To help understand and minimize the drawbacks of using bots, we can broadly categorize them into two distinct groups: **transactional** (or stateless) and **conversational** (stateful). What does this mean for us? Well, there are some key differences:

- Transactional or stateless bots don't require history – each request is treated as discrete, and the bot only needs to understand the user's request to take action. Transactional bots are great for automating quick tasks, where we're expecting simple outcomes, such as retrieving a current Internet bandwidth usage.

- Conversational or stateful bots rely on history and information collection to complete tasks. In this instance, bots may ask questions, parse the response, and determine the next course of action based on the response from the user. This type of bot is perfect for automating longer, more complex tasks that have multiple possible outcomes, but which can be anticipated during construction.

With this in mind, let's turn this into something more practical. We've already indicated that each bot type is better suited to certain tasks; some examples of what these tasks would look like are shown in Table 4-1.

Table 4-1. *Some practical examples of bot types*

Type of bot	Some practical examples of usage
Transactional bots	Transactional bots are not able to remember previous interactions with the user and can't maintain extended dialog with the user: • Alexa turning the lights off, playing a song, or arming/disarming house alarms • Confirming an appointment over SMS • Google Assistant checking and reporting the weather
Conversational bots	Conversational bots maintain the state of the conversation and carry information between turns of the conversation: • Making a reservation at a restaurant – the bot needs to know the size of the party, the reservation time, and seating preferences to make a valid reservation • Conducting a multiple-question survey • Interviewing users to report issues

Phew! We're almost at a point where we will start to build ours. I promise! I know it seems like we've covered a lot of theory, but it's important: adding speech capabilities is only half the battle. The deciding factor (to use a battle term?) is what we need to do to ensure that when our bot talks, it comes across as natural and works as expected for both our customers and our initial requirements.

If you would like to delve more into the theory behind building chatbots, there is a great article on the *Chatbots Magazine* web site, at `https://chatbotsmagazine.com/how-to-develop-a-chatbot-from-scratch-62bed1adab8c`.

Okay, we're finally done with the theory. Let's move onto more practical matters! We're going to construct a simple example that renders responses both verbally and visually on screen; as with any project, let's begin by setting the background to what we will be constructing in this chapter.

Setting the background

A friend of mine sent me an email, with a rather intriguing request:

> *"Hey Alex, you know I run a small online outfit selling Raspberry Pi kit, right? Well, I would really like to add something to help my customers find kit easier! I know you love experimenting with stuff. Fancy giving me a hand to create something? I'm keen to make it innovative if I can. Any ideas?"*

Okay, I confess: that was a fictitious friend, but that aside, this is just the kind of thing I love doing! Had this been a real request though, my immediate answer would be to create a chatbot, where we can add in speech capabilities. For the purposes of this book, we'll keep this simple and limit it to searching for different Raspberry Pi version 4 boards. The same principles could be used to search for other related products (we'll touch more on this toward the end of the chapter).

The product we will build is a chatbot for my fictitious friend Hazel (yes, the name should be familiar from earlier demos), who runs a company called PiShack. Our demo will be largely text-based, but include some simple elements such as displaying images and basic HTML markup within our conversation. The chatbot will be used to find the Raspberry 4 board products, then display the chosen one on screen, and provide a link and basic stock information to the customer.

Keeping things in scope

As with any project, we need to define the parameters of what should be included, to help keep things on track.

Thankfully this will be very straightforward for our demo; we'll have a basic conversation that leads the customer to choose from one of three board types. Based on what they select, we will then display an image for that board type, along with a part number and back stock availability. We will then simulate showing a link to a fictitious product page; for this demo, we won't include the product page. Suffice to say, this could be linked to any page within an existing project, as this will just be a standard link – the exact one can be generated, depending on the response from our customer.

Okay, with this in mind, let's crack on. Now that we've set the scene, we need to architect the various elements of our demo, so we can see how they will come together in more detail.

Architecting our demo

For our demo, I've chosen to keep things simple, with an emphasis on not using extra tools unless necessary. There are several reasons for this: the primary one is that introducing dependencies for our chatbot could introduce software that is incompatible with other elements within our project.

There are dozens of different chatbot libraries available, but the one I've decided to use for this project is RiveScript. Available from `https://www.rivescript.com/`, it's an open source scripting language, with a host of different interpreters for languages such as Python, Go, or, in our case,

JavaScript. Although this is something of a personal choice, there are several benefits from using this library:

- It (the interpreter, not the library) is written in pure JavaScript, so dependencies are minimal; a version is available to run under Node.js if desired, although this isn't necessary for simple use.

- Its syntax is really easy to learn – you can put together a basic configuration file very quickly, leaving you more time to fine-tune the triggers and responses for interacting with the chatbot.

- It's not produced by a large commercial company that requires you to edit XML files or complex configurations online – all you need is a text editor and your imagination!

- It's open source, so can be adapted if needed; if you have an issue, then other developers may be able to help provide fixes, or you can adapt it to your own needs if desired.

- It can be hosted on a Content Delivery Network (or CDN) link for speedy access from a local point; content delivered in this manner will also be cached, which makes it faster. If needed, we can also provide a local fallback to cover if the CDN link is nonoperational.

At this point, it's worth asking one question: what other options could I use? There are dozens out there, but many rely on complex APIs or have to be managed online. This isn't necessarily a bad thing, but it does add an extra layer of complexity when starting out with chatbots, and particularly with the Web Speech APIs! That aside, let's take a moment to cover off some of the alternatives that may be of interest, either now or in the future, in more detail.

Alternative tools available

When researching for this book, I came across dozens of different tools and libraries that offer the ability to construct chatbots – many of these I elected not to use for the demo we're about to build, primarily because they hadn't been updated for some time, involved complex setups, had to be set up online, or were tied into a proprietary offering which would make it difficult to move away from if circumstances changed.

This said, I did come across some interesting examples which were not so complex to set up and could be worth checking out:

- Wit.ai – available from `https://wit.ai/`, this Facebook-owned platform is open source and is easy to set up and use. It has various integrations available, including for Node.js, so will work fine with the Speech Recognition and Synthesis APIs.

- BotUI – this is a simple and easy-to-use framework available from `https://botui.org/`; its structure for progressing through each trigger/response is a little more rigid than RiveScript and requires each pair to be built into the main code, rather than in a configuration file.

- Botpress – if you've spent any time developing code for CMS systems, then you will have no doubt heard of WordPress. Hosted at `https://botpress.io/`, Botpress describes itself as the "WordPress of Chatbots," where anyone can create and reuse modules for chatbots. It's a mixed offering – while primarily being open source, it also has licensing available for more enterprise-level needs, so it will be a good way to advance in the future. This library also has a visual editor which makes it easy to build the initial chatbot triggers and responses, before integrating with something like Node.js.

The important thing to note is that integrating the Speech APIs into a chatbot is unlikely to be a simple matter of "flicking a switch" or setting a configuration parameter. Any such integration will require effort – how much will depend on the chatbot library we use!

Okay, the next step in getting set up is adding syntax highlighting support for our text editor. RiveScript offers plugins for some of the more popular ones such as Sublime Text or Atom. Let's quickly cover this off, before moving onto more pressing matters!

If you use a more specialist editor or one of the ones not listed at `https://www.rivescript.com/plugins#text-editors`, then feel free to skip ahead to the next section; this won't affect how the demo operates.

Adding text editor support

Although we can use pretty much any syntax highlighter when editing RiveScript files (they are just plain text files, after all), adding a dedicated one will absolutely help with making your code easier to read.

RiveScript offers several for the more popular editors, at `https://www.rivescript.com/plugins#text-editors`; this includes Atom, Sublime Text, and Emacs. Figure 4-1 shows an example of how code will look when run in Atom with the plugin installed (shown overleaf).

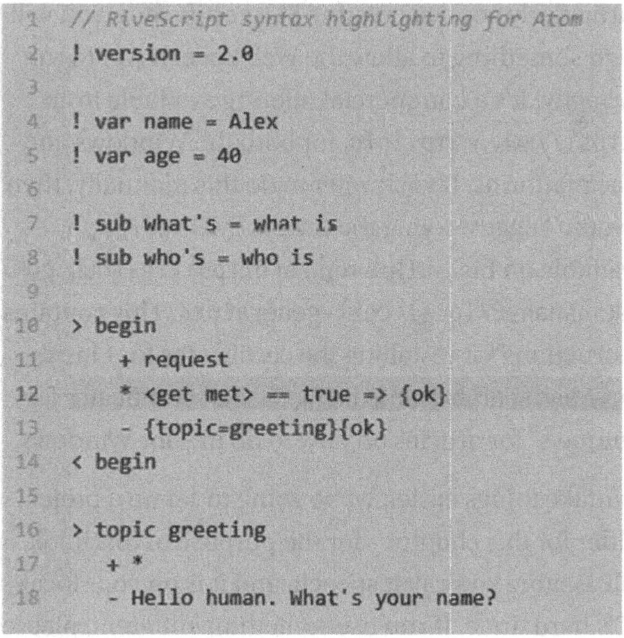

```
1   // RiveScript syntax highlighting for Atom
2   ! version = 2.0
3
4   ! var name = Alex
5   ! var age = 40
6
7   ! sub what's = what is
8   ! sub who's = who is
9
10  > begin
11      + request
12      * <get met> == true => {ok}
13      - {topic=greeting}{ok}
14  < begin
15
16  > topic greeting
17      + *
18      - Hello human. What's your name?
```

Figure 4-1. *A screenshot of RiveScript syntax in a text editor*

As I am sure you will agree, it certainly helps with reading (and subsequently understanding) the code! Assuming you've installed a suitable syntax highlighter (and screenshots later in this chapter will show examples from within Sublime Text), let's move on and complete the rest of the preparation process.

Getting tools in place

For our next project, we're going to need to avail ourselves of a few additional tools to help with development and running. Let's take a look at what we need:

- We'll need some web space which has been secured using HTTPS access – you can use web space on a test server or install a local web server such as MAMP PRO for this purpose. This web server is

particularly good at creating SSL certificates; you will
need something to allow the Web Speech API to run
correctly! It's a commercial offering available from
`https://www.mamp.info`, for both the Windows and
Mac platforms. If you prefer to do this manually, then
I would suggest trying the scripts by Daksh Shah,
available on his GitHub repo at `https://github.com/
dakshshah96/local-cert-generator/`. This contains
instructions for installing the certificates for Linux
and Mac; search online using "install certificates for
windows" for articles on how to do this for Windows.

- To make things easier, we're going to set up a project
folder for this chapter – for the purpose of this book, I
will assume you call it speech, and it is on your local
PC's hard drive. If you use something different, please
adapt steps in the demo to suit.

- The main tool we will use for building our chatbot is
the RiveScript library, available from `https://www.
rivescript.com/`. This is a JavaScript-based language
for writing chatbots, which comes in a variety of different
interfaces and is easy to learn. The library comes in CDN
format or can be installed using Node.js – to keep things
simple, we'll use the former during our demo.

Note   For the purposes of this demo, I will assume the project area
is set to work under `https://speech/`; if yours is different or you
prefer to continue using CodePen, then the demos will work in this
environment; using a local setup will give you more control.

Okay, with these three admin tasks in place, let's move on and make a start with constructing our demo!

Building our chatbot

Our demo will contain a fair amount of code, so we're going to put it together over the course of two exercises; it will give you a chance to take a breather in between before we continue with the second part. The second part will take care of configuring the chatbot with our chosen questions and answers; before we get there, let's first take a look at setting up the functionality for our chatbot.

BUILDING THE CHATBOT, PART 1: THE FUNCTIONALITY

The first step in our demo is to get hold of the latest copy of RiveScript – it's available from `https://www.rivescript.com`. For the purposes of this exercise, we'll use the CDN version available from `unpkg.com`, which is already set up in the HTML markup file.

There is a version also available for Node.js – details are listed at `https://www.rivescript.com/interpreters#js`.

Let's crack on with building the first part of our demo:

1. We'll begin by extracting a copy of the `chatbot` folder from the code download that accompanies this book; save it to the root of our project area.

2. Inside this folder, create a new file in the `js` subfolder – save this as `script.js`.

3. We'll use this to set up the functionality for our chatbot, for which we will have a fair chunk of code. Don't worry – we will go through it block by block! We'll start first by declaring the global variables that we will use throughout the demo, along with initiating an instance of RiveScript:

```
let bot = new RiveScript();
```

```
const message_container = document.querySelector
('.messages');
const form = document.querySelector('form');
const input_box = document.querySelector('input');
const question = document.querySelector('#help');
const voiceSelect = document.getElementById('voice');
```

4. Next, miss a line and then add in the following functions and function call – these take care of loading the voices into our demo:

```
function loadVoices() {
  var voices = window.speechSynthesis.getVoices();

  voices.forEach(function(voice, i) {
    var option = document.createElement('option');
    option.value = voice.name;
    option.innerHTML = voice.name;
    voiceSelect.appendChild(option);
  });
}

loadVoices();

// Chrome loads voices asynchronously.
window.speechSynthesis.onvoiceschanged = function(e) {
  loadVoices();
};
```

5. The next two functions complete the first part of our demo –
    the first looks after basic error handling, while the second is
    responsible for vocalizing content when requested. Add in the
    code below the previous step, leaving a blank line in between:

```
window.speechSynthesis.onerror = function(event) {
   console.log('Speech recognition error detected:
   ' + event.error);
   console.log('Additional information: ' + event.
   message);
};

function speak(text) {
   var msg = new SpeechSynthesisUtterance();
   msg.text = text;

   if (voiceSelect.value) {
      msg.voice = speechSynthesis.getVoices().
      filter(function(voice) {
         return voice.name == voiceSelect.value;
      })[0];
   }

   speechSynthesis.speak(msg);
}
```

6. At this point, we move onto setting up and configuring our
    chatbot – we start with declaring a constant for importing our
    triggers and responses. This next line needs to go in after the
    speak() function, leaving a blank line in between:

```
const brains = [ './js/brain.rive' ];
```

7. Next, go ahead and add in this event handler – this manages the submission of each question from anyone using the chatbot:

```
form.addEventListener('submit', (e) => {
  e.preventDefault();
  selfReply(input_box.value);
  input_box.value = ";
});
```

8. We now need to render each question (or trigger) and the appropriate response on screen – this is the responsibility of the next two functions:

```
function botReply(message){
  message_container.innerHTML += `<div
class="bot">${message}</div>`;
  location.href = '#edge';
}
```

```
function selfReply(message){
  var response;

  response = message.toLowerCase().replace(/
[.,\/#!$%\^&\*;:{}=\-_`~()]/g,"");
  message_container.innerHTML += `<div
class="self">${message}</div>`;
  location.href = '#edge';

  bot.reply("local-user", response).then
(function(reply) {
    botReply(reply);
    speak(reply);
  });
}
```

9. We're almost at the end of the script part of this demo; we have two more functions and an event handler to add in. Leave a line blank after the previous step and then add in the following:

```
function botReady(){
  bot.sortReplies();
  botReply('Hello, my name is David. How can I be of help?');
}

function botNotReady(err){
  console.log("An error has occurred.", err);
}

question.addEventListener("click", function() {
  speak("hello. my name is David. How can I be of
help?");
  bot.loadFile(brains + "?" + parseInt(Math.random()
* 100000)).then(botReady).catch(botNotReady);
});
```

10. At this point, go ahead and save the file – we can minimize it
    for now, while we move onto the next part of this demo.

At this stage, we have a semi-complete demo – if we run it now though, it won't do a great deal! The reason for this is that we still have one part remaining to add in: the questions and answers for our chatbot. Although setting up this part is relatively straightforward, there is still a fair amount of code to go through. Let's dive in and take a look in detail.

Configuring our chatbot

To get our chatbot operational, we'll be making use of the RiveScript library; it comes with different interpreters for various languages, such as Python, Go, or JavaScript.

It's an easy language to learn, although it does have one quirk that takes a little getting used to: all of the questions that we preconfigure our bot with must be in lowercase! Thankfully this isn't an issue when it comes to displaying them on screen; I will explain more at the end of this next demo, but let's focus on getting our chatbot configured and ready for use.

107

BUILDING THE CHATBOT, PART 2: THE FUNCTIONALITY

Let's complete our demo by adding in the missing questions and answers for our chatbot. We'll work through adding in each block, but to help with editing, I will also include screenshots at various points, so you can check progress:

1. First go ahead and create a blank file, saving it as `brain.rive` in the `js` subfolder of the chatbot folder we created in the first part of this demo.

2. At the top of the file, go ahead and add in this line – this forces the RiveScript compiler to work with version 2.0 of the RiveScript specification:

   ```
   ! version = 2.0
   ```

3. Our file contains a simple RiveScript function, which we use to ensure that the name of our customer is kept in title case (more on this later in this chapter). Leave a line and then add in the following code:

   ```
   > object keepname javascript
     var newName
     for (var i = 0; i < args.length; i++) {
       newName = args[i]
     }

     return newName.charAt(0).toUpperCase() + newName.slice(1)
   < object
   ```

4. Next up, we start adding in each of the statements (which come in pairs – a question and answer). You will notice that each starts with either a + or –; the former is the question or trigger, and – designates a response. Go ahead and add in the first one, where the customer may say hello to the bot and receives an appropriate response:

```
+ hello
- hello, what is your name?
```

5. The next triplet of statements is a little more complex – this time, the customer gives their name and says what they are looking for:

```
+ hi my name is * im looking for a raspberry pi 4
- <set name=<star>>Nice to meet you, <call>keepname
<star></call>. No problem, I have 3 available. Are you
looking for a particular version?
- <set name=<star>>Nice meeting you, <call>keepname
<star></call>. No problem, I have 3 available. Are you
looking for a particular version?
```

At this point, if all is well, we should have the following code in our brain.rive file, as indicated in Figure 4-2.

```
1   ! version = 2.0
2
3   > object keepname javascript
4       var newName
5       for (var i = 0; i < args.length; i++) {
6           newName = args[i]
7       }
8
9       return newName.charAt(0).toUpperCase() + newName.slice(1)
10  < object
11
12  + hello
13  - hello, what is your name?
14
15  + hi my name is * im looking for a raspberry pi 4
16  - <set name=<star>>Nice to meet you, <call>keepname <star></call>. No
    problem, I have 3 available. Are you looking for a particular version?
17  - <set name=<star>>Nice meeting you, <call>keepname <star></call>. No
    problem, I have 3 available. Are you looking for a particular version?
18
```

Figure 4-2. *The first part of our brain.rive file*

Let's continue with the next part:

6. The next question in the list contains a conditional statement –
   this time, we're asking which version the customer prefers to
   look at:

   ```
   + * versions do you have available
   - I have ones that come with 1 gigabyte 2 gigabyte
   or 4 gigabyte RAM. Which would you prefer?
   ```

7. In this next pair of statements, the customer confirms which
   version they want to see; we display an appropriate image of
   that product:

   ```
   + i would prefer the (1|2|4) gigabyte version
   - <set piversion=<star>>Excellent, here is a picture:
   <img src="img/<star>.webp">
   ```

Let's pause for a second. If all is well, Figure 4-3 shows the code we should
now have as the next part of our `brain.rive` file.

```
15   + hi my name is * im looking for a raspberry pi 4
16   - <set name=<star>>Nice to meet you, <call>keepname <star></call>. No
     problem, I have 3 available. Are you looking for a particular version?
17   - <set name=<star>>Nice meeting you, <call>keepname <star></call>. No
     problem, I have 3 available. Are you looking for a particular version?
18
19   + * Versions do you have available
20   - I have ones that come with 1 gigabyte 2 gigabyte or 4 gigabyte RAM.
     Which would you prefer?
21
22   + i would prefer the (1|2|4) gigabyte version
23   - <set piversion=<star>>Excellent, here is a picture: <img
     src="img/<star>.webp">
24
```

Figure 4-3. The second part of our brain.rive file

Let's resume adding our code:

8. Next up is a straightforward question – this time, we're checking to see if the desired product is in stock:

```
+ is this one in stock
- Yes it is: we have more than 10 available for
immediate despatch
```

9. This next part is the most complex – here, we're building up some brief details about the product and a link for the customer to navigate directly to the product page for the product:

```
+ how can i get it
- No problem, here is a link directly to the product
page for the 4 gigabyte version of the Raspberry
Pi <get version>:
^ <span class="productname"><p><h2>Raspberry Pi 4 -
<get piversion>GB RAM</h2><img src="img/<get piversion>.
webp"></p><p class="stock">More than 10 in stock</
p><p class="stockid">PSH047</p><a class="productlink"
href="rasp<get piversion>.html">Go to product page</a>
</span>
^ Just click on Add to Cart when you get there, to add it
to your basket. Is there anything else I can help with
today?
```

We can see a clearer view of how our code should look in Figure 4-4.

```
25   + is this one in stock
26   - Yes it is: we have more than 10 available for immediate despatch
27
28   + how can i get it
29   - No problem, here is a link directly to the product page for the 4
     gigabyte version of the Raspberry Pi <get piversion>:
30   ^ <span class="productname"><p><h2>Raspberry Pi 4 - <get piversion>GB
     RAM</h2><img src="img/<get piversion>.webp"></p><p class="stock">More
     than 10 in stock</p><p class="stockid">PSH047</p><a
     class="productlink" href="rasp<get piversion>.html">Go to product page
     </a></span>
31   ^ Just click on Add to Cart when you get there, to add it to your
     basket. Is there anything else I can help with today?
32
```

Figure 4-4. *The next block of code in our brain.rive file*

10. We then finish with two questions – the first acknowledges no further help is required, and the second is a generic catch-all in case our chatbot has had a problem understanding a question:

```
+ no thats fine thankyou
- You're welcome, thankyou for choosing to use PiShack's
Raspberry Pi Selector tool today

+ *
- Sorry, I did not get what you said
- I am afraid that I do not understand you
- I did not get it
- Sorry, can you please elaborate that for me?
```

We can see how the final part of our brain.rive file should look in Figure 4-5.

```
33   + no thats fine thankyou
34   - You're welcome, thankyou for choosing to use PiShack's Raspberry Pi
     Selector tool today
35
36   + *
37   - Sorry, I did not get what you said
38   - I am afraid that I do not understand you
39   - I did not get it
40   - Sorry, can you please elaborate that for me?
41
```

Figure 4-5. *The final part of our brain.rive file*

11. At this point, go ahead and save the file – we can now test the
     results! For this, browse to `https://speech/chatbot`, then
     click Ask a question, and start to enter information as shown in
     the extract in Figure 4-6.

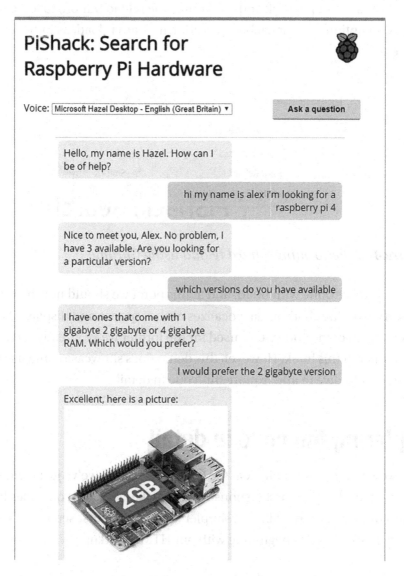

Figure 4-6. *Our completed chatbot, at the start of a conversation*

When you test your demo, you may find a particular quirk of using RiveScript – the brain.rive file is cached, which can make it harder to be sure you are running an updated version if you then make changes to it! There is a quick trick to help with this, although it only works if you are using Chrome. Simply click and hold down the reload button, to force it to display an option to clear cache and perform a hard reload, as indicated in Figure 4-7.

Figure 4-7. *Performing a hard reload using Chrome*

Okay, we're done with build, and at this point we should now have the basis of a working chatbot that vocalizes each response and displays it on screen. Much of the code we've used for the former we've already seen from earlier in this book. However, this demo does showcase some useful points, so let's dive in and explore this code in detail.

Exploring the code in detail

If we were to take a closer look at the code in the demo we've just created, I can imagine what your first response might – yikes! Yes, the code does look a little complex, but in reality it's simpler than it might first seem. Let's tear it apart block by block, beginning with our HTML markup.

Dissecting our HTML markup

Much of what is in this file is fairly straightforward – once references to the CSS styling files have been defined, we set up a #page-wrapper div to encompass all of our content. We then create a .voicechoice section to house the drop-down that allows us to choose which language to use, along with the initial button to ask a question.

Next up comes the .chat section, which we use to render our conversation with the bot; the messages are rendered in the .messages <div> element. We then have a form to submit each question, before closing out with references to the RiveScript library and our custom script.js file.

Pulling apart script.js: The Web Speech API

We've covered the easy part of our demo, which is the markup. This is where things get more interesting! The script.js and brain.rive files are where most of the magic happens – in the former, we combine the speaking/audio code with our chatbot functionality, while in the latter we store the various questions and responses for our chatbot. Let's crack open a copy of the script.js file, to see how our chatbot demo works in more detail.

We begin by initializing an instance of RiveScript as an object, before defining a series of variables, to cache various elements in our HTML markup. The first function in our code, loadVoices(), takes care of calling the Speech Synthesis API to get the various voices we will use in our code, such as English (Great Britain). It's worth noting that we *specify references* to call this function twice; this is to allow for some older browsers (particularly Chrome), which require us to load the drop-down asynchronously. In most cases, we will simply call loadVoices(); for those browsers that need it, the drop-down will be populated using the onvoiceschanged event handler from the window.SpeechSynthesis interface.

Moving on, the next function we create is the `onerror` event handler, again from the `window.SpeechSynthesis` interface; this acts as a basic catch-all for any errors that crop up when using the interface. For now, we simply render out the error type given using `event.error`, along with the `error.message`. It's worth noting that `event.error` will give a specific error code, such as audio-capture. Any `error.message` statement should be defined by us as developers; the specification does not define the exact wording to use.

A list of error codes is available on the MDN site at `https://developer.mozilla.org/en-US/docs/Web/API/SpeechRecognitionError/error`.

The final function in this part of our code breakdown is `speak()` – this is where we vocalize our content! This starts by initializing a new instance of `SynthesisUtterance`, where we then define the text to use (i.e., the response from our bot), along with the voice that should be used. Assuming no issues are found, then it is spoken by the API, using the `speechSynthesis.speak(msg)` statement.

Phew! We've done the largest part of our demo, although there is still one part left: configuring our bot! I would recommend taking a breather at this stage – perhaps go get a drink or get some fresh air. Once you're ready to continue, let's crack on with exploring the statements used to configure our bot in more detail.

Understanding how our bot is configured

Although most of the magic happens in our `script.js` file, our demo would be incomplete without the bot configuration file, `brain.rive`.

A quick look inside this file and we should recognize some elements – after all, most of it looks like plain text, with some basic JavaScript code at the start, right? Yes, you would be correct in saying this, but RiveScript has some unusual character keywords that we need to be aware of in this code. Let's go through it bit by bit, starting from the top of our code – before we do so, now is a good opportunity for a quick heads-up on how RiveScript works.

Exploring how RiveScript works: A summary

Any configurations we create using RiveScript are stored as .rive files. A common feature in .rive files is that you will see most lines starting with either an exclamation mark, a plus sign, or a minus sign, with arrow heads and carets used a couple of times, as in our example. This is important, as these define the type of statement in use. The ones we've used in our example are listed in Table 4-2.

Table 4-2. Types of special characters used in brain.rive

Character	Purpose
+ or plus sign	This denotes a trigger question from the user.
* or star	This acts as a placeholder to accept data from the user, such as a name or questions like "which versions…" or "what versions…" (as in our example).
- or minus sign	This acts as the response from the bot to our user.
() and I or brackets and pipe symbol	When used together, this denotes a choice – RiveScript will act on what it receives in a similar fashion to the star placeholder, but this time, we're limiting choice to one of three options, namely, 1, 2, or 4.
^ or arrow head	This is a newline character, where responses are best served over multiple lines.
! or exclamation mark	This denotes a RiveScript directive, such as specifying which version of the specification to use.

In most cases, we will likely use a plus or minus sign (as in our example). With this in mind, let's explore the statements one by one in more detail.

117

Dissecting the brain.rive file in detail

We start with ! version=2.0, which tells RiveScript that we're working on the 2.0 specification of the library; if this is set to a lower number (i.e., earlier version), then we risk our code not working as expected.

For now, we'll jump to what should be line 12, where we have + hello – we'll come back to the code within the > object...< object tags shortly. The code at line 12 should be self-explanatory; at this point, the user will enter hello as our initial trigger, to which the bot will respond accordingly.

The next block is a little more interesting. Here, we've specified a trigger question using the + sign; in this we use the star. A star is a placeholder for a specific piece of text given by the user – if, for example, they had used the name Mark, then the text given would equate to "hi my name is Mark im looking for a raspberry pi 4." This by itself is straightforward, but take a look at the response: what is that <call> tag I see? And what about the <set name=....> code too...?

The former is a call to what in this case will be a RiveScript/JavaScript function. Remember the code I said we would skip over at the start of this section? Well, that is the code for this function – we're using it to make sure that no matter what name is passed to it, it will always be rendered on screen with the first letter capitalized. It's worth noting that RiveScript will always format variables in lowercase when used in triggers; we use this function to display something more suitable to the user.

The next three questions follow similar principles, where trigger text is in lowercase, and we use a star placeholder in the first of this bunch of three questions. There is one exception though: the use of the pipe and brackets. Here we're specifying a number of options that could be recognized; unlike the star where anything might match the statement, the only matches allowed will be the numbers 1, 2, or 4. We then make use of whichever number is matched in the `<star>` placeholder to set a variable called `piversion` (which we use a little later on), as part of an interpolated tag to display the appropriate image for the chosen version of the Raspberry Pi board.

Moving on, the next block is the largest – it looks scary, but in reality, it's not that complex! There are two things to note: First, we `<get piversion>` and use this to render the product name and image on screen, in a small block of HTML markup. The second is the use of the ^ or the hat symbol; this allows us to split the response from our bot over several lines. I'm sure you can imagine a block of text like ours would look dreadful if combined into one line. This makes it easier for us to view it on screen.

We then close out with two triggers – the last is from the customer to confirm that's the only thing they need help with, along with an appropriate acknowledgment from the bot. The last trigger is a generic catch-all, which kicks in if there is a problem: this is likely to be if the user has entered something that doesn't match one of our pre-scripted responses. We've provided a number of alternatives that the bot can use; it will automatically pick one in turn, if it needs to use it in a conversation with a user.

Phew! That was a lengthy explanation. Well done if you managed to get this far! There was a lot to cover in this demo, but hopefully this shows you how we can make use of the Speech API to add an extra dimension when using automated chatbots. We've only touched the surface of what could be possible, let alone what we should consider; there are a few important points in the latter, so let's pause for a breather. Go get that cup of coffee or drink, and let's continue with delving into some of the areas where we could develop our demo into a more feature-complete example.

Taking things further

Over the course of this chapter, we've constructed a simple chatbot that allows us to choose from one of three Raspberry Pi 4 boards and enquire as to their availability and how we might purchase one. This is a straightforward request, but as you've probably seen, there is some room for improvement!

On that note, how might we go about fine-tuning the experience? Well, one area is the trigger questions we've used; they are somewhat rigid and do not feel as natural or intuitive as they could be in our demo. This is one area to consider. Here are a few more ideas to get you started:

- Add multiple-language support – although English is spoken widely, not everyone can speak it! It also introduces a risk of misunderstanding, due to cultural differences; being able to converse in a customer's native tongue removes that risk and makes them feel more welcome.

- Make it a two-way process – we've focused on just rendering our responses visually and verbally, but what about making it so that you can verbalize your question as well? This will particularly appeal to those who may have a handicap, where using a keyboard will be difficult or impossible.

We'll be looking at something similar when we come to build our (simple) clone of Alexa, later in this book.

- Fine-tune the phrases used – the phrases we've used serve a purpose, but I think there is room for improvement. For example, we might contract certain words, such as "I am" to "I'm," yet our chatbot doesn't allow for this! Granted this is probably more to do with how we configure our chatbot, but don't forget what we put in there will ultimately affect how it comes out as speech.

- Include other products – it's important to consider how best we would go about doing this and the changes needed to Speech Synthesis config; the changes need to be such that it makes it easier to add other products in the future, with the minimum of fuss.

I am sure there will be more that we can or might want to do to develop our project, but for now, I want to concentrate on one particular change: adding language support.

One of the great things about the Web Speech APIs is that we're not limited in any way to just English. We can absolutely add in support for a host of different languages! To prove this, and for our next demo, we're going to update the original chatbot by adding French language support. Let's take a look to see what changes are needed to effect this update in more detail.

Adding language support

For this demo, we'll use an existing copy of the original chatbot, but add in language support – I've chosen French as it's one I can speak. We can easily adapt the code to use a different language, or more than one language as needed. There are a few steps we will go through to update our code. Let's take a look at what is required in more detail.

The demo makes use of flag icons from `www.gosquared.com/resources/flag-icons/` – you can use your own if you prefer using something different.

Updating our demo

To update our demo, we would need to perform four changes:

1. The first is to update our markup and styling so that we add in flags for each country we use – in this case, US English and French.

2. We need to update the Speech Synthesis configuration to accept our language choice, based on setting a variable.

3. Next come translations – we have to create a translated version of the `brain.rive` configuration file into each new language and reconfigure our `script.js` file to import each version as appropriate.

4. The last change required will be to add event handlers to set `SpeechSynthesisUtterance.lang` to our chosen language, as appropriate.

With this in mind, let's dive in and set up our demo! As mentioned earlier, we will be adding in French language support – feel free to change this to another language if you prefer, but you will need to manually update the translated text in the `brain.rive` file.

ADDING LANGUAGE SUPPORT

Before we begin, there are a couple of things we need to do:

1. Take a copy of the `chatbot` folder you created from the
    original demo earlier in this chapter, and save it as `chat
    language` at the root of our project folder.

2. From a copy of the code download that accompanies this book,
    extract the `brain config` folder and copy the contents into
    the `js` subfolder under the `chat language` folder. These
    contain updated versions of our `brain.rive` file, in English
    and French.

3. From that same code download, go ahead and extract the `img`
    folder – save it over the top of the `img` folder within the `chat
    language` folder. This will add the two flag icons that we will
    use in our demo.

Once you've completed this, continue with these steps:

1. The first set of changes we need to make will be in our
    markup – we're going to introduce two flags as language
    selectors. Open `index.html`, look for the line of code starting
    `<button id="help"...`, and then add in this block of code
    immediately before it:

    ```
    <section class="flags">
      <span class="en-us"><img src="img/en-us.png"
      alt="en-us">EN</span>|
      <span class="fr-fr"><img src="img/fr-fr.png"
      alt="fr fr">FR</span>
    </section>
    ```

2. Next, add in the disabled attribute to the `<button>` tag, as indicated:

    ```
    <button id="help" disabled>Ask a question</button>
    ```

3. Go ahead and save this file – keep it open, but it can be minImized for now.

4. At this point, switch to the `scripts.js` file – we have a few changes to make here, starting with defining some additional variables. After the first line of code, add in this declaration, as highlighted:

    ```
    let bot = new RiveScript();
    let langSupport, intro, brains;
    ```

5. Next, we need to cache some more elements as variables – for this, go ahead and add in the following four lines of code, immediately after the `const question =...` line:

    ```
    const voiceSelect = document.getElementById('voice');
    const english = document.querySelector(".en-us");
    const french = document.querySelector(".fr-fr");
    const voice = document.querySelector(".voicechoice");
    ```

6. Now that we're introducing multi-language support, we can't hard-code our initial greetings. Instead, we will provide them as variables, so after the previous block of code leave a line and add in these two declarations:

    ```
    const enIntro = "Hello. my name is Hazel. How can I be
    of help?";
    const frIntro = "Bonjour. Je m'appelle Hélène. Comment
    puis-je vois aider?";
    ```

7. Scroll down until you reach the speak() function. Up until now, the language was implicitly set as 'en-us'; this needs to change! For this, look for the speakSynthesis.speak statement and then alter the last part of this function as indicated:

```
    })[0];
  }
```

msg.lang = langSupport;

```
  speechSynthesis.speak(msg);
}
```

8. Next, go ahead and delete the line starting with const brains = [..., and replace with this:

```
function setLanguage(langUsed, selIndex, langIntro) {
  voiceSelect.selectedIndex = selIndex;
  langSupport = langUsed;
  intro = langIntro;
  brains = [ './js/brain-' + langSupport + '.rive' ];
  question.disabled = false;
}
```

9. We now need to add in two functions to take care of what happens when we click the flags – for this, leave a line and then drop in the following code:

```
english.addEventListener("click", function() {
  setLanguage('en-us', 3, enIntro);
  question.innerHTML = "Ask a question";
});

french.addEventListener("click", function() {
  setLanguage('fr-fr', 8, frIntro);
  question.innerHTML = "Poser une question";
});
```

10. There are two more changes to make before we're done with editing this file – the next change is to alter the botReady() function. Scroll down to it and then edit as highlighted in the following:

```
function botReady(){
  bot.sortReplies();
  botReply(intro);
}
```

11. The last change to make will be similar – here we need to alter how we call our opening salutation. Scroll down to the question event handler and then update the speak() call as indicated:

```
question.addEventListener("click", function() {
  speak(intro);
  bot.loadFile(brains + "?" + parseInt(Math.random()
  * 100000)).then(botReady).catch(botNotReady);
});
```

12. Save the file – we can minimize it for now.

13. Next, fire up the styles.css file, and add the following styles at the end of the file:

```
/* flags */
section.flags {
  width: 150px;
  float: right;
  margin-top: -30px;
}

section.flags img { vertical-align: middle; padding-
right: 5px;}

section.flags img:hover { cursor: pointer; }

button { width: 30%; padding: 10px 15px; }
```

14. At this point, go ahead and save the file – we can now test the results! For this, browse to `https://speech/chatbot`, then click Ask a question, and start to enter information as shown in the extract in Figure 4-8.

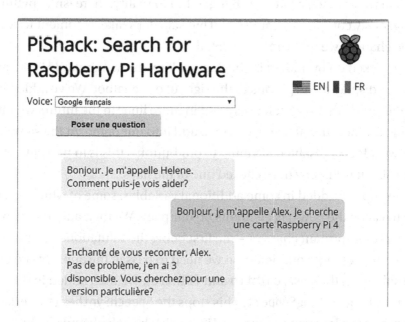

Figure 4-8. *Our updated demo, now with French language support*

Phew! Another monster demo! It seems like a lot, but in reality much of the code will be a one-off change; that will be the code we need to adapt to convert to using different languages.

Once this is done, then it is a matter of simply adding the flag (and markup for it), potentially a little styling, and the event handlers needed for each additional flag. Granted our code could be written more efficiently to automatically recognize new flags and handle them correctly, but hey, we have to start somewhere!

Dissecting the code

Okay, changing tack for a moment, we covered a good few changes in our latest update, so how does it all fit in? At first glance, it does indeed look like we've made a fair few changes, but in reality, there isn't anything outrageously complex in our demo. That said, let's take a moment to recap on the changes we made in more detail.

We kicked off by adding in the flag markup; this is standard HTML and serves to display the flag icons to the right of our chatbot. We've added in a container for this – we can easily add in more lines in the future, which point to any additional flags we care to add into our demo. At the same time, we added a disabled attribute to our button – this is to prevent people from using it until they have clicked one of the flags.

Next up, we added in some additional variables, some of which will be used to cache the new flag elements on our page. We then added in two of the most important changes – the first being the salutations. We can't hard-code these into our demo, so we need to pass in the appropriate text as variables (in this case, `enIntro` and `frIntro`). We then added in this line: `msg.lang = langSupport;` This stops the `SpeechSynthesis` interface from assuming language support is US English by default and will be whatever comes when clicking our chosen flag.

The next three changes are more substantial – here we set a common setLanguage() function that changes the `voiceSelect` drop-down to our chosen language (for French, it selects Google French, and so on). We then set the appropriate BCP47 code for the SpeechSynthesis interface (e.g., `"fr-fr"` for French) and use this to define which of our brain configuration files we should use (in this instance, it would be `brain-fr-fr.rive`). If all is good, we then remove the disabled attribute from the Ask a question button, so it is ready for our customer to use.

The next two event handlers call the `setLanguage()` function we've just defined, into which we pass the appropriate BCP47 code, the index of the voice to use, and our opening salutation. At the same time, we also update the text on our "Ask a question" button, to be either in English or the French equivalent, depending on which button is selected. Although these both work in a similar fashion, we've set them to pass in appropriate values for the chosen language – these would be duplicated for any additional languages we decide to add in to our demo.

The remaining two changes are very straightforward – as we can't hard-code the opening salutations, we have to pass in the text as variables. Here we make use of a common intro variable, into which we will have already passed in the text from our specific language variables earlier in the demo.

Summary

Chatbots are a technology that is definitely here to stay – research indicates that their use will explode over the next few years, so it is important to make sure they can be as effective as possible and that customer engagement levels do not drop as a result! We've covered some important points about how we can add in the Speech Synthesis API to provide that extra edge when using chatbots; let's take a moment to review what we have learned in this chapter.

We kicked off with some basic theory about why we should use a chatbot, the different types available, and some of the downsides to using them, before setting the scene for this chapter's project demo. We spent a little time architecting the various elements of our demo, before touching on some of the alternatives that we may consider using in the future.

We then moved onto the important stage of building our bot – we first added in text editor syntax support, before running through the main steps of building and configuring our bot. Once built, we then explored the code we created in detail, including working through the configuration file that makes our bot operate correctly. We then rounded out this chapter with a look at some of the things we could do to improve our bot, with special emphasis on adding extra language support to our demo.

Phew! A whistle-stop tour through chatbots, for sure! We'll be revisiting some of the topics covered in this chapter later, when we try to build an Alexa clone, but let's do something a little less demanding for a bit. How many times have you come across requests to leave feedback on a site? Usually this might be through an email or even a review section. Chances are, though, we have to provide our feedback in written form. That is so old-school. What if we could do it verbally and have the site convert it to text for us? Yes, it might seem like the height of laziness, but hey, I'm all for innovation! Intrigued? Well, stay with me, and I will reveal all in the next chapter.

CHAPTER 5

Project: Leaving Review Feedback

How often have you felt the need to leave feedback about a shopping experience? Hopefully you've done so at least once; I suspect though there may be a seed of doubt as to whether someone will pick up on it and do something about it!

Irrespective of what feedback you leave, chances are you have to type in your comments; what if you could do so using your voice? Yes, novel as it may seem, this is a perfect way to show off using the Speech APIs. In this chapter, we'll set up a basic product page and add in voice feedback capabilities, which will automatically transcribe our comments into written text.

Setting the scene

Almost every e-commerce site you come across when browsing will have some form of feedback mechanism – it might be a purpose-built affair or something provided as a third-party service from a partner or supplier. At the risk of sounding blasé, it almost doesn't matter how it is provided. Any company that transacts on the Internet should provide some form of mechanism; otherwise, they are likely to lose customers very quickly!

© Alex Libby 2020
A. Libby, *Introducing the HTML5 Web Speech API*,
https://doi.org/10.1007/978-1-4842-5735-7_5

In most cases, feedback forms are typically ones where you have to type out your response – there's nothing wrong with this, but it is an old-school way of doing things. Indeed, one might ask, "What other alternatives are there?" Well, you could use a questionnaire, but ultimately, it's the qualitative feedback provided that is just as, if not more, important!

What if we could turn things on their head and provide it verbally? Yes, you heard me correctly – rather than spend time laboriously typing it out, let's articulate it verbally. Sounds complicated, right? Well, perhaps not. We've already covered the basic tool needed for this, in the form of the Speech Recognition API. Let's take a look at what is involved in setting this up and how this could become a really powerful tool.

Keeping things in scope

To make this project work, you might be thinking that we need lots of extra tools, right? Wrong, we don't need any! Before I explain why, let's quickly cover off what we will include in this project and what will fall out of scope:

- We will limit our demo to recording and transcribing spoken feedback and then rendering it on screen – the latter will be with an appropriate date and time stamp.

- Our demo will initially focus on transcribing feedback in English, but will look at providing support for at least one other language, later in this chapter.

- We won't be recording any of the content left in our review into a database or submission by email; that falls outside of the scope of this demo.

With this in mind, let's take a look at the architecture for our demo, to see what is involved in more detail.

Architecting our demo

At the start of the previous section, I made what might seem a bold claim that we wouldn't need any additional software in order to set up our feedback: it's time to make good on that promise! Well, here goes.

In a sense, we don't need any extra software – the core functionality can be provided by using the Speech Recognition API and configuring it using standard features to record and transcribe spoken content. If however we did want to do things such as recording that feedback for later perusal, then yes, we would clearly need a suitable storage system and appropriate middleware to parse and store the content. However, that falls outside of the scope of this book – we'll focus on just getting content transcribed and rendered on screen.

Building our review panel

Now that we've covered the basic parts of our architecture, let's begin building our demo – we'll focus on constructing the core review panel first, before exploring how to add in multi-language support later in the book.

It's important to note that we will focus mainly on the JavaScript required to make our demo work – all of the HTML and CSS styling will come preconfigured, directly from the code download that accompanies this book.

BUILDING THE REVIEW PANEL

The first stage in this chapter's project is to construct the review panel, but before we get started, there is one thing we need to do. Go ahead and extract a copy of the reviews folder from the code download that accompanies this book – save it to our project area.

With this in place, let's make a start coding our demo:

If you run into any trouble during this demo, then there is a finished version available in the code download that accompanies this book – it's in the reviews folder, under the finished version subfolder.

1. We'll start by opening a new file and then saving it as `scripts.js` to the `js` subfolder inside the `reviews` folder.

2. We have a good chunk of code to add, which we will do so block by block – the first is a set of variables that reference various elements in the DOM, plus one we will use as a placeholder for working out if we are speaking:

```
var transcript = document.getElementById('transcript');
var log = document.getElementById('log');
var start = document.getElementById('speechButton');
var clearbtn = document.getElementById('clearall-btn');
var submitbtn = document.getElementById('submit-btn');
var review = document.getElementById('reviews');
var unsupported = document.getElementById('unsupported');
var speaking = false;
```

3. Next, we need to set up the basic frame of our script – this we use to work out if our browser supports the Speech Recognition API. Leave a blank line after the variables and then add this block:

```
window.SpeechRecognition = window.SpeechRecognition ||
window.webkitSpeechRecognition || null;

if (window.SpeechRecognition === null) {
  unsupported.classList.remove('hidden');
  start.classList.add('hidden');
} else {
  ...add code in here...
}
```

4. We can now start to add our demo code – we begin by initialing
    and configuring an instance of the Speech Recognition API. Go
    ahead and replace the ...add code in here... line with this:

```
var recognition = new window.SpeechRecognition();

// Recogniser doesn't stop listening even if the user pauses
recognition.continuous = true;
```

5. With an instance of the API now initialized, we can start to
    respond to events. The first one is the onresult handler; for this,
    leave a line after the code from step 3 and then add in this
    event handler:

```
// Start recognising
recognition.onresult = function(event) {
  transcript.textContent = ";
  for (var i = event.resultIndex; i < event.results.length;
  i++) {
    if (event.results[i].isFinal) {
      transcript.textContent = event.results[i][0].transcript;
    } else {
      transcript.textContent += event.results[i][0].transcript;
    }
  }
};
```

6. Next up, we need to trap for any instance where (heaven forbid)
    we get an error – for this, go ahead and leave a line blank after
    the onresult handler and then add in this code:

```
// Listen for errors
recognition.onerror = function(event) {
  log.innerHTML = 'Recognition error: ' + event.message +
  '<br />' + log.innerHTML;
};
```

7. We're now at one of the most important parts of this demo – a means to start and stop recording our feedback! We have two more event handlers to add, so let's add in the first, which will fire when we start or stop recording. Leave a line blank after the code from step 5 and then add in this:

```
start.addEventListener('click', function() {
  if (!speaking) {
    speaking = true;
    start.classList.toggle('stop');

    recognition.interimResults = document.query
    Selector('input[name="recognition-type"]
    [value="interim"]').checked;
    try {
      recognition.start();
      log.innerHTML = 'Start speaking now - click to stop';
    } catch (ex) {
      log.innerHTML = 'Recognition error:' + ex.message;
    }
  } else {
    recognition.stop();
    start.classList.toggle('stop');
    log.innerHTML = 'Recognition stopped - click to speak';
    speaking = false;
  }
});
```

8. The second event handler takes care of submitting our transcribed recording as feedback – for this, leave a line blank after the start handler and drop in this code:

```
submitbtn.addEventListener('click', function() {
  let p = document.createElement('p');
  var textnode = document.createTextNode(transcript.value);
  p.appendChild(textnode);
  review.appendChild(p);
```

```
let today = dayjs().format('ddd, MMMM D YYYY [at] H:HH');
let s = document.createElement('small');
textnode = document.createTextNode(today);
s.appendChild(textnode);
review.appendChild(s);

let hr = document.createElement('hr');
review.appendChild(hr);
transcript.textContent = ";
});

clearbtn.addEventListener('click', function() {
  transcript.textContent = ";
});
```

9. We're almost there. All that remains is to save our code, so go ahead and do that now. Once done, fire up your browser, and then browse to `https://speech/reviews/`. If all is well, we should see something akin to the screenshot in Figure 5-1.

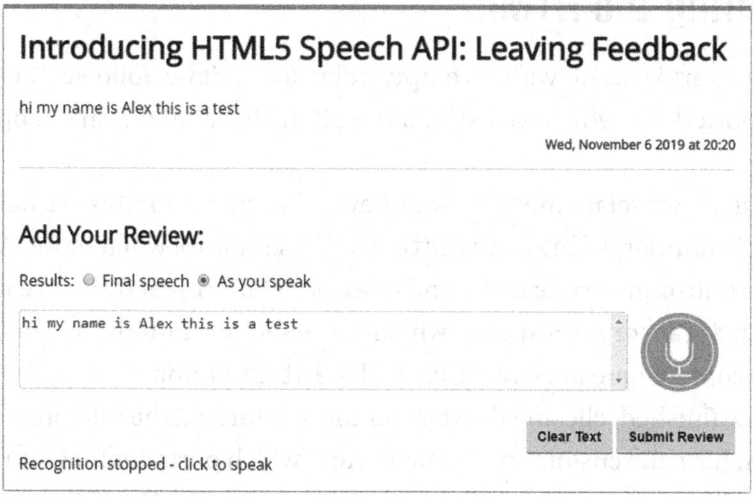

Figure 5-1. *Our finished review system*

137

At this point, we should now have a working demo, where we can talk into a microphone and the Recognition Speech API transcribes it into written content. Although it seems like we've written a fair chunk of code, the basic principles are the same as the ones we first met back in Chapter 1, and started to develop in Chapter 2. To see what I mean, let's dive into the code, to see how it all hangs together, in more detail.

Breaking apart the code in detail

As I am sure someone once said, we must start somewhere – there is no better place than the HTML markup that was preconfigured for our demo.

If we take a closer look, there shouldn't be anything outrageously complex; the demo uses standard HTML and CSS to construct our basic form page. This aside, let's take a quick look at what has been set up for us in more detail.

Exploring the HTML

The core part kicks off with an empty <div> for reviews, followed by the unsupported div, which we use to advise if the browser doesn't support the API.

Next up, we set up the "Add Your Review" section – for this, we have two radio buttons, `#final` and `#interim`. These control whether the API renders transcribed code at the end or as we speak, respectively. We then have our `#transcript` text area, which we've set to read-only; we start adding content here once we've clicked the `start` button.

Once finished, clicking the start button will turn off the microphone. We then have the customary submit button, which posts content into the reviews div on screen. This is finished off by a call to the DayJS library – this is used to format dates posted in each review. We will come back to this shortly, when we dissect the script for this demo.

Exploring the JavaScript

In contrast, our JavaScript code is clearly more complex – this might put you off, but fear not. It's not anything we've not used before, at least within the confines of the API! Let's break down the code in more detail, to see how it all fits together.

We kick off by declaring references to various elements in our markup, before determining whether our browser can support the API, with a call to window.SpeechRecognition. If this is rendered as null, we display a suitably worded message; otherwise, we begin by initializing an instance of the API as recognition. At the same time, we set the .continuous property to true, to prevent the API from stopping listening after a period of time or in the event of inactivity.

The first event handler we use (and arguably the most important) is onresult – this takes care of transcribing our spoken content. It's important to revisit this one and, in particular, the use of event.results[i][0].transcript.

We can see a screenshot of this function in Figure 5-2.

```
22    // Start recognising
23    recognition.onresult = function(event) {
24      transcript.textContent = '';
25      for (var i = event.resultIndex; i < event.results.length; i++) {
26        if (event.results[i].isFinal) {
27          transcript.textContent = event.results[i][0].transcript; |
28        } else {
29          transcript.textContent += event.results[i][0].transcript;
30        }
31      }
32    };
```

Figure 5-2. *The onResult function from our demo*

Once we've iterated through all of the results, any that contain content are returned as an object of type SpeechRecognitionResultList; this contains SpeechRecognitionResult objects, which can be accessed like an array using getter properties.

The first [0] returns the SpeechRecognitionResult at position 0 – this is effectively the final answer, which should be rendered on screen. However, if the speechRecognition.maxAlternatives property had been set, we would see the alternatives which are stored within SpeechRecognitionAlternative objects. In our case, the maxAlternatives property has not been set, so what is displayed on screen will be the final answer only.

The next event handler is a simple one in comparison – here we're intercepting onerror and rendering any error generated on screen, along with the appropriate message.

This might range from something like no-speech to aborted – you can see a complete list available on the Mozilla MDN site at https://developer.mozilla.org/en-US/docs/Web/API/SpeechRecognitionError/error.

Moving on, we have the first of three event handlers that are used to record, transcribe, and submit (or display) our feedback. The first, start, is attached to the microphone button; we work out if we are already speaking. If not, we then activate the microphone, before determining if we should display interim results or the final article. We then run a try...catch block, inside of which we run recognition .start() to start recording our speech. When done, we stop the Speech Recognition API and flip the styles back, ready to start recording again.

The second event handler, tied to submitbtn, allows us to submit our content on screen into the feedback area. We first create a paragraph dynamically using createElement('p'), before assigning it the contents of transcript.value. We then calculate and format the date of recording using the DayJS library – we could have of course used standard JavaScript, but date manipulation can be awkward when using JavaScript!

The DayJS library is available for download at `https://github.com/iamkun/dayjs`, if you would like to learn more about this library.

This, along with the contents of transcript, is then appended to the review area in the DOM using `review.appendChild(s)`, before we add a dynamically generated horizontal rule element to separate it from the next review feedback. In the third and final event handler, we use `clearbtn` to trigger emptying the contents of the transcript text area, so it is ready for the next comment to be recorded.

Now, it's great that we have a working demo, but what about hosting in a more realistic context, such as a product page? If we've planned our demo correctly, it should be a matter of copying the code into the wider template, and we shouldn't have to alter the code too much. Let's dive in and see what happens...

Adding it to a product page

For our next demo, we're going to merge the reviews demo into a basic product page for a nascent Raspberry Pi retailer – I've created a very basic one which certainly won't win any awards, but should suffice to see our review panel working in a more practical context! Let's dive in and take a look.

DEMO: MERGING THE REVIEW PANEL

Before we get started, we need to open the source folders for both the reviews demo and the product page demo in your text editor – copies of both are in the merge folder that is in the code download that accompanies this book.

For the purposes of this demo, I will use the folder names productpage and reviews, to distinguish between the original source demos.

Make sure both folders are open in your text editor before continuing with these steps:

1. The first change we need to make is with the index.html file in the reviews folder – look for this line: `<div id="reviews">`

2. Copy from this line down to (and including) `<div id="log">`
   `Click the microphone to start speaking</div>`.
   Then paste it below this line – `<h1>Product Reviews</h1>` –
   in the index .html file, within the productpage folder.

3. Next, go ahead and remove this line from the productpage folder's index.html file:

   `<p>Insert reviews block here</p>`

4. Our review panel uses the DayJS library to format the date of posting the review – for this we need to transfer across the call to the DayJS library. Go ahead and add this line:

   ```
   <script src="https://cdnjs.cloudflare.com/ajax/libs/
   dayjs/1.8.16/dayjs.min.js"></script>
   ```

above the call to the scripts file in the productpage folder:

```
<script src="js/scripts.js"></script>
```

5. We now need to update the styling to allow for the added
    review panel – for this, go ahead and copy all of the styles from
    the review version of the styles.css file into the productpage
    folder's CSS file.

6. We're almost done. Go ahead and copy the contents of the
    scripts.js file from the reviews folder into the top of the
    scripts.js file in the productpage folder.

7. We need to copy across the mic.png image for our microphone
    button – copy the img folder from the reviews folder into the
    productpage folder.

8. The final step is to remove these two lines:

```
<h1>Product Reviews</h1>
<p>Insert reviews block here</p>
```

9. Go ahead and save the file – we can now preview our results. For this,
    browse to https://speech/productpage/. If all is well, we should
    see something akin to the screenshot shown in Figure 5-3.

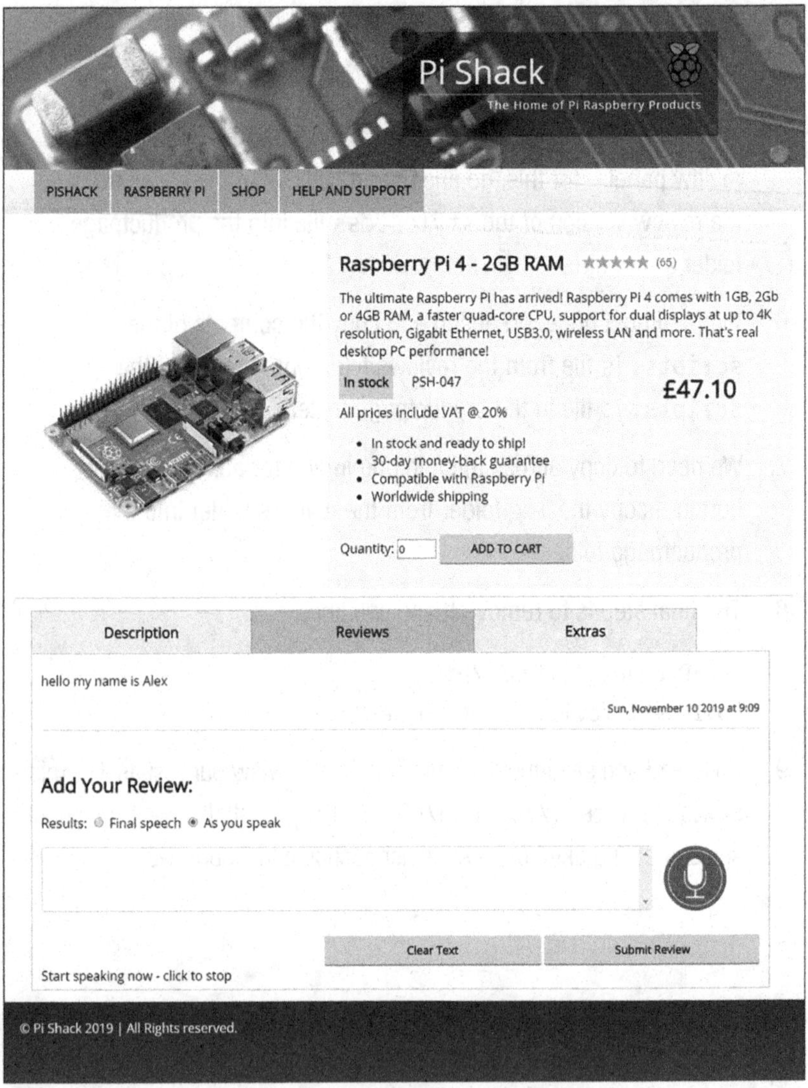

Figure 5-3. The merged review panel

Unfortunately, the screenshot doesn't do it justice – to get a feel for how it would work in action, I would recommend running the demo from the code download that accompanies this book. It's in the productpage folder and ideally should be run as a secured URL. None of the code should be unfamiliar; although the merged version will be a little rough around the edges, it gives us a perfect opportunity to optimize code such as the CSS styling!

Okay, let's move on. We've constructed our review system; at this point, we should have something that allows us to record feedback in English and display it on screen in an appropriate manner. Trouble is, in the modern age of the Internet, not everyone speaks English! It means that our demo will only be really effective in English-speaking markets or where customers can speak it as a second language.

Fortunately, this is easy to fix – we've already used some of the principles of how, in the previous chapter! With this in mind, let's dive in and see what we need to do to allow our review system to accept and transcribe more than just English...

Adding language support

In this modern age where we should embrace different cultures, it's important to show support for customers whose first language isn't English. Yet adding support for extra languages can be something of a double-edged sword – it may be very easy to add support *technically*, but which languages should one choose to support?

The answer (in part) will depend on support from Google – it provides support if customers are using Chrome. A list of countries supported by Google (under the BCP47 protocol) is available at `https://cloud.google.com/speech-to-text/docs/languages`. But this isn't the end of it – there are more questions we should ask, which include the following:

- Which browsers are our customers using? This is important as it depends a lot on which browser your customers are using: if it is Chrome (or latest versions of Edge), then support will be reasonably good – Google offers a range of different languages as part of this support. If however your customers prefer IE or Safari, then providing language support will be a moot point, as the API isn't supported on either browser!

- How do we risk not alienating customers if we decide not to offer support for a specific language? Clearly a language only spoken by a handful of customers isn't one that will be added on the grounds of economic viability; yet, what if that customer happens to be one who is a substantial revenue earner for you? Is it a case of "they who shout loudest get heard first"? Yes, I know this is something of an extreme example, but it goes to show that prioritization is key!

- Assuming we add in support for more languages, do you have the resource available to support customers who make use of the feature? After all, if they take the trouble to leave feedback in their own language, it somewhat destroys the whole purpose of having this option if the only language we can respond in is English. Yes, we could use a service such as Google Translate, but this is a poor substitute for offering a response from a real member of your team!

As we can see, simply adding in support technically is only part of the puzzle; to solve it (and offer the best support for our customers), we must consider the whole picture. We've touched on some of the questions we could ask, so it's time we got technical. Let's dive in and consider the code we need to add or adapt to allow our review system to cater for more languages.

Updating the demo

For our next demo, we're going to add in support for customers who speak French – we could add in any number of different languages, but French happens to be the one I can speak! (Okay, it's been a while since I've had to speak it full-time, but I digress…)

There are a few changes we need to make to our demo – in summary, these are as follows:

- We need to source appropriate flag icons – for our demo, we'll use the ones we had back in Chapter 3. If however you would like to try different languages, then a site such as `https://www.gosquared.com/resources/flag-icons/` will be a good place to start.

- We'll need to add in markup and styling to host these flags – bear in mind that if we were to add in more than just French, we might have to consider relocating elements, to make additional space, or altering styles so they fit correctly.

- We need to alter the configuration options when we use the Speech Recognition API, so that it is not hard-coded to the default of US English, but can accept other languages on request.

- We need to add in event handlers to allow customers to select a language and update the API configuration options accordingly.

This might seem a lot, but in reality, the changes are very easy to make. To see what I mean, let's dive in and make a start on updating our demo.

ADDING LANGUAGE SUPPORT

The first change we need to make is to our markup:

1. We'll start by opening a copy of index.html and then looking for this block:

```
<div class="button-wrapper">
  <div id="speechButton" class="start"></div>
</div>
```

2. Immediately below it, insert the following code for our flags:

```
<section class="flags">
  <span class="intro">Choose language:</span>
  <span class="en-us"><img src="img/en-us.png"
   alt="en-us">EN</span>|
  <span class="fr-fr"><img src="img/fr-fr.png"
   alt="fr-fr">FR</span>
</section>
```

3. Go ahead and save the file – we can close it, as it is not needed. Next, crack open scripts.js and then scroll down to this line:

```
var unsupported = document.getElementById('unsupported');
```

4. Immediately below it, go ahead and add these variable declarations – make sure to leave a line blank after the const french... statement:

```
var speaking = false;
var chosenLang = 'en-us';
const english = document.querySelector("span.en-us");
const french = document.querySelector("span.fr-fr");
```

5. Scroll down a few lines. Then below `recognition.`
    `continuous = true`, go ahead and add this line:

    ```
    recognition.lang = chosenLang;
    ```

6. Next, look for the `clearbtn` event handler – leave a blank
    line below it and then add in this event handler, to take care of
    setting English as our chosen language:

    ```
    english.addEventListener("click", function() {
      recognition.lang = 'en-us';
      english.style.fontWeight = 'bold';
      french.style.fontWeight = 'normal';
    });
    ```

7. We have one more event handler to add in – this one takes care
    of setting French, when selected:

    ```
    french.addEventListener("click", function() {
      recognition.lang = 'fr-fr';
    english.style.fontWeight = 'normal';
    french.style.fontWeight = 'bold';
    });
    ```

8. Go ahead and save the file – it is no longer needed, so can be
    closed at this point. Once closed, crack open `styles.css`, and
    add the following rules at the bottom of the stylesheet:

    ```
    /* CSS Changes */
    span.intro {
    padding-right: 10px;
    vertical-align: baseline;
    }

    /* flags */
    section > span.en-us,
    section > span.fr-fr {
    padding: 2px 5px 0 0;
    }
    ```

```
section > span.en-us > img,
section > span.fr-fr > img {
vertical-align: middle;
padding: 3px;
}

section > span.en-us > img:hover,
section > span.fr-fr > img:hover {
cursor: pointer;
}
```

9. Save this file, and close it. At this point, we can now test the
    results! For this, browse to `https://speech/reviewslang`,
    then click Ask a question, and start to enter information as
    shown in the extract in Figure 5-4.

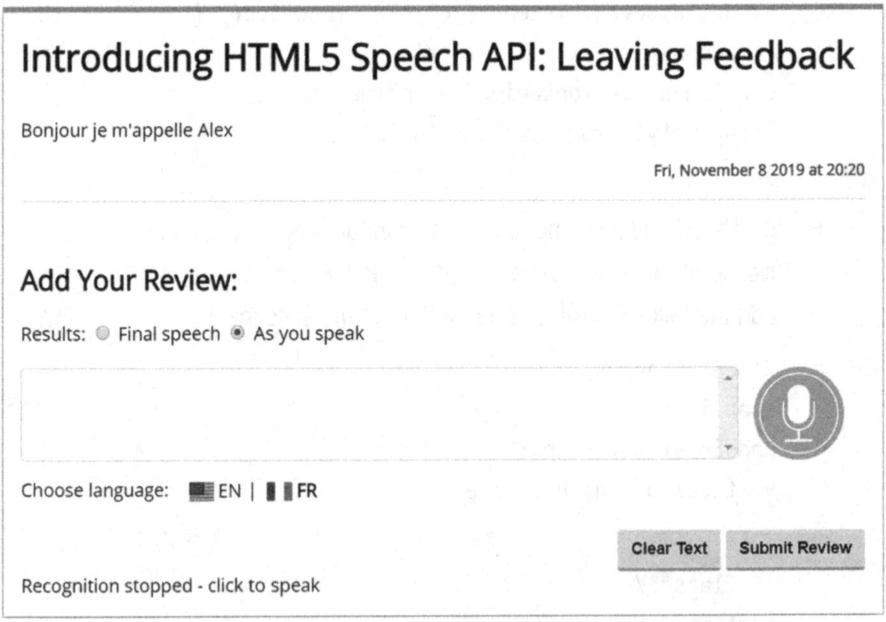

Introducing HTML5 Speech API: Leaving Feedback

Bonjour je m'appelle Alex

Fri, November 8 2019 at 20:20

Add Your Review:

Results: ○ Final speech ● As you speak

Choose language: ▆▆ EN | ▊ ▊ FR

Clear Text   Submit Review

Recognition stopped - click to speak

Figure 5-4. *Our updated demo, with French as an option*

See how easy it was to adapt our demo to allow us to speak French? The great thing about this is that the SpeechRecognition API supports a host of different languages, so we can drop in support for more languages very easily.

It's important to note though that we've hard-coded a lot of what is needed in this demo; if we were to add in more languages, it would be worth optimizing our code, so we can reuse existing styles more effectively. This said, there were a couple of important changes made to support extra languages in this demo, so let's take a moment to go through the code in more detail.

Dissecting the code

Over the course of the last couple of pages, we made several changes to our code. The first was to add in appropriate markup as scaffolding for our chosen flags (in this case, both US English and French). We then switched to the `scripts.js` file and added in some variables – two to help with configuring the API (`speaking` and `chosenLang`) and two as references to elements in the DOM: `english` and `french`.

Next up, we had to alter the default language for our instance of the API – as we can't now use the default of `'us-en'` (or US English), we need to tell it which language should be used. For this, we assigned the value of `chosenLang` to `recognition.lang`; this was set to `'en-us'` as default (so maintaining the status quo). However, this will now be updateable through the use of the next two event handlers, for `english` and `french`. Here we set the `recognition.lang` to `'en-us'` or `'fr-fr'`, depending on which flag is clicked; we also set the EN or FR text on screen to bold and deselect the other flag's text.

We then rounded out the demo with some simple styling changes, to allow for the presence of the flags. These fitted perfectly under the `transcript` textarea element, but if we were to add in more, then we might want to consider the wider implications to the UI and move some of the other elements around for a better fit.

Okay, let's change tack. Over the course of this chapter, we've made use of the Speech Recognition to implement the beginnings of a useful feedback mechanism, which could be adapted for use on any web site wanting to offer customers a chance to leave comments. This is a great way to get comments that we can use to help improve our offer, but it can come with a few gotchas that we need to consider. Let's just say they could come back to bite us if we're not careful! To see what I mean, let's take a look at the wider picture in more detail.

Leaving reviews: A postscript

As with any new technology, there frequently come some downsides – after all, this is still relatively new technology, and there are bound to be changes before the standard is finalized! This said, there are three points of note, to which we should pay special attention:

- One of the first things we need to consider is how customers might react, particularly if they've had a poor experience! As part of any UX design, we should consider implementing some house rules. What if customers used profanities in their comments, for example? They might feel justified in expressing their opinions if they've had less than a perfect experience, but we clearly don't want our review comments littered with unsavory words!

- A second issue to consider is one of spamming – yes, it might seem a little odd, but with the advent of technology, there is technically nothing to stop people from spamming your feedback mechanism! Whether this does become a reality, only time will tell, but it is nevertheless something to think about when implementing a voice-activated review system for your web site.

- The reliance on Google to support functionality for some browsers will be a concern – not because Google is likely to go out of business any time soon, but the simple fact that they may want to begin monetizing support that is currently offered for free. It does mean that we are somewhat at the mercy of Google when it comes to support; there may come a time when a language might not be supported, so we will have to react quickly to minimize any issues if support is removed.

In short, there may not be much we can do about these points, but we can build in some protection. For example, we might ask that users must log in to leave a review or build in something to monitor for instances of particular words that we could try to filter out when transcribing our content.

Also, that support? Well, we hardcoded our entries to prove our demo works, but this isn't very efficient. Instead, we could make our code more dynamic – it can do a search for any entries present in a configuration file. Based on what it finds, it iterates through them and builds up the content automatically. It means that as long as media such as flags are present, all we need to do is turn support on or off; our code will work out automatically which languages to support and add the appropriate entries to our web page.

Okay, we're almost at the end of this chapter, but there is one more thing to consider – what about developing our solution further? Of course, this is all dependent on both your requirements and how creative your imagination is; to get you started, let's take a look at a few ideas on how you can add to your solution to help develop the experience for your customers.

Taking things further

Okay, we've built a basic demo, which allows us to talk in either English or French and for it to transcribe and post our comments in written form. The question is "Where next?" Well, there are a few things we could do. Let's take a look:

- One element that is clearly missing from our demo is a rating – this is a good opportunity to allow customers to provide an objective figure, in addition to qualitative feedback. We could simply implement a suitable mechanism, such as the RateIt plugin from `https://github.com/gjunge/rateit.js`, but what about doing this verbally? How we achieve this will depend on the structure used, but it should be possible to provide the rating verbally and for it to be translated into the appropriate star rating. As an example, adding a rating could look like the example screenshot shown in Figure 5-5.

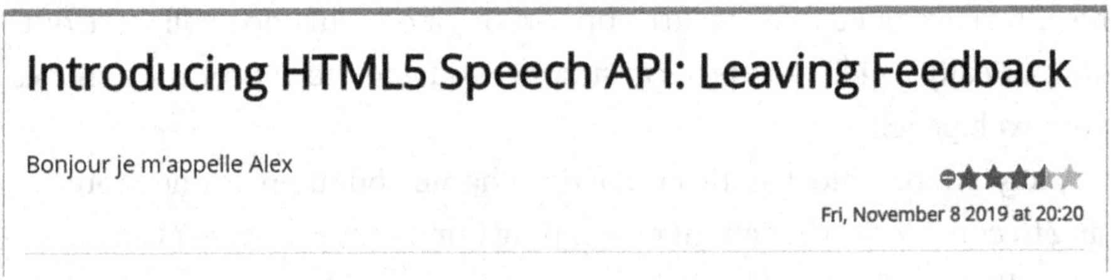

Introducing HTML5 Speech API: Leaving Feedback

Bonjour je m'appelle Alex

Fri, November 8 2019 at 20:20

Figure 5-5. Our mocked-up rating stars

- Our demo allows us to post reviews on a page, but this is only part of the story – we should absolutely look at using that feedback and potentially responding to the customer if this is appropriate. The latter though means we would need at least one method of getting in contact with them, such as an email address. How could we achieve this? One method might be to encourage customers to register for an account, so we can get that email address – this will of course have implications for privacy legislation such as GDPR, which we will need to consider.

- If resourcing to support management of feedback from customers is an issue, then we could consider using an API such as Google Translate to at least convert our transcribed content into English or our native tongue (if it isn't English). This does come with a cost – we can only hope to get a sense of what Google Translate provides as machine-translated content won't be perfect!

These are just a few ideas to get you started – we could even look at adding extras such as avatars, if the type of site we operate is suitable for such an extra! It goes without saying though that if we do add in extra options, then these need to be tested thoroughly, to be sure that they offer value and don't appear as a gimmick to our customers.

Summary

Customer feedback is essential for any business, no matter how small or large the operation – ultimately the success of our business will depend on the comments received and how we respond or the action we take to improve ourselves. Clearly it's important to make the process of giving feedback as easy as possible – what better way than to leave verbal comments? We've covered the basic steps to achieve this over the course of this chapter; let's take a moment to review what we have learned in more detail.

We kicked off by introducing the theme for this chapter, before quickly setting the scene and determining both how we will scope and build our demo. We then moved onto constructing the form, before exploring how the code worked in detail while making note of similarities from earlier chapters.

We then took a look at how we could incorporate this into a more real-world example, before delving into the subject of language support – we covered the steps required to alter our demo, before exploring some final points about the downsides of providing verbal feedback and where we can develop our project to introduce new features for our customers.

Okay, we're not stopping here; it's time to move on to our next chapter! Hands up how many of you own a smart assistant such as Google Assistant, Siri, or Amazon Alexa? Bill Gates, one of the co-founders of Microsoft, once said that voice and speech will become a standard part of the web interface – with the advent of Siri, Alexa, and Google Assistant, he was not wrong! We already have many of the techniques in place to build a simple version of Alexa for a web site. Intrigued on how? Stay with me, and I will reveal all and more in the next chapter.

CHAPTER 6

Project: Building Alexa

"Alexa, what time is it…?"

For some of you, I'll bet that is an all too common a phrase in your household – I suspect it's a case of not if, but how many!

Over the last few years, the growth of smart assistants (or SAs) such as Amazon Alexa or Google Assistant has exploded; gone are the days when we had to trawl web sites or search through newspapers or books to get that scrap of information. Indeed, one of the co-founders of Microsoft, Bill Gates, once said that he believed voice and speech output will become a standard part of the [web] interface – with the advent of Siri, Alexa, and Google Assistant, he was not wrong!

This got me thinking – we've already been introduced to the two core technologies that lie at the heart of smart assistants, namely, speech synthesis and recognition. Could we build something that mimics how assistants such as Alexa work? It may not be as powerful as the hardware equivalent is, but it could use both APIs to create something useful. As long as we make it modular, then we can add features, to help develop it into something more worthwhile in the future.

With that in mind, and over the course of this chapter, we'll make use of the Speech Recognition and Synthesis APIs to create a simple Alexa-style voice assistant; we'll learn how to make it modular, so that it's easy to add further skills to help expand its capabilities.

© Alex Libby 2020
A. Libby, *Introducing the HTML5 Web Speech API*,
https://doi.org/10.1007/978-1-4842-5735-7_6

Setting the scene

Our next project is going to be a simpler one – it's an opportunity to relax a little, as I know what's coming up later in the book is going to be intensive! Let me introduce you to Rachel – she will be able to tell the time in your local area, in New York (more on that later), get the weather, and more.

We'll start with some simple tasks to illustrate how easy it is to add features in. Let's begin by taking a look at how we will architect our demo in more detail.

Architecting our demo

We've already been introduced to the two APIs that feature at the core of this project; by now, they should start to look a little familiar. However, for this project, we're going to add a little twist.

Instead of hard-coding both the Speech Recognition and Synthesis APIs by hand, we're going to make use of a library to do some of the work for us. This will be one of a handful that we'll make use of, so let's take a look at the list in full:

- Annyang – this library is a wrapper around the Speech Recognition API that we've used thus far in this book; it's available from `https://www.talater.com/annyang/`.

- SpeechKITT – this is a GUI that works in tandem with annyang and can be downloaded from `https://github.com/TalAter/SpeechKITT`. The GUI library is a couple of years old, but offers native support for annyang and still works perfectly fine for our needs.

Just in case you're wondering about the reference to KITT in the GUI library, the library was named after the '80s US show *Knight Rider*. You can even see a picture of the lead actor, David Hasselhoff, on the GitHub page for SpeechKITT!

- Luxon – used for dates and times, along with time zone support; this is available from `https://moment.github.io/luxon/index.html`.

- OpenWeatherMap – one of the requests we make relates to getting the weather; for this, we will make use of the API available from `https://openweathermap.org/`.

- Pixabay – if you happen to own a smart assistant already, this is something you might not expect to see in a demo like this; after all, smart assistants can't show pictures unless you happen to configure your smart assistant to use your PC as the display mechanism! We've included it here to explore how we might use a service such as Pixabay to display images; we will talk more about whether this is the right approach later in the chapter.

- jQuery – this is a necessary evil. We're making use of it to work around a limitation with the SpeechKITT GUI. We'll explore more on why later in the chapter.

In addition, I would recommend having the JSON Editor Online web page (`https://jsoneditoronline.org/`) open in your browser; it's a great JSON editor and will be useful for browsing the raw data returned from some of the services we use.

Our demo will showcase a handful of straightforward requests; we can use this as a basis for adding in more features that use different APIs. It's something we'll explore later in this chapter, but for now, let's crack on with coding our demo.

Building our demo

In terms of coding our demo, it will seem like a walk in the park, compared to previous projects! Our demo will be very simple in terms of structure – outside of some markup and styling needed for presentation, there will only be one element added. This will be done dynamically and will be used to trigger all of the requests we make.

Let's crack on and get the markup set up, before we take a look at how the code that we write will bring our demo to life.

Creating the markup

Our first task is to set up the markup for this little demo – this one is very straightforward. We don't even need to provide a placeholder for our microphone trigger, as this will be created dynamically for us by the SpeechKITT GUI. Let's dive in and take a look at the code in more detail, beginning with our markup.

SETTING UP THE MARKUP

To set up the markup, go ahead with these steps:

1. We'll begin by creating a new folder for our project – save it as rachel at the root of our project area.

2. Next, go ahead and create a new file for our base markup; add in the following code:

```
<!DOCTYPE html>
<html>
<head>
    <title>Introducing HTML5 Speech API: Building an Alexa
    Clone</title>
```

```
<link href="https://fonts.googleapis.com/
css?family=Open+Sans
&display=swap" rel="stylesheet">
</head>
<body>
  <div id="page-wrapper">
    <h2>Introducing HTML5 Speech API: Building an Alexa-
    style Smart Assistant</h2>
    <section>
        Rachel's voice: <select name="voice" id="voice">
        </select>
    </section>
  </div>
  <script src="js/annyang.min.js"></script>
  <script src="js/speechkitt.min.js"></script>
  <script src="js/jquery.min.js"></script>
  <script src="js/luxon.min.js"></script>
  <script src="js/scripts.js"></script>
</body>
</html>
```

3. Save the file as index.html – we can close it for now. The
    next exercise will take care of adding the script functionality.

4. We have one last step to do – we need to copy across some
    JavaScript files and CSS styling from the code download that
    accompanies this book. Go ahead and extract copies of the
    following files, and put them into subfolders under our rachel
    folder that we created earlier:

    •   styles.css – into a new css subfolder

    •   The following into a new js subfolder: annyang.js,
        jquery.min.js, luxon.min.js, and speechkitt.
        min.js

5. At this point you can close any open files. Leave yourself a blank file open, ready to make a start on the next exercise which will be along shortly.

We now have our markup in place – there is nothing complex or unusual about the code. We've simply set up our basic framework and included a handful of JavaScript and CSS files; the magic will come when we start to develop the script that brings our demo to life.

Making our demo come to life

Before we get started on adding our JavaScript code, there is one small task we need to do – sign up for a free account at `https://home.openweathermap.org/users/sign_up`.

This will take a couple of hours to be activated by the team at OpenWeather; you can assume it is set up once you get a welcome email with the key from the OpenWeather team. You may want to factor this in before you get stuck into developing the code! Assuming you've signed up and had email confirmation to say that your account is now active, let's make a start on our demo.

DEMO: ADDING FUNCTIONALITY

To set up our demo, follow through these steps:

1. First, we need to create a new file for our script – for this, go ahead and create `scripts.js` in the `js` subfolder under the `rachel` folder we created in the previous exercise.

2. We can now begin to add code. There is a lot to cover, which we will do block by block. The first block takes care of loading Rachel's voice – add the following code in at the top of the `scripts.js` file:

```
const voiceSelect = document.getElementById('voice');

function loadVoices() {
  var voices = window.speechSynthesis.getVoices();

  voices.forEach(function(voice, i) {
      var option = document.createElement('option');
      option.value = voice.name;
      option.innerHTML = voice.name;
      voiceSelect.appendChild(option);
  });
}

loadVoices();

// Chrome loads voices asynchronously.
window.speechSynthesis.onvoiceschanged = function(e) {
  loadVoices();
};
```

3. With Rachel's voice loaded, we can now get her to talk and flag if any errors crop up. Leave a line blank after the previous step, and then add in this function to manage basic error handling:

```
window.speechSynthesis.onerror = function(event) {
  console.log('Speech recognition error detected:
  ' + event.error);
  console.log('Additional information: ' + event.message);
};
```

4. This next function makes Rachel talk – go ahead and add the following code in after the previous function, leaving a blank line in between:

```
function speak(text) {
  var msg = new SpeechSynthesisUtterance();
  msg.text = text;

  if (voiceSelect.value) {
    msg.voice = speechSynthesis.getVoices().
    filter(function(voice) {
      return voice.name == voiceSelect.value;
    })[0];
  }
  speechSynthesis.speak(msg);
}
```

5. We come to the interesting part – now that Rachel can talk, it's time she said something! The first example will be to articulate the current time:

```
// Rachel, what time is it now?
var timeNow = function() {
  var localtime = luxon.DateTime.local().
  toLocaleString(luxon.DateTime.TIME_SIMPLE);
  speak("The time is " + localtime);
}
```

The time mentioned will be local to wherever you live in the world.

---

6. This next task is to articulate the time in a different location – I chose New York, which happens to be the home of Apress Publishing. Go ahead and drop the following code in after the previous step, leaving an empty line in between:

```
// Rachel, what time is it in New York?
var timeinnewyork = function() {
```

```
var NYTime = luxon.DateTime.local().setZone('America/
New_York').toLocaleString(luxon.DateTime.TIME_WITH_
LONG_OFFSET);
  speak("The time in New York is " + NYTime);
}
```

7. We've covered the time in two different locations, but what about the date? No problem, here's the code:

```
// Rachel, what is today's date?
var DateNow = function() {
  var localdate = luxon.DateTime.local().
  toLocaleString(luxon.DateTime.DATE_SIMPLE);
  speak("The date is " + localdate);
}
```

8. I love a good joke, so it only seems sensible to see if we can include a couple in this demo; if you own a real Alexa, then I'm sure you will have seen emails suggesting you ask it for a joke too! Here's the first:

```
// Rachel tell a funny joke:
var telljoke = function() {
  speak("Why do we tell actors to break a leg? Because
  every play has a cast");
}
```

9. This next joke will seem a little more fitting for us designers and developers, at least from the use of font types; go ahead and add in this code after the code from the previous step, leaving a blank line in between:

```
var tellsecondjoke = function() {
  speak('Helvetica and Times New Roman walk into a bar.
  The bar tender shouts "Get Out of here - we don\'t
  serve your type!"');
}
```

10. Another obvious thing to ask Rachel would be the weather – for
    the purposes of this demo, I've hard-coded it to be one of my
    favorite holiday destinations, or the city of Copenhagen. For this,
    go ahead and add a blank line after the code from step 9 and
    then drop in this code:

You will need to replace <INSERT YOUR APP ID HERE> with the API key from
OpenWeather, as per the beginning of this exercise.

```
// Rachel, what is the weather in Copenhagen?
var weather = function() {
  var yourappid = "<INSERT YOUR APP KEY HERE>";

  $.ajax({
    method:'GET',
    crossDomain: true,
    url: 'https://api.openweathermap.org/data/2.5/weather
?q=copenhagen,dk&appid=' + yourappid,
    dataType: "json",
    async: true,
    success: function(response){
      speak("The temperature in Copenhagen is currently:
      " + parseInt(response.main.temp - 273.15) + "
      degrees");
    }
  });
}
```

11.   This next function takes care of getting some example data
        from Wikipedia – as it so happens, I had an email from Amazon
        suggesting this very topic, for my Alexa! Leave a blank line
        under the previous function and then add in this code – note
        that the url value should be on one line and not spread over two
        as shown in the following:

```
// Rachel, Wikipedia "artificial intelligence"
var wikipedia = function() {
  $.ajax({
    method:'GET',
    crossDomain: true,
    url: 'https://en.wikipedia.org/api/rest_v1/page/summary
    /Artificial_intelligence',
    dataType: "json",
    async: true,
    success: function(response){
      speak("Here is the extract from Wikipedia on
      artificial intelligence: " + response.extract);
    }
  });
}
```

12.   For this last option, we're going to come back to this one later in
        the chapter – add it in for now, and all will become clear soon:

```
// Rachel, show me a picture of...
var flickr = function() { console.log("This to follow"); }
```

13.   We're almost at the end of this exercise. This last part takes
        care of initializing annyang and SpeechKITT. Leave a blank line
        as before, and then drop in this code:

```
if (annyang) {
  var commands = {
    'Rachel what time is it': timeNow,
    'Rachel tell a joke': telljoke,
    'Rachel tell another joke': tellsecondjoke,
    'Rachel what time is it in New York': timeinnewyork,
    'Rachel what is the weather like in Copenhagen': weather,
    'Rachel wikipedia artificial intelligence': wikipedia,
    'Rachel show me a picture of some orchids': flickr
  }

  // Add our commands to annyang, then tell KITT to use
  annyang:
  annyang.addCommands(commands);
  SpeechKITT.annyang();

  // Define a stylesheet for KITT to use
  SpeechKITT.setStylesheet('css/styles.css');

  // Render KITT's interface
  SpeechKITT.vroom();
}

$(document).ready(function() {
  $("#skitt-ui").insertAfter($("h2"));
});
```

14. Go ahead and save the file – we can now preview the results of our work! Browse to https://speech/rachel/ in your browser; if all is well, we should see something akin to the screenshot shown in Figure 6-1.

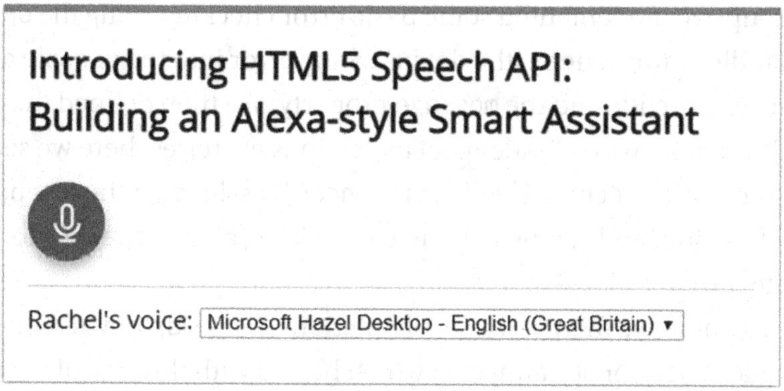

Figure 6-1. *Our finished result – meet "Rachel" in all her glory...*

At this stage, we now have a functioning demo – Rachel has come to life and is able to respond to some simple requests. Although the code we've used isn't particularly complex and should by now be relatively familiar, our demo highlights some key points we should consider more closely. Before we do so, let's dive in and take a look at the code in more detail.

Breaking apart the code

In comparison to some of the demos from earlier in this book (and those yet to come), this one will seem like a walk in the park! We've been able to reuse some of the code from earlier projects, namely, the Speech Synthesis API; the rest is from the annyang library that we introduced earlier in this chapter.

The main focus of this code sits in the scripts.js file – here, we kicked off by caching a reference to the voice drop-down used in our markup, before calling the loadVoices() function to load in the voices from Google into this drop-down element. As before, we've also included the onvoiceschanged function – some earlier versions of Chrome loaded voices asynchronously, which can only be done using this method. (It will be less of an issue now with more recent versions of Chrome, so this function has been included for compatibility.)

169

Next up, we implemented some basic error checking using the onerror
event handler – this renders the details of any error into the console area,
using the error code and the message property. We then defined the
speak() function, which is identical to previous exercises; here we set a
new instance of SpeechSynthesisUtterance(), assigned it the text passed
into the function, and set the voice to use, before calling .speak() to
articulate the text.

At this point, we then had a set of functions. Let's skip down to the
initialization function for annyang, which begins with this line of code: if
(annyang) {. It's here that we set up the instance to annyang and told it to
use the SpeechKITT GUI and our specified styles.css stylesheet.

It's worth noting that SpeechKITT uses the .vroom() method to start
up; this is a reference to the inspiration for this GUI and can easily be
replaced with render(), which does the same thing.

We now have a basic configuration in place – if we revert back to
around line 40 (var timeNow = function() {), we can see the first of
several simple functions that will be called each time annyang recognizes
when a request has been made, such as this one (Figure 6-2).

```
39   // Rachel, what time is it now?
40   var timeNow = function() {
41       var localtime = luxon.DateTime
42                       .local()
43                       .toLocaleString(luxon.DateTime.TIME_SIMPLE);
44       speak("The time is " + localtime);
45   }
```

Figure 6-2. The first function to be called by annyang

If I had said "Rachel, what time is it?", annyang would call this `timeNow()` function and display the response, which will be the local time for where you live. The function calls are defined in the `var commands = {...}` object toward the end of the script – these will be executed as and when annyang determines that one matches the response from our user.

Okay, let's move on, I would say that this is the end of the explanation, but if only! In truth, the project has revealed a number of issues and areas for further exploration; let's begin with the first which is something of a styling challenge. If you had run annyang's example demo (shown at `https://github.com/TalAter/SpeechKITT` as a separate demo), you would have noticed that the trigger sits at the bottom of the screen, which doesn't always fit what people need! It's due to a configuration issue (or limitation – depending on your view). Let's dive in and I will explain all.

Solving a styling problem

In our project, I am sure that you will have noticed the small usage of jQuery at the bottom of the script file and that earlier I alluded to this being a "necessary evil" – there is good reason for this, so let me explain what I mean.

If we had run our demo using the original CSS styling provided from the SpeechKITT web site, you would have found that the microphone trigger sits at the bottom-left corner of our screen.

No amount of moving it using CSS on its own will help – this particular element is generated dynamically, so for it to be properly moved, we need to use JavaScript or jQuery! As a matter of convenience, I've used jQuery in this instance do this job; this keeps it very neat and tidy, although this is at the expense of importing a large library. Whether this works for you is a different matter though. This will depend on if you happen to be using jQuery already. If not, then pure JavaScript would be preferable, although the code to do this isn't quite so concise! We can see the source of our problem illustrated in Figure 6-3, where the microphone element is highlighted in our console.

```
⌖  🗀  |    Elements    Console    Sources    Network    Performance    Memory    Application    Security    A

<!doctype html>
<html>
▶ <head>…</head>
▼ <body>
     <script src="//cdnjs.cloudflare.com/ajax/libs/annyang/2.4.0/annyang.min.js"></script>
     <script src="//cdnjs.cloudflare.com/ajax/libs/SpeechKITT/1.0.0/speechkitt.min.js"></script>
   ▶ <script>…</script>
.. ▶ <div id="skitt-ui" class="skitt-ui--not-listening" style="display: none;">…</div> == $0
     <link rel="stylesheet" href="//cdnjs.cloudflare.com/ajax/libs/SpeechKITT/1.0.0/themes/flat.css"
     style-sheet">
   </body>
</html>
```

Figure 6-3. *The microphone trigger from the original SpeechKITT demo*

However, doing a simple element move isn't the end of it – there are a couple of other changes we had to make, in order for us to style our demo as we wanted to do. The other changes we made are all CSS-related. In no particular order, they are

- We dropped the two media queries from the original demo – these were getting in the way and affected the specific format used for styling our demo. I am sure that media queries would be useful, but the ones from the original demo don't fit this particular example, so would need to be revised anyway!

- We then removed this rule – the reason for this is a little more complex:

```
#skitt-ui {  display: block !important; }
```

I'm not a fan of using the !important directive, as it frequently gets used and abused for the wrong reasons! I was keen to remove at least one of them if I could – the one against #skitt-ui was the more likely candidate.

There was one more block where we needed to make changes – in the #skitt-ui rule, the following entries (highlighted) were removed:

```
#skitt-ui {
  height: 50px;
  display: inline-block;
  background-color: #2980B9;
  z-index: 200;
  border-radius: 25px;
  outline: none;
    position: fixed;
    bottom: 20px;
    left: 20px;
  border: none;
  box-shadow: rgba(0,0,0,0.2) 0px 4px 8px;
  cursor: default;
  font-family: Lato, Helvetica, Arial, sans-serif;
  font-size: 16px
}
```

Making these changes meant that we could effectively reposition our microphone trigger anywhere on screen and not worry about its positioning!

Okay, let's change tack. Up until now, we've explored how to add in a number of verbal examples, where we can articulate the response back to our user verbally, such as the current time or weather.

We do though have a choice to make: what about visual content? Yes, it's not something you might expect with a standard Alexa (although not impossible), but as we're working in a browser, we can consider whether we want to display content on screen. This is something we'll make use of more in the next project, but for now, how about displaying something simple, from say a site such as Flickr or Pixabay.com?

Adding new features

Now that Rachel is set up and operational, we can add in all manner of different features. The only limiting factors are our imagination and whether we can make it work for us.

This does raise a good question though: what kind of features should we add? In most cases, one could argue that they should be verbal only – it does depend on how close we want to mimic a real smart assistant (and no, I don't mean one of a human kind, either!) On the other hand, it's possible to say that this doesn't apply, as you can create all manner of skills that are not all verbally based. Choices, choices...

That aside, and for our next exercise, we're going to take a little poetic license and assume that we can make use of our PC's screen as well as accept verbal input. We're going to display a random image from a picture library; this will be of orchids (this happens to be my favorite flower, but you can use any category, such as cars, camera, people, and etc.). Rachel will pull back a list of images from the picture library site and display one at random on screen. Let's take a look at the changes we need to make in more detail.

ADDING AN IMAGE

To add in a picture option, go ahead with these steps:

1. We'll start by editing our `script.js` file – we already have a placeholder function for this, so go ahead and look for this line of code:

```
console.log("This to follow");
```

2. Remove the comment, and then drop in this code:

```
// Rachel, show me a picture of some orchids

var pixabay = function() {
```

```
var API_KEY = '<INSERT APP ID HERE>';
var URL = "https://pixabay.com/api/?key=" + API_KEY +
"&q=" + encodeURIComponent('orchids');

$.getJSON(URL, function(data){
  function getRandomInt(max) {
    return Math.floor(Math.random() * Math.floor(max));
  }

  if (parseInt(data.totalHits) > 0) {
    var randomImg = getRandomInt(20);
    console.log(randomImg);
    $("<div class='imgPreview'><img src=" + data.
    hits[randomImg].largeImageURL +"></div>").
    insertAfter($("#skitt-ui"));
  } else {
    console.log('No hits');
  }
});
};
```

3. Save the file – we don't need it to remain open, so you can close it.

4. Next, switch to the `styles.css` file, and scroll all the way to the bottom.

5. Go ahead and drop in this code, and then save the file:

```
/* Additions to allow for image */
.imgPreview { margin-left: auto; margin-right: auto;
 display: block; width: 300px; margin-top: 20px; }

.imgPreview img { width: 300px; }
```

175

6. We can now preview the results of our change – for this, browse to
    `https://speech/rachel`, and then click the white microphone.
    Articulate "Rachel, show me a picture of some orchids" into your
    microphone. If all is well, we should see a random image appear,
    similar to the screenshot shown in Figure 6-4.

Figure 6-4. Displaying a picture from Pixabay as an added feature

A nice, easy change to make. Granted not all changes could be this
simple, but with a little creativity, I'm sure we can find more that could be
added in a similar manner!

This said, it does highlight a couple of useful points about the modular
nature of this code and how easy it is to add in new features. Keeping this
in mind, let's revisit this code in more detail, to see how we effected this
change to our demo.

Exploring the code in detail

For this demo to work, I needed to choose a picture library with a useable API – I did consider Flickr, but their current API didn't make it very easy to add into our demo! I chose Pixabay instead, as theirs is simpler; they may not have quite as many images or be as well known as Flickr, but that isn't critical for the purposes of this demo.

The first change we made when we set up Rachel at the start of this chapter; this was to add in the command to execute the function that returns our image:

```
var commands = {
    ...
    'Rachel show me a picture of some orchids': pixabay
};
```

To allow the code to continue working at that time, we put a placeholder function in that rendered a message to the console. However, in this exercise, we replaced that console log message with a URL that would form the basis for our request to Pixabay – the category being encoded, to allow for the use of quotes in the URL.

We then used an AJAX call to get the list of images – it could return any number of URLs, but as long as it returned at least one, we then chose a random number between 1 and 20 and used this to display the largeImageURL property from the returned JSON object. This was then used to create an empty div element on screen, inside which we rendered our chosen image.

Okay, let's move on. So far, our demo has been operating in US English. This is perfectly okay, but not everyone speaks English; what about including support for other languages? Thankfully this is relatively easy to do – it does mean making some changes, so let's dive in and take a closer look.

Adding support for different languages

When working with the Speech Recognition or Synthesis API, we've already seen in some of our earlier projects that adding in language support is relatively straightforward. Yes, there may be a few changes to make, but nothing too onerous. The same applies to the annyang library we've used in this chapter.

For our next demo, I'm going to get Rachel to start speaking French (primarily because that's the language I can speak, so I can check it works) – if you prefer to use a different language, please feel free to update the text accordingly.

ADDING SUPPORT FOR LANGUAGES

We have a few changes to make, so let's get started:

1. First, take a copy of the now completed rachel folder, and save it as rachel-language at the root of our project area.

2. The first change we need to make is to replace the speak(text) function – for this, go ahead and replace the existing version with this code:

```
function speak(text) {
  var msg = new SpeechSynthesisUtterance();
  msg.text = text;
  msg.lang = 'fr-fr';

  speechSynthesis.speak(msg);
}
```

3. Next, scroll down a little until you see the timeNow function – replace the speak... line with this:

```
speak("Le temps est maintenant " + localtime);
```

4. We need to do something similar for the `timeinnewyork` function – go ahead and replace the `speak...` line with this:

```
speak("TLe temps à New York est maintenant " + NYTime);
```

5. The dateNow function also needs to be updated – for this, replace the `speak...` line with this line of code:

```
speak("Le date aujourd'hui est " + localdate);
```

We'll skip past the two joke functions for now – I will explain more at the end of this exercise.

---

6. Next up is the `weather()` function – for this, replace the `speak...` line as indicated:

```
speak("La température à Copenhague est maintenant :
" + parseInt(response.main.temp - 273.15) + " degrees");
```

7. We need to something similar with the `wikipedia()` function – go ahead and alter it as shown:

```
success: function(response){
    speak("Voici l'extrait de Wikipedia sur l'intelligence
    artificielle: " + response.extract);
}
```

8. The final change is to alter the name given in the var commands ={...} block – for this, we will use Hélène, as this is more French. Change each instance of the word Rachel with Hélène, so you have this:

```
var commands = {
    'Hélène quelle heure est-il': timeNow,
'Hélène raconte une blague': telljoke,
'Hélène raconte une autre blague': tellsecondjoke,
```

```
'Hélène quelle heure est-il à New York': timeinnewyork,
'Hélène quel temps fait-il à Copenhague': weather,
'Hélène wikipedia intelligence artificielle': wikipedia,
'Hélène montre-moi une photo d\'orchidées': flickr
  }
```

9. We're almost done. The last two things we need to check or change are the language and making sure we have localized the annyang library. Scroll to the bottom of the `scripts.js` library, and look for this line:

```
// Add our commands to annyang
annyang.addCommands(commands);
```

10. Go ahead and add in this `.setLanguage` command, immediately below that line:

```
annyang.setLanguage('fr-FR');
```

11. The last change is to localize our speechKITT library – for this, close the scripts.js (as we're done with that for now), and open speechKITT

    `.min.js`.

12. Find this line: `u="What can I help you with?"` Replace it as indicated:

```
u="Qu\'est-ce que je peux vous aider?"
```

You can see a screenshot of how it should look in Figure 6-5.

```
d="Activate Voice Control",u="Qu\'est-ce que je peux vous aider?",g=[
ef=o:((s=document.createElement("link")).rel="stylesheet",s.href=o,s.
unction(){if(h()){var t=document.getElementById("skitt-listening-text
tt-listening-text__instructions");(t=document.createElement("span")).
```

Figure 6-5. Updating the speechKITT.min.js file...

I would recommend doing a search and replace – it will be much easier!

13. Okay, go ahead and save and then close that file; we can now preview the results. Fire up your browser, and then browse to `https://speech/rachel-language`. If all is well, we should see the screenshot shown in Figure 6-6, where the microphone symbol has already been clicked, ready for speaking.

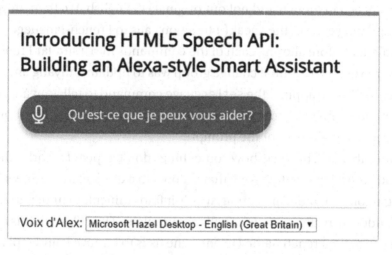

Introducing HTML5 Speech API:
Building an Alexa-style Smart Assistant

Qu'est-ce que je peux vous aider?

Voix d'Alex: Microsoft Hazel Desktop - English (Great Britain) ▾

Figure 6-6. *Our updated French-language version of "Rachel"*

At this point, we now have a demo. Let's try running the Pixabay command to see how Rachel responds. By rights, we should get a random image of some orchids back, surely...? There's nothing wrong with that assumption; it's perfectly valid, only except this time, we get back the square root of absolutely...nothing. What gives?

Breaking down the code

There is a very good reason for our demo appearing not to work – it might seem a little crazy, but there isn't actually anything wrong with our code as such! Yes, I know it seems a little weird, but trust me on this: the code is syntactically valid. Before I reveal the root cause, let's quickly cover off the changes we made to localize our demo.

Our demo had four distinct areas where changes were needed. Our first change was to replace the speak(text) { function, so that it would return speech in French and not our original US English. We then moved onto updating each of the speak() function calls to French-language equivalents, before altering each of the commands into a similar French-language version. Our final change group was to update annyang and SpeechKITT – we applied the setLanguage command to tell annyang to respond to French commands and updated speechKITT.min.js to show localized text in French for the prompt.

Now, that lack of voice, how come things don't appear to work, when the code is perfectly valid? Well, that is down to a quirk with the Speech Recognition API: there are certain words it finds difficult to understand and render correctly, so instead will remain silent. The culprit in this case is the use of the French name Hélène – the fix is to remove it and replace it with a different name. In this case I would suggest something like "Alex"; it's very much a case of trial and error, before you find something that works. The rest of the code works fine, so simply removing "Hélène" will work just as well.

It's arguable as to whether this is a bug as such – it's more around the fact that the API is still a work in progress, so still requires some technical development before it has fully matured and is able to articulate these errant words. It does also explain why, by the time you've finished with updating this demo, you may end up with two or three names in use – "Rachel" from the original demo, "Hélène" in this one, and whatever you choose to use to replace it!

Okay, let's move on. We've explored how we can use annyang to simplify implementing the Speech Recognition API (and as an alternative to hard-coding it manually). Where next? There are a few things we can do to help improve and develop our code further, so let's take a moment to explore how we can update it in more detail.

Improving performance

Hopefully by now, if you've updated the demo, we have a working version of Rachel, localized for French use (or your own language, if you've elected to use something else). It's a simple demo which shows how easy it is to work with a language that is different from English – our demo does however unmask a few things that we should consider correcting! Let's take a look in more detail:

- Our demo makes use of five different script files, including the core one we created – this is a little excessive! We should absolutely consider reducing our reliance on libraries if we can: a quick win would be to change the jQuery code at the end of scripts.js to be vanilla JavaScript. (I used jQuery for convenience only!)

- If you take a closer look at the code for the French version of our demo, you will see that I've not updated the two joke entries. This is deliberate; the jokes I've chosen will not likely translate that well into French, so we should consider replacing them with French jokes or with something else entirely. It's an important point – clearly not everything will translate across to a different language in the same way, for a tool whose default language is US English!

- I would absolutely consider rationalizing the JSON code used for the calls to OpenWeather and Wikipedia; the core code is functionally the same, but the response back will of course be different. This is a good example where we can modularize this particular option to be shared across multiple commands, should we decide to add in more that make use of it.

- Should we even use annyang? I know this might sound crazy (given that this chapter has been about using it), but its use does come at a cost. We can of course merge our minified files, but we should consider whether this is worth the expense of lugging around a large file or if we should write our code manually and drop the use of annyang.

- There is a little slipup in our code. Have you spotted where? If you look closely, we've specified a function to call time for New York. Trouble is it's based on GMT+5 – this is fine for the United Kingdom (where I'm based), but not for France! This is something we need to allow for when localizing our application; not only do we need to change languages but we also need to make sure that our features also make sense.

- We've also made use of the Pixabay picture library in our demo – there is nothing technically wrong with this, but is this something we should use, given that most things a smart assistant will do are likely to be verbal? Of course, we could argue that some of the things they can do do rely on using a PC or laptop. I guess it all depends on how closely you want to mimic a real device!

This is just a few things for us to consider changing – I'm sure you will likely find more! It does go to show that in demos such as ours, we can't simply rely on updating text when localizing code. We also need to consider aspects where values change because our country has changed (such as time zones). It does also mean that if your target country has a propensity to do things differently (e.g., use more mobile devices), then this needs to be factored into our demo as well.

Okay, let's move on. Assuming we make these changes, where next? Well, this kind of functionality is absolutely open to being expanded. Let's take a look at a few ideas, to help get you started.

Taking things further

"Aha, where next?" I wonder. Well, the world is our oyster, as they say. I'm not sure where that saying came from, but as it implies, we are free to add in all manner of different features, as long as we can code something that is technically feasible.

To help with this, I've scoured through a few emails I've received over the last 6 months, for ideas as to how we might be able to expand what we can offer. Here is a list of a few ideas, to get your creative juices flowing:

- Play local radio station – this isn't so easy; if you can get the URL of your favorite radio station's online player, you could potentially fire a request remotely and use a little JavaScript to automatically click any play buttons that you might come across.

- Find your nearest supermarket/local store – this might need to rely on one of the APIs from Google, but if you want to avoid using that behemoth, you can use the geolocation APIs already available in the browser, to hard-code values for you. Once in, it's a simple matter of using the Haversine formula (which we will see in use in the next chapter), to work out the distance. It may not be as pretty, but it will at least allow you to code something to prove it works!

- Find a recipe containing X, where X is your favorite food – for this, I would suggest firing a request to Google to see what it comes back with, or you can try using a service such as the Spoonacular API (`https://spoonacular.com/food-api`), in a similar fashion to how we use an API in the next chapter.

- Turn the background color of a page element in a browser into a different color (simulate turning the light into a different color) – okay, this is a simple one, but it's the principle that counts! It was inspired by the range of smart bulbs you can now get, such as the Philips Hue system; you can see a demo of how to achieve this at `https://mdn.github.io/web-speech-api/speech-color-changer/`.

- Count syllables in a word – yes, this indeed comes from an email sent by Amazon; a (partial) screenshot is shown in Figure 6-7.

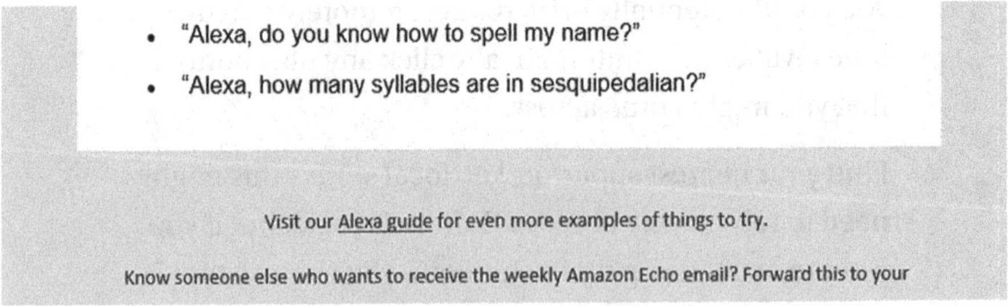

- "Alexa, do you know how to spell my name?"
- "Alexa, how many syllables are in sesquipedalian?"

Visit our Alexa guide for even more examples of things to try.

Know someone else who wants to receive the weekly Amazon Echo email? Forward this to your

Figure 6-7.   (Partial) email from Amazon

It might sound unusual, but in reality, it isn't that difficult – we could use a function similar to this, to count the syllables in our chosen word:

```
function new_count(word) {
  word = word.toLowerCase();
  if(word.length <= 3) { return 1; }
  word = word.replace(/(?:[^laeiouy]es|ed|[^laeiouy]e)$/, ");
  word = word.replace(/^y/, ");
  return word.match(/[aeiouy]{1,2}/g).length;
  }

console.log(new_count('sesquipedalian'));   // the answer is 5
```

In case you're wondering what sesquipedalian means, it is somewhat ironic in this context. It can mean having many syllables, which is very apt here!

- A somewhat more complex feature would be to try adding products to Amazon's web cart – it does involve signing up for one of their APIs; if you're curious, take a look at the documentation available at https://docs. aws.amazon.com/AWSECommerceService/latest/DG/ AddingItemstoaCart.html for more details.

Hopefully this has given you something to think about – we are really only limited by our imagination and how far we want to take things! The key to making this work is to keep things as modular as possible – if we consider changing the commands block to accept commands from a JSON file, then we can leave our core code untouched and work on editing the JSON file for any updates.

Summary

The creation of a smart assistant might seem like a complex process, but in reality, the core technologies are very straightforward to set up! Over the course of this chapter, we've explored how we can use the Speech APIs to create a working (if not basic) version of a smart assistant – we've assigned to it a number of features, but can always add to them in the future. We've touched on using some interesting concepts in this chapter, so let's take a moment to review what we have learned.

We kicked off by setting the scene for the chapter and exploring how we would architect our demo; we touched on using an alternative speech library, to provide a little variety to our demo.

Next up came the build process, where we added the markup and script to make it come to life; we then took it apart before understanding the featurette that initially prevented our demo from articulating any responses. We then moved onto exploring how we can add new features, by using the addition of an image as our example, before touching on how to add language support to our demo. We then rounded out the chapter with a brief view on some crucial changes we should make as well as how we can develop our demo into something more useful as a production application.

And rest! Yes, that was a simple chapter, but deliberately so. We have a monster coming up shortly! Our next chapter will explore the use of some API services to get data, when using the Speech APIs. Anyone for food? I'll explain that request, and more, in the next chapter...

CHAPTER 7

Project: Finding a Restaurant

"I'm getting hungry with all this coding... Surely it must be time, right...?"

Yes, it's time for some food! Rather than stay in, I want to go out. Trouble is, where to? What style of food do I fancy? We could take a look online, but that is so old-school. Why not simply ask our computer to tell us which nearby restaurants serve the food we fancy?

Yes, we can use the power of the Speech APIs and the Zomato restaurant search service to do the work for us. Over the course of this chapter, we'll explore how we can use the APIs with other services to create some innovative apps to help satisfy that craving and keep you fueled and ready for more coding.

Setting the scene

While researching for the Raspberry Pi board demo back in Chapter 3, it got me thinking, *Could we use the Speech APIs to create a more useful application that gets its source dynamically?* Okay, the answer is almost certainly going to be more of a case of how, not if, but stay with me. All will become clear very shortly.

© Alex Libby 2020
A. Libby, *Introducing the HTML5 Web Speech API*,
https://doi.org/10.1007/978-1-4842-5735-7_7

If we take another look at the code from that demo, you will see that it is largely all hard-coded; after all, it was more about the Speech APIs than finding a piece of technology named after my two favorite foods...but I digress! To make using the Speech APIs more useful, we should try tying it to a data source such as JSON or a SQL.

This just happens to be the subject for our next project. Over the course of this chapter, we're going to create a simple app to find suitable places to eat in the beautiful city of Prague, in the Czech Republic. Why Prague? Well, I happened to visit it on holiday before I started writing this book – it is such a beautiful city, with gorgeous architecture and, of course, lots of restaurants to visit.

Okay, with that in mind, we need to make a start with building our app; the first stage is to set the parameters of what we will include in our demo, so let's dive in and take a look at this in more detail.

Setting the parameters of our project

As with any project, we need to set the boundaries of what we will include as our minimum viable product, at least for the purposes of this book.

It's particularly important for this demo, as it has the potential to develop into something much bigger; at the same time, we need to be aware that it won't be production-ready, but will at least give us the opportunity to develop something more suitable for production use.

So, with this in mind, let us set the scene for our demo. Allow me to introduce you to "Gofer Good Food" – a proof of concept bot application for finding great restaurants in and around Prague. This is the kind of app that could be made available as a free download by the local tourist office; for convenience, we will create our initial MVP as a desktop version to explore how it might work. Fortunately, we've already used one of the technologies that we need, from earlier in the book. Let's take a look at the full list of features, in addition to the Speech APIs:

- We will use the Zomato.js API for finding our restaurants – although we're using Prague as our example, the same principles could work with any city or area supported by the API.

- All responses during the search phase will be audio-based – this covers both our requests to find suitable restaurants and the responses from our app.

- Any responses which show the details of the restaurant (such as maps, telephone numbers, etc.) will be rendered on screen.

- We will make use of a service to provide a basic map facility, showing where we are located in the city (we'll cover extending this to the restaurants later in the chapter).

- Use a currency conversion process to show local prices in a currency of your choice – for this book, we'll keep it to US dollars, but the principles will be the same for other currencies.

- We'll work out where you are located using longitude and latitude values and use these to work out how far away your chosen restaurant is located.

Great! There's plenty for us to get started – I am sure that there are more ideas we can come up with to develop this further. We'll touch on some ideas later in this chapter. For now, we'll crack on with determining the business logic for our app, but before we do so, there is something important we need to cover off: setting expectations around how our proof of concept will work.

Setting expectations

At this point, I can probably hear the voice in you say this: *"Uh-oh, what you do mean by...expectations...?"* It's a fair question, but there is a good reason why we've called this demo a proof of concept. Let me explain more.

We can never hope to do a full-sized demo such as this justice, in the limited space we have available in this book; indeed, we could easily fill the pages of an entire book in its own right! We also have the added complication that the two core technologies in use (the chatbot framework and the Speech APIs) are somewhat like chalk and cheese – neither offers native support for each other, but with a little persuasion, they can be made to work together.

It does mean though that things may not be 100% perfect – but if they were, then life would be boring, right? I'm very much the kind of person who believes in pushing the boat out to see how far things can go; yes, we might find they don't work, but we don't know until we try!

Allowing for this, I would strongly recommend approaching this project with an open mind – the Speech APIs work well with different frameworks, so it's very much a case of working out if something is feasible and how far one can go with it. This next project won't be production-ready, but should offer us lots of opportunities to develop the principle further into something more fully-fledged that real people can use!

Okay, enough of the forewarning. Let's turn our attention to determining the business logic for this application, so we can see how it will work in reality and where we might have opportunities for development at a later date.

Determining the business logic

For the purposes of this project, we could ask for all manner of details when it comes to determining which restaurants to return back to our user – the thing is though, once you've asked one, it's the same process to ask others!

With this in mind, we're going to focus on asking just two questions: the first will be which cuisine type the customer wants and the second the price range. This way, we can keep the selection fairly wide, and it provides a great opportunity for you to extend it at a later date. We'll start by initiating the request through one button, but use a separate one to enable the microphone for each response – the latter will be kept nearer the bottom of the app, so as not to obscure the results for our customer (it's a UX styling reason, not a technical one!)

Okay, let's move on. Now that we've worked out the basics of what we will do, it's time to get technical and work out how we're going to power our demo. We've already made use of the two key APIs needed for this application, but we need others; let's take a look at the tools we need to use for our project in more detail.

Architecting our project

We could use a variety of different tools to complete this project – all of which will have their own features or drawbacks, but for the purposes of this demo, I've elected to use the following services:

- Zomato – they've collated the details of thousands of restaurants worldwide and provide an API-based service, where we can get details such as cuisine, typical prices, reviews, and the like. We'll make use of their free API, to get the details we need for our app. The data comes in JSON format – for convenience, we'll use jQuery to consume and present the data. We can equally use vanilla JavaScript as well.

Note Using this API does require signing up for their service at `https://developers.zomato.com/api`; this is free, as long as you stay within the boundaries of their daily usage rate.

- RiveScript – we made use of this back in Chapter 3; this time around, we will make the speech two-way, using both the Speech Synthesis and Recognition APIs.

- Google Maps – although I'm personally not a fan of having to use Google, they do provide a great mapping service; we can embed it into our demo, so that we can see where we are located in Prague.

- We'll make use of the free currency converter API at `https://www.exchangerate-api.com/`, to convert from local currency to US dollars – we could hard-code this if we wanted to, but adding in the API call will make things more interesting for us!

- We'll also make use of the SessionStorage API to temporarily store values from the restaurant searches, so that our bot can use them. There is a logistical reason for doing this; we will explore this in more detail toward the end of the chapter.

- As a bonus – and if space permits – we will briefly touch on using a Click to Call approach when displaying telephone numbers. Most mobiles will do this automatically, but we can increase our chances if we take some simple steps to reformat telephone numbers correctly.

At this point, there are a couple of limitations that we need to be aware of:

- For the Zomato API, we will host a copy of the JSON file locally. The only reason for this is speed: the JSON file is a weighty beast at over 6,500 lines! Don't worry. We won't modify it. I will explain what changes need to be made to switch over to using the version hosted by Zomato at the end of the project.

- Our hosted version will only use the first 20 names returned; we will go into what changes would be needed to expand this later in the chapter.

Okay, now that we know what technologies we are going to use, it's time to get stuck into writing code! To help make things simple, we'll break this down into several stages: the first is setting up the basic files and folders we need, so let's take a look at what is involved in more detail.

Setting up the initial markup and styling

As we will soon see, there is a fairly substantial amount of code in this demo. For the purposes of this demo, we will skip over the HTML markup and styling; this is standard code, based on code we've used in previous demos. Instead, we will focus entirely on the critical part, the JavaScript to see what's needed to make our application operate as expected.

SETTING UP THE BASICS

There are a few things we need to cover off before we get into the real meat of our code. Let's take a look at this in more detail:

1. We'll begin by extracting a copy of the zomato folder from the code download folder that accompanies this book – go ahead and save it in our project area.

If you see any references to "mini-project area" in the subsequent demos within this chapter, they refer to this zomato folder.

2. We've used a geolocation SVG by Freepik from the Flaticon web site at `https://www.flaticon.com/free-icon/ placeholder-filled-point_58960` – this I've included in the code download. If you would like to use an alternative, please alter the code accordingly.

3. I would recommend having a JSON editor available – there is a great one you can use online at `https:// onlinejsoneditor.com/`. The JSON file produced by Zomato is enormous, so having something available that will allow us to filter the data will be a great help!

4. You will need the API key from Zomato that we mentioned at the start of this exercise.

Okay, with these in place, let's crack on with our demo.

Initializing our project

The majority of the work needed to get our demo operational will be in creating our script file – this will cover both of the Speech APIs and our call to the Zomato data.

INITIALIZING THE PROJECT

The first step is to set up a blank file for our code – go ahead and crack open your text editor, then create a new file, and save it as `script.js` within the js subfolder of our mini-project folder, before continuing with these steps:

1. We have a fair amount of code to add – the first section will set up the basic function and add in a number of variable declarations. Go ahead and add in the following code as indicated:

```
/*jshint esversion: 6 */

(function () {
  "use strict";

  let bot = new RiveScript();

  const message_container = document.querySelector('.messages');
  const question = document.querySelector('#help');
  const voiceSelect = document.getElementById('voice');
  const mylat = document.querySelector("span.lat");
  const mylon = document.querySelector("span.lon");
  const output = document.querySelector(".output_result");

  var cuisineType = sessionStorage.getItem("cuisine");
  var rating = sessionStorage.getItem("priceRange");
  var restCount = 0;
  var takeaway = "";

  /**************************************************/
}());
```

2. Next, we will add in a simple function to take care of working out where we are located in Prague. Leave a blank line after the takeaway variable declaration, and then add in the following code:

```
mylat.innerHTML = "50.0904752";
mylon.innerHTML = "14.3889708";

  /*function getLocation() {
  navigator.geolocation.getCurrentPosition((loc) => {
    mylat.innerHTML = loc.coords.latitude;
    mylon.innerHTML = loc.coords.longitude;
  })
}

getLocation();*/
```

You will notice that this is commented out – this is deliberate. We will reveal why later in this chapter.

---

3. At this point, we've set up the initial declarations – go ahead and save the file.

4. Keep the file open as we will continue in the next exercise.

At first glance, you might think that only four steps seems like a really short exercise! It's a good point, but hey, we needed to start somewhere, and I am sure you will not thank me for jumping in at the deep end, right? Don't worry – we still have plenty more code to cover. Let's move onto the next part, where we begin to make our bot talk back to us.

Making our bot talk

Okay, that last comment might sound like we're encouraging a recalcitrant child to continually misbehave, but that could not be further from the truth! In reality, this next demo is about giving our app the capability to talk. It's a two-stage process, where we define how our app should speak; the "what to say" comes in a later demo.

ADDING SPEECH CAPABILITIES

With that in mind, let's make a start:

1. After the comment line at the end of the previous block, leave a line blank and then add in this function – it will take care of loading voices into our demo:

    ```
    function loadVoices() {
        var voices = window.speechSynthesis.getVoices();

        voices.forEach(function(voice, i) {
            var option = document.createElement('option');
            option.value = voice.name;
            option.innerHTML = voice.name;
            voiceSelect.appendChild(option);
        });
    }

    loadVoices();
    ```

2. We need to add in a second function – for some versions of Chrome, voices have to be loaded asynchronously, so add in this event handler:

    ```
    // Chrome loads voices asynchronously.
    window.speechSynthesis.onvoiceschanged = function(e) {
        loadVoices();
    };
    ```

3. The next function takes care of rendering error messages in the browser's console, if our application throws any during operation. For this, leave a blank line, and then add in the following code:

```
window.speechSynthesis.onerror = function(event) {
  console.log('Speech recognition error detected: ' +
  event.error);
  console.log('Additional information: ' + event.message);
};
```

4. The crux of this part of the application comes next – here we
    articulate each message provided by our bot, as and when
    requested in the code. For this, add in the following code below
    the onerror event handler:

```
function speak(text) {
    var msg = new SpeechSynthesisUtterance();
    msg.text = text;

    if (voiceSelect.value) {
      msg.voice = speechSynthesis.getVoices().
      filter(function(voice) {
        return voice.name == voiceSelect.value;
      })[0];
    }

    speechSynthesis.speak(msg);
  }
```

The rest of this section switches to the code that we need to
add in for our bot – we'll begin by declaring a reference to the
brain.rive file that we use to configure our bot. For this, add
in the next three lines after the closing bracket of the previous
function, leaving a blank line in between:

```
const brains = [
  './js/brain.rive'
];
```

5. We've seen the next two functions before, albeit a simpler
    version of the first — we need to add in code to handle how
    responses are rendered on screen by our bot. Go ahead and
    add in the following code below the brains const declaration:

```
function botReply(message){
  if (message.indexOf("No problem") != -1) {

    $.when(getRestaurants()).then(function() {
      restCount = sessionStorage.getItem("restCount");
      message = "No problem, here is the " + restCount +
      " I've found:";
      message_container.innerHTML += `<div class="bot">
      ${message}</div>`;
    }).then(function(){
      $(".here").css("display", "block");
      output.textContent = "";
    });
  } else {
    message_container.innerHTML += `<div class="bot">
    ${message}</div>`;
  }

  location.href = '#edge';
}
```

6. Next, we need to add in the function that will take care of
    rendering our responses on screen, when interacting with the bot:

```
function selfReply(message){
  var response;

  response = message.toLowerCase().replace
            (/[.,\/#!$%\^&\*;:{}=\-_`~()]/g,"");

  if (response.indexOf("No problem") != 1) {
    restCount = sessionStorage.getItem("restCount");
```

```
    message = "No problem, here is the " + restCount + "
        I've found:";
}

message_container.innerHTML += `<div class="self">
${message}</div>`;
location.href = '#edge';

bot.reply("local-user", response).then(function(reply) {
    botReply(reply);
    speak(reply);
});
}
```

7. With those two functions out of the way, we need to add in three more to manage the initialization of our bot – the first is this one:

```
function botReady(){
    bot.sortReplies();
    botReply('Hi there! Hungry? Looking for a restaurant here
    in Prague?');
}
```

8. The second takes care of what should happen if the bot is not able to be initialized:

```
function botNotReady(err){
    console.log("An error has occurred.", err);
}
```

9. Our bot can't be initialized automatically (we will explain why later) – to get around this, we need to add in an event handler for the Start a search button. For this, go ahead and add in the following code:

```
question.addEventListener("click", function() {
    speak("Hi there! Hungry? Looking for a restaurant here
    in Prague?");
    bot.loadFile(brains + "?" + parseInt(Math.random() *
    100000)).then(botReady).catch(botNotReady);
});

/**************************************************/
```

10. We're done with this section. Go ahead and save the code.
    Leave the file open though, as we will continue with the next
    part shortly.

Okay, so we're done with the first part, but there's still plenty to go! At this point we should now have the basic container function in place, along with our initial variables and the first part of the process in making our bot talk.

The next part of this project is where things get a little more complex – before we can allow our bot to articulate what it has found, we have first to get it to find something to talk about! Yes, the next part is where we go digging for details of restaurants that match our criteria. Let's dive in and take a look at the mechanics of how in more detail.

Getting the restaurant details

This next section is where things get more interesting – it's where we can really begin to show off how the Speech APIs can work with other services that we can consume.

Over the course of the next few pages, we're going to work our way through getting details of selected restaurants using the aforementioned Zomato service and assemble the results in a format that can be displayed on screen.

SEARCHING FOR RESTAURANTS

Let's make a start with adding in the code:

1. The first part we need to add takes care of working out the
    distance between two points of latitude and longitude, so we
    can indicate how far away the restaurant is from our present
    location. For this, leave a blank line underneath the previous
    event handler, and then add in this function:

```
function distance(lat1, lon1, lat2, lon2) {
    var p = 0.017453292519943295;     // Math.PI / 180
    var c = Math.cos;
    var a = 0.5 - c((lat2 - lat1) * p)/2 +
            c(lat1 * p) * c(lat2 * p) *
            (1 - c((lon2 - lon1) * p))/2;

    return 12742 * Math.asin(Math.sqrt(a)); // 2 * R;
    R = 6371 km
}
```

2. Next comes the critical part of this section – the call to Zomato
    to get details of restaurants that fit our selection criteria. For
    this, we have a somewhat lengthy function to add in, so we'll
    break it into sections; go ahead and add in this part first:

```
function getRestaurants() {
  $.ajax({
    method:'GET',
    crossDomain: true,
    url: 'js/restaurants-prague.json',
    dataType: "json",
    async: true,
    headers: {
```

```
    "user-key": "c697ba51c6b29523f885bb3a8b279c93"
  },
  success: function(response){

< ADD IN CODE HERE >

  }
  });
}
/***************************************************/
```

3. We can now add in the three blocks of code which we need to make this work – the first is used to filter the JSON file based on our selection criteria. Go ahead and drop the following lines of code in, replacing the <ADD IN CODE HERE> comment from the previous step:

```
/* filter on cuisine type and user rating */
var returnedData = $.grep(response.restaurants, function
(element, index) {
  return ((element.restaurant.cuisines == cuisineType) &&
  (element.restaurant.price_range == rating));
});
```

4. The next block of code takes care of storing the number of restaurants found as a sessionStorage value – this is used to update the response back from our bot. Go ahead and add in these lines of code below the grep function, leaving a line blank in between:

```
// Work out how many restaurants and store in session Storage
restCount = (returnedData.length == 1 ? "1 restaurant" :
returnedData.length + " restaurants");
sessionStorage.setItem('restCountValue', restCount);
```

5. Next up is the real meat of this part of the demo – here we retrieve the various values from our filtered JSON data and render them on screen. This takes the form of a nested set of for... statements – go ahead and add in the following code after the previous step, leaving a blank line in between:

```
for(var i=0; i<returnedData.length; i++){
  var distanceaway = distance(mylat.innerHTML, mylon.
  innerHTML, returnedData[i].restaurant.location.latitude,
  returnedData[i].restaurant.location.longitude);

  for(var x=0; x<returnedData[i].restaurant.highlights.
  length; x++){
    if (returnedData[i].restaurant.highlights[x] ==
    "Takeaway Available") {
      takeaway = "Yes";
    }
  }

  var newDiv = $("<div class='card'>");
    newDiv.append(
      $("<div class='card-body'>").append(
      $("<span>").html("<img src=" + returnedData[i].
      restaurant.thumb + "><h1><a href=" +
      returnedData[i].restaurant.menu_url +
      ">"+returnedData[i].restaurant.name+"</a></h1><img
      class='rating_img' src='./img/" + returnedData[i].
      restaurant.price_range + ".png'><span
      class='distance'><img src='./img/location.svg'>" +
      distanceaway.toFixed(2) + " kms</span>"),
      $("<p>").html("Tel. Nos: " + returnedData[i].
      restaurant.phone_numbers),
      $("<p>").html("Rating: <span class='av_rating'>" +
      returnedData[i].restaurant.user_rating.aggregate_
      rating + " / 5 </span>"),
```

```
$("<p>").text("Address: " + returnedData[i].restaurant
.location.address),
$("<p>").text("Cuisine: " + returnedData[i].restaurant.
cuisines),
$("<p>").text("Average cost for two: " + returnedData[i].
restaurant.average_cost_for_two + " " + returnedData[i].
restaurant.currency + " (or USD " + amt + ")"),

$("<p>").text("Is takeaway available: " + takeaway),
$("<p>").text("Latitude: " + returnedData[i].restaurant
.location.latitude),
$("<p>").text("Longitude: " + returnedData[i].restaurant
.location.longitude),
$("<p>").html("<a href=" + returnedData[i].restaurant.
url + ">Link to Restaurant</a>")
  )
);
$(".here").append(newDiv);

// reset
distanceaway = 0;
}
```

6. Phew! That was some function, huh? Don't worry – we're at the end of this section. We have one more section to add in to complete this file. Go ahead and save your work thus far – you can keep the file open, as we will be back shortly to add in the remaining code.

Okay, we're making good progress. The bulk of the code for this file is complete. We have one section left to do, before switching to configure our bot – and that is to add in the Speech Recognition API.

We'll be using this to dictate our choices to the app – it means that rather than enter text in (as we did in previous demos from earlier in the book), we can now simply speak and the app will translate it into written text. Let's dive in and take a look at how we can reuse code from earlier demos into something a little more practical.

Adding speech input capabilities

For the last part of the script.js file, we need to add in code to allow our bot to recognize verbal commands from us; hopefully you will recognize much of the code from earlier demos, even though we've repurposed it into our app!

In reality, much of the basic framework for the Speech Recognition API (and its sister, the Speech Synthesis API) is unlikely to change dramatically from project to project; it might look different, but if you look at the code closely, you will see the same constructs appear, such as speechstart and result. With this in mind, let's take a look at how we can reuse our code from earlier demos to complete this part of the project.

ADDING SPEECH

Okay, let's crack on and add in the final part of the code for our script.js file:

1. We'll begin by leaving a blank line under the previous comment and then adding in this getUserMedia call:

```
navigator.mediaDevices.getUserMedia({ audio: true
}).then(function(stream) {

<ADD CODE IN HERE >

    }).catch(function(err) {
    console.log(err);
  });
```

2. Next, leave a blank line, and then replace the phrase <ADD CODE IN HERE> with these variable and property declarations:

```
const SpeechRecognition = window.SpeechRecognition ||
window.webkitSpeechRecognition;
const recognition = new SpeechRecognition();

recognition.interimResults = false;
recognition.maxAlternatives = 1;
recognition.continous = true;
```

3. Next up come the event handlers that take care of managing the Speech Recognition service or responding to events as they occur. The first deals with starting the service when we click the Click and talk to me! button:

```
document.querySelector("section.speech > button")
.addEventListener("click", () => {
  let recogLang = "en-US";
  recognition.lang = recogLang.value;
  recognition.start();
});
```

4. The next event handler we need to add in takes care of detecting the presence of speech, that is, we've started to talk. For this, leave a blank line, and then add in the following code:

```
recognition.addEventListener("speechstart", () => {
  console.log = "Speech has been detected.";
});
```

5. In the same vein, we have an event handler to take care of when the Speech Recognition service detects a word or phrase that has been properly recognized and returned back to our app. We use this as a trigger for our bot to display the next question – for this, go ahead and add in this code:

```
recognition.addEventListener("result", (e) => {
  console.log = "Result has been detected.";

  let last = e.results.length - 1;
  let text = e.results[last][0].transcript;
  output.textContent = text;
  selfReply(output.textContent);
});
```

6. We have two event handlers left. When we're done talking, we need to signal this to the API; the speechend event handler takes care of this for us:

```
recognition.addEventListener("speechend", () => {
  recognition.stop();
});
```

7. In the event of any errors, we need something to display a suitable error message in our browser's console area. For this, we use the aptly-named error event – go ahead and add in the following code after the previous event handler:

```
recognition.addEventListener("error", (e) => {
  console.textContent = "Error: " + e.error;
});
```

8. We're done with this file now – go ahead and save your work and then close it for now. The remaining code we will add in a separate file.

Phew! We're done – at least with this file! Granted it was a lot to work through, but setting it up so that we could have tested changes earlier would have been tricky and made the steps for assembly a lot more complex. Still, if you managed to get this far, then well done. Take a breather and get yourself a drink as celebration!

Okay, back to reality, we have one more section to take care of, which is telling our bot what to say. Although we have a good few steps to work through, I promise you the code will be a lot simpler, so without further ado, let's dive in and take a look.

Configuring the bot

This next section should be somewhat familiar to you, at least in terms of constructs – it's time to set up the various responses for our bot to articulate to us as customers. We'll be using the RiveScript bot framework for this, in a similar fashion to the demo from earlier in the book; this time around, we will extend the use of some of the features we first used back in that demo.

ADDING SPEECH

Okay, let's get started:

1. The first step in configuring our bot is to open a new file and then add this statement – this tells our bot to use version 2 of the RiveScript interpreter:

    ```
    ! version = 2.0
    ```

2. Next, leave a blank line, and then add in this first function – this takes care of substituting one of the food types with a format that can be recognized by Zomato and rendering it into sessionStorage in the right case before continuing with the next question:

    ```
    > object foodtype javascript
    var newFood
    for (var i = 0; i < args.length; i++) { newFood = args[i] }

    if (newFood == "local") { newFood = "Czech" }
    newFood = newFood.charAt(0).toUpperCase() + newFood.slice(1)
    sessionStorage.setItem("cuisine", newFood)
    ```

```
   return "Do you have a price range in mind - budget,
   midrange, or expensive?"
< object
```

3. We have a second function to add in – for this, leave a blank
    line and then add in this code, to take care of storing the right
    value for the available price range values offered by Zomato:

```
> object rating javascript
    var priceRange
    for (var i = 0; i < args.length; i++) {
      priceRange = args[i]
    }

    if (priceRange == "budget") { priceRange = 1}
    if (priceRange == "midrange") { priceRange = 2}
    if (priceRange == "highend") { priceRange = 3}
    sessionStorage.setItem("priceRange", priceRange)

    return "Ok let us see what I can find..."
< object
```

4. Our third (and final) function gets the number of restaurants
    found by Zomato, which is then rendered as part of the
    conversation with the bot:

```
> object restCount javascript
    return sessionStorage.getItem("restCountValue")
< object
```

5. Next up, we need to start adding in the statements that
    simulate the conversation we will have with the bot. For this,
    we will actually start with the response from the first question –
    go ahead and leave a blank line, and then add in this code:

```
+ search restaurants
- Ok. Searching for a restaurant - what cuisine would you
like? Indian, Italian or something else?
```

6.   We now need to take care of the desired food type – for this,
     go ahead and add in the following code after the previous step,
     leaving a blank line in between:

```
+ i would prefer (chinese|indian|local|mexican) please
- <call>foodtype <star></call>
```

7.   The final question we need to ask is around the price range –
     for this, go ahead and add in the following code, leaving a blank
     line in between:

```
+ (budget|midrange|expensive)
- <call>rating <star></call>
^ I have found a selection of restaurants for you! Would
you like to see the restaurants I've found?
```

8.   The last step is to confirm that we want to see the available
     restaurants that fit our chosen criteria – for this, leave a blank
     line, and then add in the following code:

```
+ yes please
- No problem, here is the <call>restCount</call> I've found:
```

9.   We have one final block to add in – this is a generic catch-all,
     in the event that we either don't say the right text or the API
     doesn't recognize something we've said. Leave a line, and then
     drop in the following code:

```
+ *
- Sorry, I did not get what you said
- I am afraid that I do not understand you
- I did not get it
- Sorry, can you please elaborate that for me?
```

10. At this point, we're done with editing. Save the file as `brain.rive`
     in the `js` subfolder of our mini-project area and then close it.

We're almost at a point where we can test our project, but before doing so, there is one more part we need to fix. Yes, I did indeed say that we had finished with `script.js`, but if you take a really close look, you might see a problem.

Okay, I confess "problem" might be too strong a word, but nevertheless, if we don't do this next section, then it's likely you will see (or USDundefined) appear in the final result! Yes, we put in a variable `distanceaway` to display the converted amount in US dollars in step 5 of the "search restaurant details" demo, but haven't put something in to perform that conversion... D'oh!

Don't worry. It's an easy fix. It allows us to make use of another API, so let's take a look at how this feature fits into our overall demo in more detail.

Converting currencies into US dollars

If we take a closer look at the code (as indicated in Figure 7-1), we can indeed see the `distanceaway` variable being referenced – a quick search of the rest of the file won't show any other reference to it.

```
d(
eturnedData[i].restaurant.thumb + "><h1><a href=" + returnedData|
img class='rating_img' src='/img/' + returnedData[i].restaurant.
mg/location.svg'>"    distanceaway.toFixed(2)    " kms</span>"),
urnedData[i].restaurant.phone_numbers),
ss='av_rating'>"+returnedData[i].restaurant.user_rating.aggregat(
pnedData[i].restaurant.location.address)
```

Figure 7-1. *The distanceaway variable being used...*

It's an easy fix, so let's make a start on adding it in as our next demo.

DISPLAYING USD CONVERSION

To fix the issue, go ahead and follow these steps:

1. We'll begin by reopening the script.js file and then looking for the comment line that sits just before the distance function.

2. Leave a blank line underneath it, and then add in this variable declaration:

   ```
   var amt;
   ```

3. Under that declaration, leave a blank line, and then drop in this function:

   ```
   $.getJSON('https://api.exchangerate-api.com/v4/latest/
   CZK', function(data) {
     var currencies = [];
     $.each(data.rates, function(currency, rate) {
       if (currency == "USD") {
         amt = (rate * 300).toFixed(2);
       }
     });
   })
   ```

4. Go ahead and save the file – we can close it. Your demo is now finally complete!

Okay, our code really is complete this time! With the final function in place, let's turn our attention to testing the demo, so you can see how both of the Speech APIs can interact with other services used in this demo.

Testing the demo

Here comes the most interesting part, and perhaps the most nerve-wracking: it's time to test our demo!

For this, you will need to browse to `https://speech/restaurant`; when launching the demo for the first time, we will see something akin to the screenshot shown in Figure 7-2.

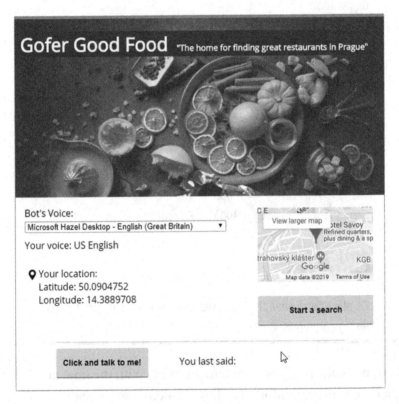

Figure 7-2. *Our completed demo, ready to accept input*

To operate it, I would suggest using this approach, where your responses are indicated in bold text:

- Click Start a search. Then wait for the initial welcome message to appear and be spoken.

- Say **search restaurants** when prompted.

- At the request for type of cuisine, say **I would prefer local please**.

- When prompted for the price range, say **midrange**.

- When the bot confirms it has found some results, say **yes, please**.

It might sound like we're steering the test toward a known scenario and not anticipating what a user might say, but this is deliberate. This has the benefit of exposing both how well the demo works technically and whether the questions posed by the user would be natural – in this case, I suspect there is room for improvement!

Leaving that aside for the moment, we can begin to see how the demo works in Figure 7-3.

Figure 7-3. *The first part of our demo in action...*

If we progress through each step, we can see what the final result looks like in Figure 7-4, shown overleaf.

Figure 7-4. *The second part of our demo in action*

As we can see from the screenshot in Figure 7-4, we've included basic details for each restaurant, along with a link that will take the customer back to the Zomato web site for that restaurant – this being useful to view extra details, such as opening hours and reviews. The details we've added here can absolutely be adjusted – each is fetched from within the JSON object for that restaurant and displayed as text (or within HTML markup), as appropriate.

We'll touch on expanding this later in this chapter.

Okay, now for the important part? How does our code work? We've covered some useful APIs within the course of this demo, so let's take a moment to review what we've used in more detail, before we take a look at how we could improve our code as part of any future development.

Dissecting our code in detail

Over the course of this chapter, we've covered a substantial amount of code – the bulk of it lies in our `script.js` and `brain.rive` configuration files. Much of it uses principles we've covered in earlier demos, so should be starting to look familiar by now!

However, given that the two core technologies used don't provide native support for each other, it's worth taking some time to explore how we've managed to get the two communicating to each other in more detail. With that in mind, let's first take a look at the HTML markup in more detail, before moving onto the script.js and brain.rive files in turn.

Dissecting our HTML markup

Much of what is in this file is fairly straightforward – once references to the CSS styling files have been defined, we set up a #page-wrapper div to encompass all of our content. We then create a .voicechoice section to house the drop-down that allows us to choose which language the bot should use, along with displaying the default voice set for the customer.

Next up comes the .location section, which we use to render hard-coded values representing the longitude and latitude coordinates of our chosen hotel, as well as a (working) Google Maps image showing where the hotel is in Prague.

We then have the #help section which is where the conversation is hosted; the last entry is then reformatted by our script file to host the results found from the Zomato data (more on this later). We then round out this part of the demo with the .speech section, which contains the button to fire the Speech Recognition service, as well as a suitably located .output area to display our responses.

Breaking apart the main script file

This is where things get more interesting and start to come together – our script.js file hosts most of the code needed to run our demo. We kick off with a block of variable declarations; this contains a commented-out block of code which we will use to provide our location using the HTML5 Geolocation API (more on this later in this chapter).

The Speech Synthesis API and our bot

With the declarations out of the way, we then have the loadVoices() function, which is used to load the voices provided by Google into the .output_result drop-down box that we set up in our markup file. Note how we have also provided an event handler for the onvoiceschanged event– some versions of Chrome required that these voices be loaded asynchronously, although that should be less of an issue with more recent versions of Chrome. We then move onto the speak() function, which is where we configure a new instance of the SpeechSynthesisUtterance interface, before providing it with the selected voice from the voiceSelect drop-down and the text to say from the msg variable.

Next up, we move into the code needed for our bot to operate – we begin with a declaration that stores a reference to our brain.rive file before running the botReply() and selfReply() functions. These are a little more complex, so here is a breakdown of what they do, starting with the botReply function, which we use to render responses from our chatbot:

- All messages displayed on screen from our bot are passed through the message placeholder variable – we first examine the contents of this.

- If the message variable contains the text "No problem," we use this as a trigger to first search the JSON provided by Zomato, before storing a count of the number of restaurants returned.

- We then adjust the message accordingly, before building up the markup and rendering both on screen in the .here div and resetting the .output_log div.

- If, however, we have not found an instance of "No problem," then we simply display the message on screen and move to the next response from the customer.

In case you're wondering why we use "No problem," it's simple: we need to use a trigger phrase to intercept and alter the message back to the user. It doesn't feature any other text elsewhere in our demo!

The other of our two Reply functions is the `selfReply` – this is the one used to transform the text of our answers into something that can be processed by our bot. In order, this is what happens:

- We first assign the response variable – this is used to store a copy of the text of our request, before turning it into lowercase and removing punctuation or special characters from it (these have to be omitted for RiveScript to operate correctly).

- We then check the contents of the message – as before, if it contains "No problem," we intercept it and alter it to display the restaurant count value which we get from session storage.

- We then reformat the message with appropriate markup before rendering it on screen and pushing it to the speak function to be echoed verbally.

We then round out this part of our demo with two system functions and an event handler – the first two are used to prepare the bot for running (`botReady`), and what happens if the bot is not available (`botNotReady`). We then use both in the question event handler, which loads the `brain.rive` file before initializing our demo.

Fetching the restaurant data

This next section may seem the most complex, but in reality, much of it is taken up by the AJAX request we make to load the data into our demo. We kick off with two functions: The first calls a service provided by ExchangeRate-API.com, to get the US dollar equivalent for each price we use. The second, distance, is used to calculate how far away each restaurant is from our present location.

The core part of this section is the getRestaurants() function – this is where we load our JSON file, before using $.grep to filter out any restaurant that does **not** match our requirements. We then work out how many restaurants are returned (restCount), before storing this as a value in Session Storage. We then iterate through each restaurant, to first work out the distance from our location (distanceaway), then if it offers takeaway, and rendering the results as individual cards which are appended to the .here element on screen.

Usage of the Speech Recognition API

The final section of the script file contains the code we've used to recognize our verbal commands – much of it is reused from earlier demos, so should begin to look familiar at this stage! Nevertheless, it's still worth going through it in more detail, as a recap.

We kick off by using getUserMedia to allow us access to our microphone from the browser – once this is initialized, we then define a SpeechRecognition object, based on which version is supported by our browser. At the same time, we set a number of properties, including interimResults and continuous.

We then have a set of event handlers to manage what happens when we talk. The first initializes the service when we hit the button located at the bottom of our demo. We then have speechStart and result, which identify if anything has been spoken or if we have a result that has been recognized by the service, respectively. Within the result event handler, we get a copy of the transcript and assign this to the text variable, before displaying it on screen and passing it to our bot to articulate it verbally. The remaining two event handlers, speechend and error, take care of when we've finished talking or if we have an error that crops up during usage of our demo.

Exploring the bot configuration file

The final part of our code is the `brain.rive` configuration file we use for our bot – in comparison to the script file, it will seem like a leisurely walk in the park!

We start by declaring which version of the RiveScript interpreter should be used – in this project we use version 2. This is followed by three RiveScript functions – these are termed as objects in RiveScript, but work in the same way as standard functions. In the first, we iterate through any parameters passed, before substituting instances of `local` for `Czech` (needed for Zomato) and then storing a reformatted version in Session Storage. We then return back the next sentence to use, which asks which price range our customer wants to use.

The second function works in a similar fashion – this time though, we convert the price range specified by our customer into a number. The latter is needed for Zomato to operate correctly. We round out this function by returning confirmation that our bot will search the database for us. In the third function, we simply get back the value of the number of restaurants found, which we then articulate on screen to our customer.

The rest of the configuration file contains each of the statements we use to run our conversation with the bot – note that we've used the same + symbol to denote a trigger for our bot and the responses are specified with a – sign before each one. There are several `<call...>` statements in use; these call the functions (or objects) specified at the start of the file. The final part (starting with the * symbol) is a generic catch-all that kicks in if the bot has a problem understanding what we've said or it doesn't match what it is expecting to see on screen.

Taking things further

Now that we have a working demo, where do we go from here? Well, there are a good few options we could look at incorporating into such an application, if we were to decide to take things further. Let's take a look at a selection:

- Add in error handling and system messages – our demo relies on us saying the right commands, but with the best will in the world, we don't always get it right! The demo needs something to help inform the user when there is an issue and how best to handle it.

- Examine the statements used in our bot conversation – there are instances where we might want to look at putting in a pause, such as when we say, "OK, let us see what I can find…" At present, this jumps straight into finding an answer, which isn't very realistic!

- We've inserted the latitude and longitude values provided by Zomato as numbers, but what about converting them to a map link, using a service such as Google Maps or OpenStreetMap?

- Add in confidence levels – the Speech Recognition API is still a work in progress; it is very good at recognizing content, as long as you say it clearly. Providing some visual feedback will help encourage the user to alter their approach if the confidence levels being reported are low.

- Provide better visual cues as to what to say – we've put some limited options within our `brain.rive` file, but the demo doesn't indicate what to say at all! A great way to improve this would be to put some text in a smaller font under each of the questions, so the customer knows what to say to trigger a suitable response.

- Adding in language support – this is an almost essential prerequisite, in todays' world; it might even help to localize values such as average costs of meals into the customer's local currency, rather than provide them in a currency which isn't as familiar!

- Merge the two buttons used in the demo into one – we have to provide one to fire the Speech Synthesis API, as browsers won't allow this to fire automatically once the page is loaded. This would involve some rework of the code required to fire the speak() function, as well as testing the points where it needs to be called in code.

- There are occasions where we might not get a complete result back from our demo, so the bot ends up saying there aren't any restaurants, when this might not be the case! The JSON file is enormous, so is there a better way of making this more resilient and less prone to misreporting?

- We could even go as far as checking to see if a booking could be made directly from the app; this might be as simple as an email or phone call, but anything to help the customer will be appreciated!

Although there are indeed plenty of things we could do to improve and extend our demo, I want to pick up on three simple changes that we can make right now with little difficulty. These are to format contact numbers using the tel: format, adding a geolocation-based feature, and extending the amount of data we show to the customer. These are simple changes we can effect, so without further ado, let's dive in and take a look, beginning with the formatting of contact details.

226

Formatting telephone numbers

For the first of the three changes we'll be covering, I want to explore how the phone numbers listed in the demo are formatted.

Yes, I know this might sound a little silly, but bear with me on this, and all will become clear.

This isn't something we are likely to do from a laptop or desktop, but for those users who access the Internet from smart devices, we can automatically format numbers to allow them to be called directly from the page. This is known as the "Click to Call" service – with a few simple changes, we can set all of our numbers to be displayed accordingly.

Let's take a look at the changes we would need to effect:

- The number should be provided in the international dialing format, with the plus symbol, country code, area code, and number. Using the Naše maso restaurant featured in Figure 7-4, we would write our link thus:

  ```
  <a href="tel:+420-2-22312533">+ 420 (2)-22312533</a>
  ```

- Although it's not obligatory, adding hyphens as shown in this example will help with better detection.

- Mobile browsers should detect numbers automatically, although Mobile Safari will go further and convert them to the right format automatically. If you want to disable it so that you can maintain a consistent format across all browsers, then add this meta tag at the head of the HTML markup:

  ```
  <meta name="format-detection" content="telephone=no">
  ```

These are simple changes we can make to our demo and will provide an extra touch to anyone using the application on a device that can make or receive phone calls.

Okay, let's change tack. The second of our three changes is centered around location; our demo is currently hard-coded to one hotel to prove it works, but isn't useful if you can't stay there! Let's adapt the code to make it more dynamic. We'll do this in the next exercise.

Adding location-based facilities

Our demo used hard-coded details of the Hotel Savoy, based on the outskirts of Prague – it's a gorgeous hotel I was lucky enough to be able to stay in, but as a five-star outfit, I know that not everyone can afford it! So, to allow for this, we should make our location values more dynamic – there is no better way to do this than by using the Geolocation API.

Support for this API is not an issue within desktop browsers; it is covered by all of the major browsers, as indicated in Figure 7-5.

Current aligned	Usage relative	Date relative		Apply filters	Show all
IE	Edge	Firefox	Chrome	Safari	Opera
					10.1
					11.5-12.1
6-8		2-3	4	3.1-4	15
9-10	12-17	3.5-69	5-77	5-12.1	16-63
11	18	70	78	13	64
	76	71-72	79-81	TP	

Figure 7-5. *Support for the HTML Geolocation API*
Source: caniuse.com

There is no real concern either for mobile devices; all except Opera Mini are known to offer native support this API. (Opera Mini shows minimal usage, so this is not likely to be an issue either!)

With this in mind, let's take a look at how we can update our demo – we've already done some of the hard work needed, so let's look at what is required to complete it and get it operational.

DEMO: ADDING LOCATION-BASED DETAILS

Adding in basic geolocation is very easy, at least to give us current longitude and latitude values. To do this, follow these steps:

1. As a quick test, open up a browser's console area, and then drop in this code:

```
navigator.geolocation.getCurrentPosition(function(location) {
    console.log(location.coords.latitude);
    console.log(location.coords.longitude);
    console.log(location.coords.accuracy);
});
navigator.geolocation.getCurrentPosition((loc) => {
    console.log('The location in lat lon format is: [', loc.
    coords.latitude, ',', loc.coords.longitude, ']');
```

2. This should give us values similar to the ones we originally hard-coded in our demo.

3. Now that we've tested it, we need to adjust our code – we've already included the function part of this code in our demo, although we've not enabled it. To do so, look for these lines and comment them out:

```
mylat.innerHTML = "50.0904752";
mylon.innerHTML = "14.3889708";
```

4. Next, remove the comments around the block that immediately follows, from `function getLocation()`... down to (and including) the `getLocation()` function call.

5. Save the changes – your code is now location aware and won't rely on fixed values. If you refresh the demo, you will see new numbers appear for the distance values for each restaurant the app displays on screen.

The downside of doing this means that we will need to effect changes elsewhere; otherwise, we might get some abnormally high values as it will calculate based on wherever you are in the world, which is unlikely to be in Prague!

The great thing though about this demo is that we can change it to report on restaurants in any of thousands of locations worldwide, so there is bound to be something available near to where you live.

Displaying more details about restaurants

Our third and final change is more a matter of taste – there is a whole host of different values we could incorporate into our demo! This might include examples such as opening times, online delivery, or if table reservations are available; it's a matter of perusing the raw JSON data and choosing which details we want to display.

To help with this, I would recommend copying the raw JSON file into a JSON editor and then using it to browse through the data. An online one such as JSON Editor Online (`https://jsoneditoronline.org/`) works perfectly well for this purpose, as indicated in Figure 7-6.

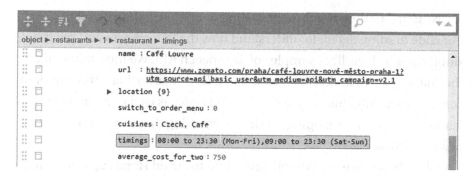

Figure 7-6. *JSON Editor Online in use*

If you use JSON Editor Online, you can click each key value (to the left of the colon in the highlighted example) and get the full path to that value within the file. In the case of the highlighted example, we would end up with this code, which we could put into our demo:

```
$("<p>").text(
  "Latitude: " + returnedData[i].restaurant.timings
),
```

There's a whole host of other values you can try, so feel free to browse through the file and decide which to try!

Summary

Wow, that was some monster project! The Speech APIs are one of those technologies though that can be used in all manner of situations such as finding restaurant details. We've covered some useful techniques throughout this chapter, so let's pause for a moment to review what we've learned.

We kicked off by setting the scene, parameters, and business logic to use in our project, before exploring how we would architect our demo and setting some expectations as to its usage. We then moved onto setting up the initial markup for our project, before adding in the various sections of our script, such as the facilities to speak or finding the restaurant details.

Next up, we then ran through testing our demo, before dissecting our code in some detail, to understand how the latter works and see the similarities with earlier examples of the Speech API. We then rounded out the chapter with a look at how we could take things further – this explored some ideas around improving our existing code, as well as adding new features as part of developing this into something that can be put in front of real customers.

Okay, let's move on. We still have more to cover! Hands up how many of you use an online music streaming service, such as Deezer or Spotify? I'll bet there will be a fair few of you to whom this applies: what if we could use our voice to control how we play our music? Yes, you heard me right. Keep with me, and I will reveal all in the next chapter.

CHAPTER 8

Project: Finding and Playing Music

I love listening to music – there is something to be said for plugging into your favorite artist while spending hours developing code or writing books. As long as I have a drink to hand too, then I'm happy. But I digress.

Prior to digitizing my entire music collection and discovering the joys of online music streaming, I used to wade through hundreds of CDs. Let's just say it was something of an eclectic collection; it didn't matter what it was – there was something about dropping in a CD and hitting play. Those days are now long gone, since converting to using Spotify – it's a lot easier to find my music, and I certainly don't have to worry about space!

Since converting to using Spotify, it got me thinking, *Would it be possible to control it using my voice?* Over the course of my research, I've not found anyone yet who has done something similar, at least with Spotify; would that mean no one has managed to do it, or had the desire to do so? I wonder. As I'm a keen fan of pushing the boat out and exploring what I would hope to be uncharted waters, I thought, *Why not give it a go?*

© Alex Libby 2020
A. Libby, *Introducing the HTML5 Web Speech API*,
https://doi.org/10.1007/978-1-4842-5735-7_8

Setting the background to our project

Over the course of this chapter, we're going to assemble a quick and dirty app to play back a chosen album, using the Spotify API from within our browser. As part of this, we will add in these features:

- The app will have (almost) full control by voice, using the Speech Recognition API – the only parts not controllable will be the initial authorization process and the first playback from the real Spotify client (more on this anon).

- We will be able to do basic tasks such as play or pause music, skip forward or backward a track, and add the album to your saved albums list in Spotify.

- We will display a track listing, along with the lengths of each track, plus a list of albums from the same artist – the latter will include the album name and image.

- We will provide an option to search for artists of a similar name – the results will show their name and Spotify ID, which we will use to get their albums as well.

This is only a small subset of what we can achieve using the Spotify API – there is a whole stack of other things we can do, but space constraints mean we can't cover everything!

Hopefully this will give you a balanced mix of functions we can control using our voice and a feel for how we can use the Spotify API in this context; as a preview, you can see a screenshot of the completed demo in Figure 8-1.

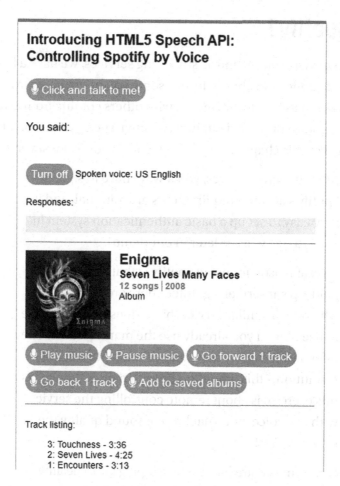

Figure 8-1. *A preview of our finished demo*

Okay, let's move on. I am sure you will be asking one question: why Spotify, when we have a host of other services available that we could use, such as Deezer, Google Play Music, or even Amazon Music? It's a good question, so let's take a look at the reasons for choosing to use Spotify.

Why Spotify?

When working with online music streaming services, we have a fairly healthy list of options to choose from – some you might know from TV advertising such as Spotify or Deezer, with others coming from established companies who've branched out into this area, such as Amazon or Google Play Music. For this chapter, I've elected to use Spotify, for several reasons:

- As with many services, you always have to sign up – Spotify's account requirements are minimal, and it is very easy to set up a basic authentication system in code (as we will see later in our demo).

- A great reason for using Spotify is that I'm already a paid-up subscriber – granted there are other outlets who offer a similar service, but it doesn't make sense to use them if you already use the market leader. They offer a wide variety of music, although it's not high resolution – this limitation doesn't matter though, as this exercise is about remote controlling the service with our voice, not what level of sound quality the service offers!

- Online music streaming is developing into a healthy market, with the likes of Deezer, Spotify, and Amazon Music, but most of them had one thing in common – they all seem to make it difficult to interact with each service's API using standard client-side technologies! The only exception to this was Spotify – as you will see shortly, we'll be making use of a third-party wrapper library to help with running our code, one of a limited number available for Spotify. (Indeed, one service wouldn't even let me log into their API area...)

Okay, let's move on. Now that we've covered off which music service we will use, we need to explore how we're going to construct our demo. We'll be making use of a number of tools, in addition to Spotify and the Speech APIs (naturally!), so let's dive in and take a look at what we will be using to construct our demo in more detail.

Architecting our demo

For the purposes of building our demo, we'll be making use of several tools, in addition to Spotify and the Speech APIs. The ones I've elected to use are as follows:

- Vue.js for the authorization skeleton code – I could use tools such as React, but this adds complexity which isn't necessary. Vue.js keeps things nice and simple and doesn't require the use of server-side tools such as Node.js by default, to show off the basics of operating with Spotify. A good example of authorizing access to Spotify is in the CodePen demo by Lee Martin at `https://codepen.io/leemartin/pen/EOxxYR` – we'll be using this as the basis for our demo.

We will talk more about the authorization part of the process shortly.

- We could interact with Spotify's API directly, but to keep things simple, we will make use of a wrapper library by José Perez, which is available from `https://github.com/JMPerez/spotify-web-api-js`.

- jQuery – this is purely for convenience; in an ideal world, we would refactor our code to use either Vue or vanilla JavaScript! For transparency, we'll be using the latest version of jQuery which is 3.4.1 at the time of writing. Other versions of jQuery can be used, although you will need to test to ensure your code still works.

Okay, with our main tools in place, we can now start coding! But – I hear you say – what's this about authorizing? Yes, as with any API, we need to be authorized users to access the service; the service provider needs a way to track usage and maintain a decent level of service for all users. Although this does not affect our use of the Speech APIs, it's nevertheless a key part of our demo, so let's dive in and take a quick look at our options in more detail.

Authorizing our demo

When working with the Spotify API, a key critical part of our app will be the authorization process between us and Spotify; this is to allow registered access to the APIs so we can stream music.

This is a two-part process. The first, where we register the app with Spotify, we will cover later; for now, let's assume this has taken place and take a look at the various ways in which authorization can happen when working with Spotify.

Choosing a method

Assuming we've registered our app with Spotify, there are three ways we can be authorized to use the Spotify API. They are as follows:

- Authorize ourselves as a user, which can be periodically refreshed – use the **Authorization Code** method.

- Set up temporary authorization for a user – use the **Implicit Grant** method.

- Set up authorization for an app, which can be
  periodically refreshed – use the **Client Credentials
  Flow** method.

We can see how these compare in Table 8-1.

Table 8-1. *Methods of authorizing access to Spotify API*

Flow	Access user resources	Requires secret key (server side)	Access token refresh
Authorization Code	Yes	Yes	Yes
Client Credentials	No	Yes	No
Implicit Grant	Yes	No	No

Source: Spotify Developer Portal

For the purposes of our demo, we will use the Implicit Grant Flow
option – this is designed for clients that are written entirely in JavaScript and
do not require the use of server-side code to operate. There is indeed a server-
side option available in the form of spotify-web-api-node, but to show off
how the Speech APIs work, running it server side just adds an extra layer of
complexity that isn't needed. After all, why complicate matters, right?

The implications of using our chosen method

For our demo, we've chosen to use the Implicit Grant Flow method for
authorizing access – this standard was created as RFC-6749 by the Internet
Engineering Task Force, or IEFT. Making use of this method is the best
choice in our case, for several reasons:

- Implicit Grant Flow is for clients that are implemented entirely using JavaScript and running in the resource owner's browser.

- You do not need any server-side code to use it – this removes the need for complex server-side tools, such as Node.js.

- Rate limits for requests are improved, but there is no refresh token provided.

You can see a more in-depth discussion on how this method works on the IETF web site, at `https://tools.ietf.org/html/rfc6749#section-4.2`.

What does this mean for us? We get direct access to the Spotify Accounts service, with an access token supplied by the API that will start with something akin to `https://accounts.spotify.com/authorize`.

The whole process is carried out client side and does not involve secret keys, but the access tokens are short-lived and need to be refreshed manually with no option available to extend them when they have expired. The full request will include parameters in the query string, which we can see listed in Table 8-2 (and later in our demo).

Table 8-2. *The various properties required for Implicit Flow*
authorization

Query parameter	Value
client_id	*Required.* The client ID provided to you by Spotify at the point of registration.
response_type	*Required.* Set it to "token."
redirect_uri	*Required.* The registered URI to redirect to after the user grants/denies permission.
state	*Optional, but strongly recommended.* The state can be useful for correlating requests and responses – using a value can give extra assurance that a connection is a genuine request.
scope	*Optional.* A space-separated list of scopes.
show_dialog	*Optional.* Forces the user to approve the app again, if it has already been approved.

Source: Spotify Developer Portal

The best way to understand how it all fits together, short of seeing it
operating, is to see it as a flow chart – we can see how the flow operates in
Figure 8-2.

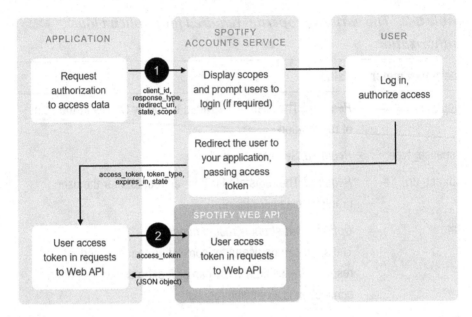

Figure 8-2. *The authorization process for our demo*
Source: Spotify Developer Portal

It's important to understand though that choosing a method will come with some constraints – after all, it's unlikely we get anything for free, without something that might affect how we do things!

Fortunately, the constraints are not too severe, and the effects of them could be reduced if we decided to use one of the other authorization methods available from Spotify. That's another story though. In the meantime, let's take a look at how the constraints might affect our demo in more detail.

Constraints of using this method

Although our chosen method keeps things simple and is the best fit for our needs, there are still some constraints that we need to be aware of, which means that we can't completely control everything by voice. Let's take a look at what they are:

- Before we run our demo, we will need to fire up Spotify
  and run a song for a few seconds (it's something we have
  to do periodically). If we don't run Spotify at all, you will
  get errors appear in console, and albums will not play.

- We need to use the browser version of Spotify for this
  demo to work; if you try using the desktop app, you will
  find the two do not interact with each other, and you
  may also find a different album playing in the desktop
  app that doesn't relate to the one playing in your demo!

- When running the authorization part of the demo,
  we have to click the Accept button for Spotify to allow
  access. Unfortunately, this isn't accessible via speech
  from within our demo, hence why we can't completely
  control things using our voice!

Okay, now that we've covered off the basics of authorizing access to
Spotify, it really is time to start developing code. I know it might seem like
a long wait before we do so, but the Spotify API isn't as easy as it should be;
we've had to cover some important points around how to get access to the API.

Now that we've covered this, we can get stuck into setting up our app;
the first task is to set up an integration so that Spotify recognizes calls from
our app as genuine and provides the appropriate content.

Setting up prerequisites

When working with APIs, we frequently have to set up some form of
account or integration – it's a necessary evil, but nevertheless important so
that the service provider can manage demand and keep access secure for
registered users.

It's no different for using Spotify – the first stage in our demo is to set
up an integration, so let's dive in and take a look at the steps required to
create the integration for our app.

DEALING WITH PREREQUISITES

To set up the integration, follow these steps:

1. We'll begin by downloading a copy of the code download that accompanies this book – go ahead and save the `spotify` folder into our project area. This will contain the relevant styles and Vue.js and jQuery libraries in place, ready for us to use.

2. Next, we need to sign into Spotify's developer dashboard area at `https://developer.spotify.com/dashboard/` – for this, you will need to create a free account, or you can use your existing one if you are already an existing subscriber to the service.

3. Once logged in, click Create a Client ID – you will see a modal appear, similar to the (partial) screenshot shown in Figure 8-3.

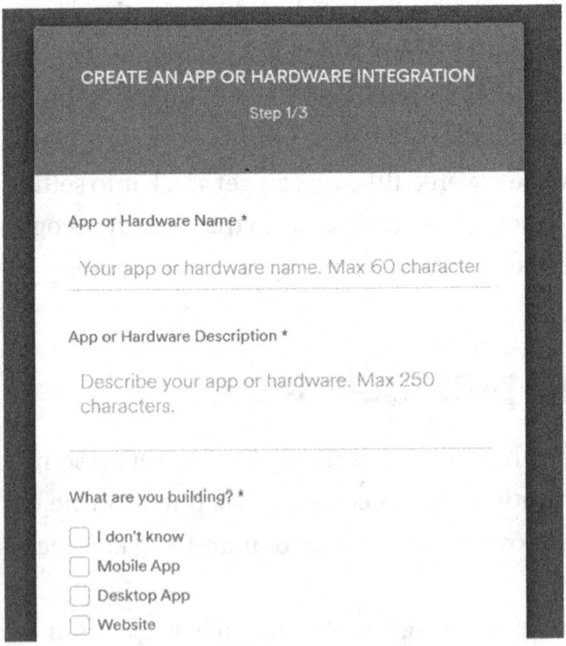

Figure 8-3. *Create a Client ID modal on display*

4. Go ahead and fill out the details requested (indicated by the red star) – you can use the following as a guide to help you through the wizard:

- Are you developing a commercial integration? – **No**

(We are working in a purely developmental capacity at present, but if you do decide to go commercial, then please make sure you set up an integration accordingly. It's important to note that you can't edit this option once the integration has been enabled).

- I understand that this app is not for commercial use – **No**

- I understand that I cannot migrate… – **No**

- I understand and agree with…. – **No**

5. Hit Submit. At this point, the details will be displayed, and you will be presented with your app's dashboard.

6. You will see a link marked SHOW CLIENT SECRET, along with your client ID. Click the link, and then make a note of both IDs, as we will use both later in our demo.

We're now ready to start developing code! Before we do so, there are a couple of things to note:

- We'll make use of a Spotify icon from the Flaticon web site – this is purely for creating a favicon for our site. The icon I've used is available from https://www. flaticon.com/free-icon/spotify-logo_49097.

- The Favicon site at https://favicon.io/favicon-converter/ is very handy for setting up the code needed to display favicons correctly – we'll be incorporating code generated from this site into our app.

Adding in a favicon is entirely voluntary; you can of course decide not to use it, and it won't affect how your demo runs! I've done it purely to stop our app from throwing an error about not finding a suitable icon.

You may find that if you test code after each demo, not all of it works. Don't be alarmed; this is to be expected! We're covering a lot of code, so we need to do it in sections – it will all work out at the end of the final demo.

At this stage, with all of the prerequisites in place, we are now ready to start writing code. There is a fair amount of code to go through, so we will do it in stages – the first task is to set up the basic authorization framework, so that we can begin to add in code to interact with Spotify's API.

Creating the framework

We really are now at a stage where we can write some code! With our app integration all set up and ready to be used, we can turn our attention to setting up code for our app. There is a fair amount of code to work through over the course of this project, so I've split it into a three-stage process; the first stage takes care of the basic authorization process.

To help with not reinventing the wheel, I will make use of a CodePen demo by Lee Martin (you can see the original at `https://codepen.io/ leemartin/pen/EOxxYR?editors=1010`). This uses the Vue.js framework to lay out the code. Don't worry if you're not familiar with this framework – at a basic level, it maintains a split between markup and JavaScript code. We will go through each part in detail after the exercise.

SETTING UP OUR SKELETON CODE

To get our authorization framework set up and ready to rock and roll, go ahead with these steps:

1. We'll begin by cracking open a copy of `index.html` and then scrolling down to (or looking for) the comment marked `<!--INSERT CODE HERE -->`.

2. We have a fair amount of code to add, so we will do this in stages – first, remove the comment, and then add a couple of blank lines.

3. Next, go ahead and insert this block – this will take care of the markup around our speech facility:

```
<main id="app">
  <h2>Introducing HTML5 Speech API: <br>Controlling
  Spotify by Voice</h2>
  <template v-if="me">
    <div id="speech">
      <button>
          <i class="fa fa-microphone"></i> Click and talk
          to me!
      </button>       .

      <p class="output">You said: <br><strong
      class="output_result"></strong></p>
      <span class="voice">Spoken voice: US English</span>
      <p>Responses:</p>
      <div class="response">
        <span class="output_log"></span>
      </div>
    </div>
```

4.   We have a few more blocks to cover – the next one we need to add
will look after the display of our playing album, by providing details
such as an image, artist, and track count. Leave a line blank after
the previous block, and then add in the following code:

```
<div id="currentalbum">
<span class="albumimage"><img src="img/100.png" /></span>
<span class="albumartist"></span>
<span class="albumname"></span>
<span class="trackcount"></span>
<span class="year"></span>
<span class="albumtype"></span>
<span class="albumID"></span>
<span class="artistID"></span>
</div>
```

5.   The next block isn't needed for the authorization process, but
it's easier to add it in now – this one will set up the buttons
needed to control the music playing. Go ahead and add in the
following code, leaving a blank line after the previous block:

```
<button @click="playmusic"><i class="fa
fa-microphone"></i> Play music</button>
<button @click="pausemusic"><i class="fa
fa-microphone"></i> Pause music</button>
<button @click="playnexttrack"><i class="fa
fa-microphone"></i> Go forward 1 track</button>
<button @click="playprevioustrack"><i class="fa
fa-microphone"></i> Go back 1 track</button>
<button @click="addtosavedalbums"><i class="fa
fa-microphone"></i> Add to saved albums</button>
```

6. We're making good progress. This next section sets up a placeholder for the track listing, for the album we are playing through our demo. Go ahead and add in the following lines of code, leaving a blank line after the previous block first:

```
<div id="albumlist">
  <p>Track listing:</p>
  <ul></ul>
</div>
```

7. This next section looks after the display of other albums by the same artist – leave a blank line after the previous block, and then drop in this code:

```
<div id="otheralbums">
  <span>Other albums by Artist:</span><button
  @click="getalbumsbyartist"><i class="fa fa-microphone">
  </i> Get Albums</button>
  <ul></ul>
</div>
```

8. We also have a section to display other artists of a similar name – for this, add in the following code, after the previous block:

```
<div id="artistlisting">
  Search for Artist: <input v-model="searchartist">
  <button @click="searchartistsbyname"><i class="fa
  fa-microphone"></i> Search</button>
  <span>Chosen artist: {{searchartist}}</span>
  <div id="artistlist"><ul></ul></div>
</div>
```

9. We're almost done with the markup. There are two more
    sections left to add in: a hidden info block that confirms you are
    logged in and the closing code for our Vue template. Go ahead
    and add in the following code after the previous step, leaving a
    blank line in between:

```
    <div id="info">{{ me }}</div>
  </template>
  <template v-else>
    <button @click="login">Login with Spotify</button>
  </template>
</main>
```

10. At this point, save the file – leave it open for now. We'll take a
    quick breather, but will continue with the code shortly.

We now have our markup in place, ready for use – it won't do a
great deal though, as we've yet to add in the scripting code to make it
operational.

We will add this in shortly. Feel free to go get a cup of coffee or drink
and take a breather though, as we still have plenty of code to add in!
Assuming you're good to go, let's continue with the next part of our demo,
to add in that authorization code.

Getting authorization from Spotify

In our next demo, we should start to see things happen – this is where
we add in the code to initiate a request for authorization and hopefully
get it approved! Okay, that sounds more complex than it really is, as it all
happens in the background, with only a single click of a button needed
from us. To see what I mean, let's add in the code as part of our next demo.

MAKING OUR AUTHENTICATION PROCESS OPERATIONAL

To get our demo to authorize access with Spotify, go ahead with these steps:

1. The first task in this demo is to add in a couple of blank lines after the closing `</main>` tag from the previous demo and then drop in this code – this will give us the basic Vue object that we will use to initiate authorization to Spotify:

```
<script>
  const app = new Vue({
    el: '#app',
    data() {
      return {
        client_id: 'bf253330696448f696dc45889f3fd61c',
        scopes: 'user-top-read playlist-read-
        collaborative playlist-read-collaborative
        playlist-modify-public playlist-read-private
        playlist-modify-private streaming app-remote-
        control user-modify-playback-state user-read-
        currently-playing user-read-playback-state user-
        library-modify',
        redirect_uri: 'https://speech/spotify',
        me: null,
        albumname: 'Not listed',
        searchartist: null,
        createplist: null
      }
    },
    methods: {
      <!--ADD IN ADDITIONAL METHODS HERE -->
    }
  })
</script>
```

2. We need to add in a few more configuration functions – the first is the actual call to Spotify to request authorization. Go ahead and add in the following code inside the methods object, replacing the comment marked `<!-- ADD IN ADDITIONAL METHODS HERE -->`:

```
login() {
  let popup = window.open(`https://accounts.
  spotify.com/authorize?client_id=${this.client_
  id}&response_type=token&redirect_uri=${this.redirect_
  uri}&scope=${this.scopes}&show_dialog=true`, 'Login
  with Spotify', 'width=600,height=800')

          window.spotifyCallback = (payload) => {
            popup.close()

            fetch('https://api.spotify.com/v1/me', {
            headers: {
                'Authorization': `Bearer ${payload}`
              }
            }).then(response => {
              return response.json()
            }).then(data => {
              this.me = data
            })
            spotifyApi = new SpotifyWebApi({
            clientId: '<ADD IN CLIENT ID HERE>',
            clientSecret: '<ADD IN CLIENT SECRET HERE>'
          });
          spotifyApi.setAccessToken(payload);
          }
      },
```

You will see the presence of a few lines of code that relate to the clientID and clientSecret values; there is a reason they are needed here, even though they are not used for the authorization process. We'll go through the significance of this after this demo.

3. We have one more object to add in – this triggers the call to initiate the request to Spotify. For this, add in the following code immediately after the closing }, from the previous block, and before the closing }) of our Vue object:

```
mounted() {
        this.token = window.location.hash.substr(1).
                        split('&')[0].split("=")[1]

                if (this.token) {
                    // alert(this.token)
                    window.opener.spotifyCallback(this.token)
                }
        }
```

4. Go ahead and save the file, but leave it open (or minimized) – we're now ready to test our work! For this, browse to https://speech/spotify/. If all is well, we should see the initial login button displayed, as indicated in Figure 8-4.

Introducing HTML5 Speech API: Controlling Spotify by Voice

Login with Spotify

Figure 8-4. The initial login button to Spotify from our demo

If we click the Login with Spotify button, we should see a popup window appear, requesting access for our demo to use the Spotify API. A (partial) screenshot of this request is displayed in Figure 8-5.

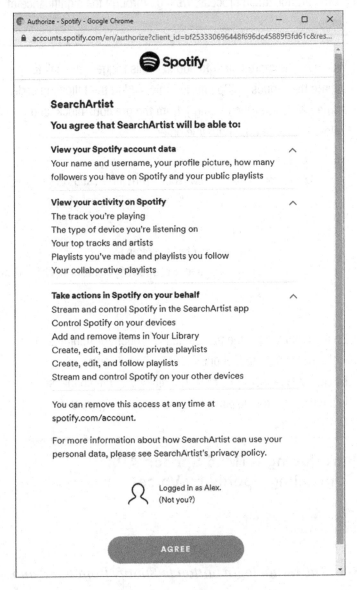

Figure 8-5. *A (partial) request to authorize our demo*

Breaking apart the code

Over the course of the last two demos, we've set up the basic framework needed to authorize access to Spotify's API; this has exposed some useful pointers, so let's take a look at the code in more detail to understand how it all fits together.

The first part of the first demo is straightforward; we set up all of our markup, including that required to operate the speech facility, later in the chapter. The only key thing to note is the use of the @ signs in step 5 of that demo; these are calls to functions within the Vue object we create in the second demo (they operate in a similar way to onclick="...." in plain JavaScript). We also make use of double curly brackets – these are just placeholders, which are substituted for real values by the Handlebars library that is bundled in with Vue.

The real crux of these two demos comes in the second part – for the uninitiated, Vue works on the principle of creating (and initializing an instance of) a configuration object. We click off by defining the app const as a new instance of Vue, into which we pass a target element ("#app"); we then define a number of values in the data object – respectively our client ID, permitted scopes, a redirect URL for authorization, and some other placeholders used for our demo.

Next up, we create a method object, into which we set up the login() object (or function); this defines a popup variable that contains the URL we use to request access. Once the Vue instance is mounted() in the demo, this initiates a callback which calls the login() object. This fires the request to Spotify, which is then processed accordingly. Assuming it is successful, we get a response back – this is hidden in the demo, as we don't need to display it all of the time. At the same time, we create a new instance of the spotify-web-api library, into which we define our clientID and clientSecret values, ready for us to start using Spotify.

Streaming content from Spotify

With our authorization process now operational, it's time to add in the code to stream content from Spotify. For this, we'll make use of the spotify-web-api-js wrapper library by José Perez; this wraps the relevant calls to each of the Spotify endpoints using a promise-based syntax.

Spoiler alert   This is a lengthy demo. Feel free to pause at any time if you need a break!

To give you a reminder of how it will look once we're done, we can see a partial screenshot of our completed app in Figure 8-6, once we've clicked Log into Spotify and OK to allow authorization.

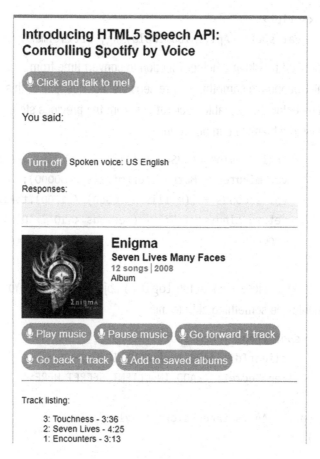

Figure 8-6. *Previewing our Spotify demo...*

Okay, let's make a start on our code.

MAKING USE OF THE SPOTIFY API

To stream content from Spotify into our demo, follow these steps:

1. Revert back to the index.html file we had open in the previous
   exercise, then scroll down to the opening <script> tag, and add
   in this line of code immediately below it, as indicated:

```
<script>
    var spotifyApi, albumIDplaying, artistimage;
```

2. We need to add in a helper function to convert time from milliseconds to something more sensible. For this, add in this code below the variable declarations from the previous step, leaving a blank line in between:

```
function msToMinAndSec(millis) {
    var minutes = Math.floor(millis / 60000);
    var seconds = ((millis % 60000) / 1000).toFixed(0);
    return minutes + ":" + (seconds < 10 ? '0' : ") +
    seconds;
}
```

3. Next, take a look back at the login() object we created. You should see something akin to this:

```
spotifyApi = new SpotifyWebApi({
    clientId: '<ADD IN CLIENT ID HERE>',
    clientSecret: '<ADD IN CLIENT SECRET HERE>'
    });
spotifyApi.setAccessToken(payload);
    }
},
```

4. We need to add in both the client ID and client Secretsvalues from our Spotify account; for this, go ahead and replace the comments with your client and secret IDs that you created earlier in this chapter.

5. The next task is to start adding in the functions that operate the various features within our demo. The first is to add in something to allow us to do the most important part: play music! For this, we have a substantial function to add in; the first part of it takes care of getting the current state from Spotify and displaying album details on screen:

```
playmusic() {
// get current playing album
spotifyApi.getMyCurrentPlaybackState()
.then(function(data) {
  spotifyApi.play(data);
  sessionStorage.setItem("chosenalbum", data.item.album.id);
  sessionStorage.setItem("chosenartist", data.item.
  artists[0] .id);

    var albumtype = data.item.album.album_type;

    $(".year").html(data.item.album.release_date.
    substring(0,4));
    $(".albumtype").html(albumtype.charAt(0).
    toUpperCase() + albumtype.slice(1));
    $(".trackcount").html(data.item.album.total_tracks +
    " tracks");
    $(".albumID").html(data.item.album.id);
    $(".artistID").html(data.item.artists[0].id);
    $("#currentalbum > span.albumname").html(data.item.
    album.name);
    $("#currentalbum > span.albumartist").html(data.
    item.artists[0].name);
    $("#currentalbum > span.albumimage > img").
    attr("src", data.item.album.images[1].url);
  }, function(err) {
    console.error(err);
  });
```

6. Next, leave a blank line – we now need to add in the closing half of the play() function. For this, drop in the following code, which looks after the display of track details and times on screen:

```
// get album tracks
spotifyApi.getAlbumTracks(sessionStorage.getItem
("chosenalbum"))
.then(function(data) {
  var tracklength;

  $("#albumlist > ul > li").remove();

  data.items.map( function(item) {
    spotifyApi.getAudioFeaturesForTrack(item.id)
    .then(function(response) {
      tracklength = response.duration_ms;
      $("#albumlist > ul").append(`<li>${item.
      track_number}: ${item.name} -
      ${msToMinAndSec(tracklength)}</li>`);
    });
  });
}, function(err) {
  console.error(err);
});
},
```

7. The next three objects we need to add in will look tiny in comparison! The first of the three is the function needed to allow us to pause music – go ahead and add this in immediately below the closing } of the function from step 6:

```
pausemusic() {
  // stop music
  spotifyApi.pause();
},
```

8. Second, in a similar vein, we need to add in something that will allow us to advance a track – go ahead and add this in immediately below the pausemusic() function:

```
playnexttrack() {
  // play next track
  spotifyApi.skipToNext();
},
```

9. For the third of these small functions, add in this code immediately below the previous block, to allow us to go back a track:

```
playprevioustrack() {
  // play previous track
  spotifyApi.skipToPrevious();
},
```

10. We're making good progress, although there is still a good amount of code to add in. The next function will allow us to search for artists by name. Go ahead and add in the following code, immediately after the closing `},` from the `playprevioustrack()` object:

```
searchartistsbyname() {
  // search artists by name
var artistquery = $("#artistlisting > input").val();

spotifyApi.searchArtists(artistquery)
  .then(function(data) {
    data.artists.items.map( function(item) {
      if (item.images.length == 0) {
        artistimage = "https://speech/spotify/img/noimage.png";
      } else {
        artistimage = item.images[2].url
      }

      $("#artistlist > ul").append(`<li><span><img src
="${artistimage}"></span><span>${item.name} - ${item.
id}</span>
```

```
</li>`);
    });
}, function(err) {
    console.error(err);
});
},
```

11. The next function we need to add in is to retrieve a list of albums by our chosen artist – this is taken care of by the following code, which we need to add in immediately below the previous object from step 10:

```
getalbumsbyartist() {
    // get albums by a certain artist
    var selectedartist = sessionStorage.
    getItem("chosenartist");

    spotifyApi.getArtistAlbums(selectedartist)
      .then(function(data) {
        data.items.map( function(item) {
            $("#otheralbums > ul").append(`<li><span>
            <img src="${item.images[2].url}"></span>
            <span>${item.name}</span></li>`);
        });
    }, function(err) {
        console.error(err);
    });
},
```

12. We're almost done. The last function to add in will take care of adding a chosen album to our saved albums in Spotify. This is a short function in comparison to others; go ahead and add in the following code below the closing } of the getalbumsbyartist() object:

```
    addtosavedalbums() {
        // add to saved albums
        var getalbum = $(".albumID").text();
        spotifyApi.addToMySavedAlbums([getalbum]);
    },
},
```

13. This last block of code is admittedly something of a cheat – we use it to help set the Spotify ID of our chosen artist into session storage. Scroll down to the closing `</script>` tag, then leave a line, and add in the following code:

```
<script>
    $(document).ready(function() {
        $("body").on("click", "#artistlist ul li", function() {
            var chosenartist = $(this).text();
            var chosen = chosenartist.split(" ");
            sessionStorage.setItem("chosenartist", chosen.
            pop());
        });
    });
</script>
```

14. At this point we can now save our work – go ahead and take a breather! This might seem a lot of code, but I promise you we've added in the bulk of our code, and that the next part (controlling our demo by voice) will be much shorter in comparison.

15. When you're ready, let's preview the results of our work – for this, browse to `https://speech/spotify/`; if all is good, we should see something akin to the screenshot shown at the start of this mammoth exercise.

At this point, we can leave the index.html file open, but minimized – we will be revisiting it in the final part of this project.

I must offer congratulations if you managed to get to this point with a working demo – that last exercise was certainly a monster! While it's nice to see that monster begin to resemble something operational, it's a good opportunity to go through the code in more detail; it shows off a few useful points which are worth more attention.

Understanding the code

We kicked off by setting up a few variables that are used in our code, such as a new placeholder for our SpotifyAPI wrapper instance and album image. We then added in a helper function to convert the time returned by Spotify for each track into something more useful, before initiating that instance of Spotify with our client details, using the wrapper library.

Next up, we added in a host of different event handlers that make use of the wrapper library; although they all work in different ways, most work on the same principle of using a promise-based syntax. A good example is the playmusic() function, which looks like this:

```
playmusic() {  // get current playing album
  spotifyApi.getMyCurrentPlaybackState()
  .then(function(data) {
    spotifyApi.play(data);
    sessionStorage.setItem("chosenalbum", data.item.album.id);
    sessionStorage.setItem("chosenartist", data.item.artists
    [0].id);

    $(".year").html(data.item.album.release_date .substring(0,4));
    $(".albumtype").html(data.item.album.album_type);
    $(".trackcount").html(data.item.album.total_tracks + "
    tracks");
    $(".albumID").html(data.item.album.id);
    ...
```

```
    albumIDplaying = data.item.album.id;        sessionStorage.
    setItem("chosenartist", data.item.artists[0].id);
  }, function(err) {
    console.error(err);
  });
```

This function is triggered when we hit the play button in our demo – we first get the current playback state from Spotify (hence why we need to run the web client for a few seconds!). We then pushed values for the current artist and album into session storage, before initiating play and piping out various values such as album image, a count of the number of tracks, and names for each track. The use of session storage is a little bit of a hack, but necessary. It forces the spotifyApi library to get the right ID for the album at the right time; otherwise, we may end up with it trying to pass a null value, and consequently get a 400 error (or no listing)!

The other functions work in a similar manner (with some exceptions) – each using a promise-based syntax to request a JSON object with data from Spotify, before pulling out the relevant data and displaying it on screen at the appropriate point.

Talking to Spotify

At last, we can get our app to recognize our voice! Yes, it might seem like we've covered a lot before we can get to the real crux of our project (and the point of this book). However, as mentioned before, the Spotify API isn't the easiest to work with; Jose's library is a great step toward abstracting a lot of the code away, but it still means we have to add a fair amount into our project.

Thankfully though, most of the code you are about to see should be reasonably familiar by now; we've used much of it from previous demos, which is good for reusability. The only real change is in the `result()` handler where we tell our demo what to do when it recognizes valid speech. We can see a preview of how things will look in Figure 8-7, once we've completed the changes.

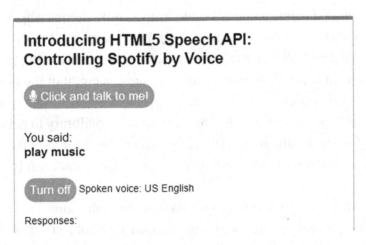

Figure 8-7. *Our Spotify demo, enabled for voice control*

With this in mind, let's dive in and take a look at the code required to enable our app to recognize verbal commands in more detail.

TALKING TO OUR DEMO

To add speech capabilities, follow these steps:

1. We'll begin by reverting back to the index.html we had open from the previous demo. Scroll down to the second `<script>` block at the bottom, and then add a blank line before the closing `});` of the `DOM.ready()` function.

2. We now need to add in the code that allows our demo to
    recognize commands by voice – we have a good amount of
    code to add in, so let's do it block by block. The first block goes
    in below the blank line we just added, which will declare a
    number of variables and properties for the Speech Recognition
    API to operate:

```
const output = $(".output_result");
navigator.mediaDevices.getUserMedia({ audio: true
}).then(function(stream) {

    const SpeechRecognition = window.SpeechRecognition ||
    window.webkitSpeechRecognition;
    const recognition = new SpeechRecognition();

    recognition.interimResults = false;
    recognition.maxAlternatives = 1;
    recognition.continuous = true;
```

3. We have a series of event listeners to add in – the first will trigger
    the Speech Recognition service once we click the Click and talk
    to me! button. For each event handler, leave a blank line after the
    previous one, and then add in the code block in turn:

```
$("body").on("click", "#speech > button", function() {
    let recogLang = "en-US";
    recognition.lang = recogLang.value;
    recognition.start();
});
```

4. The next event handler is one we've used in previous demos –
    this is triggered when the demo detects that the microphone
    is live and sounds have been detected, but not necessarily
    recognized as speech:

```
recognition.addEventListener("speechstart", () => {
  $(".output_log").text("Speech has been detected.");
});
```

5. We've seen the start of this next handler before – this determines if anything spoken is recognizable as speech and acts on it if this is the case:

```
recognition.addEventListener("result", (e) => {
  $(".output_log").html("Result has been detected.");

  let last = e.results.length - 1;
  let text = e.results[last][0].transcript;

  $(".output_result").html(text);

  /* Play music */
  if (text.indexOf("play music") != -1) {
    $("#app > button:nth-child(4)").trigger("click");
  }

  /* Pause music */
  if (text.indexOf("pause music") != -1) {
    $("#app > button:nth-child(5)").trigger("click");
  }

  /* Go forward */
  if (text.indexOf("go forward") != -1) {
    $("#app > button:nth-child(7)").trigger("click");
  }

  /* Go back */
  if (text.indexOf("go back") != -1) {
    $("#app > button:nth-child(8)").trigger("click");
  }
```

```
/* Save album */
if (text.indexOf("save album") != -1) {
  $("#app > button:nth-child(9)").trigger("click");
}

/* Get other albums */
if (text.indexOf("gct other albums") != -1) {
  $("#otheralbums > button").trigger("click");
}

/* Search artist */
if (text.indexOf("search artist") != -1) {
  $("#artistlist > input").val("enigma");
  $("#artistlist > button").trigger("click");
}

$(".output_log").html("Confidence: " + (e.results[0][0].
confidence * 100).toFixed(2) + "%");
});
```

6. We have three more event handlers to add in – this next one detects if we've stopped speaking, with the onspeechend handler being triggered if this is the case:

```
recognition.addEventListener("speechend", () => {
  recognition.stop();
});

recognition.onspeechend = function() {
  $(".output_log").html("You were quiet for a while so
  voice recognition turned itself off.");
  //console.log("off");
};
```

7. This last event handler takes care of basic error handling – in a production environment, this would be more in-depth, but for our purposes, it's enough to simply render the raw error message in the console:

```
recognition.addEventListener("error", e => {
    if (e.error == "no-speech") {
      $(".output_result").html("Error: no speech
      detected");
    } else {
      $(".output_result").html("Error: " + e.error);
    }
});
}).catch(function(err){
  console.log(err);
});
```

8. We're done with editing the file – go ahead and save it. We can now preview the results of our work; for this, browse to `https://speech/spotify/`. If all is well, we should first see something akin to the screenshot shown in Figure 8-7 at the start of this exercise.

Over the course of this last demo, we've revisited some of the functions that we saw in our first project earlier in this book; it shows how easy it is to add in speech capabilities and that much of the code can be reused with little difficulty. As with many projects, it's the results handler that is frequently changed; with that in mind, let's take a look at the code in more detail, to see how it all fitted together.

Exploring the code in detail

A lot of the code we've worked on in this demo should by now begin to look a little familiar – the beauty of the API is such that we can set up a number of stock handlers and reuse these throughout our projects. Granted some (such as the results handler – more anon) might need to change, but many such as onspeechend can remain the same across different projects. With this in mind, let's take a look at the code in more detail.

We kicked off by declaring a number of variables and properties – these include caching .output_result, defining an instance of the Speech Recognition API as SpeechRecognition, and setting the interimResults, maxAlternatives, and continuous properties for the API.

We then moved onto setting up event handlers to respond to the API – the first allows us to trigger the API using en-US as the default language. Notice that this isn't using a standard jQuery syntax for event handlers – we have to defer it, so that it can be assigned once the button is present on the page (it's not available until we've logged in).

The next handler we added in is for the speechstart event – this was lifted directly from an earlier project, which shows how easy it is to reuse code when it comes to working with the Speech APIs. We then moved onto a rather lengthy handler for the result event – it looks long, but most of this is defining what should happen when the API recognizes certain phrases. This handler transcribes the contents of the results property, before outputting it on screen and determining if any of the actions provided can be executed.

We then added in three more event handlers, which were lifted from previous projects: two to determine if we've stopped speaking (speechend and onspeechend) and the last to provide rudimentary error logging (error). It's important to note that the two speechend handlers work in slightly different ways – the first determines if we've stopped talking, and the second controls what happens when we've stopped talking and can therefore switch off the API.

Taking things further

Hopefully by now, you will have had a chance to play with the demo – granted it's a little rough and ready in places, but we should bear in mind that this chapter isn't about using Spotify, but how we can set the Speech APIs to interact with Spotify content!

Nevertheless, there are a few things we could do to improve the interface and start to add a little more polish to our app:

- One thing you may have noticed is that the sort order for the track listing doesn't appear to be right. There is a reason for this; it has to do with the insertion order of each item into the <span> element that contains the listing, once it has been retrieved from the API. To work around this, we could push the items into an object array and then sort them using the .sort method before rendering the new order on screen. (Just to confirm, the track IDs are correct – it's just the order that's not!)

- For the purists among you, you may have spotted that the track times are slightly out for some of the tracks; this is very likely due to how we are converting the original millisecond value to something more human-readable and recognizable. This may not be a real issue, but it might be worth experimenting with the function to see if this can be improved.

- Cast your mind back to earlier in the book – in a number of projects, we implemented support for an additional language (French). There should be no reason why we can't add the same support here; we would need to update the UI to reflect the changes, as well as adding the right trigger commands for each feature, such as playing music.

- One area which is sorely lacking in this demo is any form of feedback from the app – we can see what commands we issue verbally, but how about using the Speech Synthesis API to respond with confirmation that an action has taken place?

- The list of albums returned can be rather large; this is one area we could definitely improve on! Our demo shows the first 20 items returned from the API, but we should look at perhaps limiting this to the first five (?), with an option to show an extended list if desired.

- We've implemented the `navigator.mediaDevices.getUserMedia` method to initiate access to the microphone (which we used back in Chapter 1), but at present the Turn off button is not operational. Ideally, we should provide an option to turn off the speech facility, but this will need a refactoring of the code as the button won't initially be visible.

This should give you a flavor of where we could go and a few ideas to get you started. There are plenty more options we can use in José's wrapper library, so I would recommend reading through both the documentation from his site and from the Spotify Developer Portal – there is plenty to help you develop your app into something that could become a voice-enabled production solution at some point in the future.

Summary

Adding speech facilities to any application opens up a world of possibilities, particularly for those of us who are less able – or perhaps just lazy! Over the course of this chapter, we've worked on adding speech capabilities to a project that uses the Spotify API; let's take a moment to review what we've covered in this chapter.

We kicked off by setting the background to our project, before exploring the question of why we chose Spotify as our API provider. We then moved onto a quick discussion around how we would architect our project and the subject of getting access to the API authorized by Spotify (and what it would mean for our project).

We then worked through setting up the basic authentication process, having first sorted out a few prerequisites; we then turned our attention to adding in the code to allow us to stream content from Spotify. Last but by no means least, we then added in the code to allow us to interact verbally with Spotify, before exploring some ideas to help get us started on developing our project further into something that could be used in a production environment.

Okay, take a breather, folks, as we have another big project coming your way! One can't fail to notice how Internet shopping has really taken off over the last few years; more and more people are using devices to shop online, where they don't necessarily need to see the results on screen. One way to help with this is to add in speech capabilities during the checkout process – stay with me, as I show you how we can do so, in the next chapter.

CHAPTER 9

Project: Automating the Purchase Process

We're almost at the end of the book, but we have one more project in store for us! I'm sure you've spent hours trying to find a particular product, then added it to a basket, and gone through a good handful of screens to complete checkout, right? It's a real pain with more complex baskets. What if we could *automate* part of the process, using the power of our voice?

With the power of the Speech APIs, we should be able to verbally ask the site to find and add products to a basket and then check out using the Payment Request API – all without touching a single keyboard. Sound impossible? Over the course of the chapter, I will show you a good chunk of this idea may just be reality now. We'll go through the various steps required to add voice capabilities to the core part of the process, so you can see how much time and effort we can save our customers.

Setting the scene

Before we delve into the specifics of how we might achieve such a project, I want to answer one question that I am sure will be on the lips of at least some of you: why would we do something like this? Well, there are two good reasons, if not three: Amazon (or Google – depending on your affinity), accessibility, and...well, why not? Before you all think I've completely lost the plot, let me explain what I mean by that somewhat cryptic answer.

© Alex Libby 2020
A. Libby, *Introducing the HTML5 Web Speech API*,
https://doi.org/10.1007/978-1-4842-5735-7_9

The first, Amazon, or Google for that matter, is because of the invention of the smart assistant. We touched on the subject earlier in the book, of how more and more searches are being achieved without a visual display. How are they managing this? Well, it's through the use of smart assistants! Why spend time trawling through the web site, when you can get the likes of Amazon's Alexa or Apple's Siri to do the work for you?

The second, or accessibility, is a crucial factor in today's world of inclusion – we already have screen readers which can (to a greater or lesser extent) help partially sighted people around web sites. The trouble is it requires us developers to expend considerable amount of time and resource on adding ARIA-based accessibility capabilities – this is useful, but there is a risk it may not work so well for every site or restrict how we do things. Instead, why not get the web site to do the work for us? We can always start with providing basic capabilities, along with accessibility tags, but adding speech capabilities will allow us to be more flexible and offer a more personal touch.

The third and final reason of "why not?" is exactly as it says on the tin – why not? We should never feel constrained by the need to keep things safe or only do what we know; after all while, this gets boring, and we begin to lose appetite! We should absolutely look to push the boundaries of what we can achieve – it may or may not always work, but after all, you won't know until you try, right?

With that earth-shattering thought in mind, let's move on. We will shortly take a look at how we are going to architect our project for this chapter, but before we do so, let's turn our attention to how we're going to keep things in scope and make sure this project stays on track.

Keeping things in scope

It's at this point where we must be careful – building an e-commerce shop, let alone adding speech capabilities to it, can easily fill the pages of an entire book, if we're not careful!

With this mind, we're going to limit ourselves to a couple of key processes, so you can get a flavor of how a speech option can be set up and extend it to cover other areas in your own projects. The two key areas we will cover are

- Adding a product to cart – we'll set up the code for a four-product shop (this should be enough to show a little variety; it's the same process whether we sell a limited range or hundreds of products).

- Checking out by entering card details and hitting a payment button – this will simulate payment being sent and receiving a positive response in return.

We will not be going through the mechanics of how to construct our shop, as the amount of code required is too substantial to do it justice in the space that we have available in this chapter! Instead, we will assume we have a basic, but functional, shop working and proceed on the basis that we will add speech capabilities to it.

We will go through some pointers to get you started on extending the shop to cover other areas, toward the end of the chapter.

Okay, now we've set the scene, it's time to delve into the tools we will be using; we've already met and used two (in the form of the Speech APIs), but we will make use of some others within our project.

Architecting the project

As with any project, we could use any one of a variety of different tools for the job – it goes without saying that there is clearly no one tool we could (or should) use! We already know we're going to use the Speech APIs that we've seen from earlier, but to make this work, we need to introduce a handful of extra technologies. They are as follows:

- CompressPNG.com (`https://compresspng.com`) – this I've used to compress the PNG images used in this demo; it's not strictly necessary in a development capacity, but the originals were larger than needed!

- Google Fonts – we're using the Open Sans and Caveat fonts available from `https://fonts.google.com`; these can be downloaded and set up locally if needed.

- jQuery – downloaded and renamed from the jQuery CDN at `https://code.jquery.com/jquery-3.4.1.min.js`.

- Stripe – we're using a jQuery-based plugin library from Stripe, to help with formatting and managing the credit card details; this is available from `https://stripe.github.io/jquery.payment/lib/jquery.payment.js`.

- Font Awesome – for this we're using the MaxCDN link at `https://maxcdn.bootstrapcdn.com/font-awesome/4.5.0/css/font-awesome.min.css` – this is used for the basket icon in the cart.

Note   The use of jQuery is for convenience only; in an ideal world, we would look to remove it out of use and likely focus on using vanilla JavaScript or a framework such as React or Vue.

Okay, with that out of the way, let's move on. It's time to get stuck into coding! Over the next few pages, we're going to cover a fair amount of code; for reasons of space, we will focus mostly on the JavaScript used for the speech capabilities, as the HTML markup and CSS styling are standard fare. With this in mind, let's dive in and take a look at the code in closer detail.

Preparing our shopping cart

It's time to start setting things up. For our final project for this book, we're going to create a basic shop to sell a limited range of cookies – not just any ol' cookies as my mama used to say, but ones that are really soft and chewy...mmm...but I digress!

From a technical perspective, our demo will be an amalgamation of code based on two CodePen demos and speech recognition code from earlier demos; the shop is a cut-down version of a Pen by Virgil Pana from `https://codepen.io/virgilpana/pen/ZYqJXN`, with the pop-out payment form based on the Pen by Maycon Luiz at `https://codepen.io/mycnlz/pen/reLOZV`. It's possible to create something from scratch, but given the constraints on space available in this book, we wouldn't be able to do it justice!

SETTING UP THE SHOPPING CART

Leaving that aside, let's make a start with setting up our shop:

1. We'll begin by extracting a copy of the shop folder from the code download that accompanies this book; go ahead and save it to our project area.

2. Fire up your browser, and then head over to `https://speech/shop/`. If all is well, we should see the shop appear, similar to the screenshot shown in Figure 9-1.

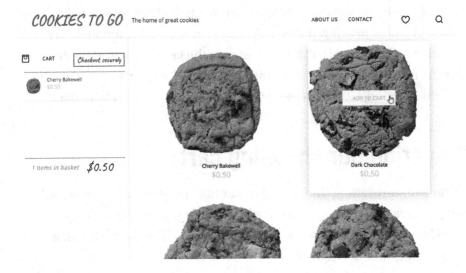

Figure 9-1. Our initial shop

Setting expectations

At this point we have a functional shop (of sorts) – granted it's not going to be perfect, but it will be sufficient for our needs. It is important to set the right expectations though, so in the interests of transparency, there are a couple of points to bear in mind throughout this chapter:

- The code is **not** production-ready – indeed, much of the functionality one would expect to see in a shop gallery and checkout process is not present. This chapter is not about building shopping carts, but establishing how we might make them available through use of verbal commands. It's for this reason that we will focus more on the techniques to do this, rather than the shop itself.

- For reasons of space, I will focus on the key parts of selecting a product from a gallery and putting it through a (simulated) purchase – one might argue that searching for a product is also essential, but that's not going to be any good if we can't add it to our basket! The key though is that the principles for "voice enabling" our site will be the same for most parts of the site, so we can always adapt existing code to work for other areas.

With this out of the way, let's turn our attention to the bit I know you're all waiting for – updating our demo! Don't worry. It's coming in just a few lines, but before we get stuck in, let's look at the steps involved in updating our demo in more detail.

Adding speech capabilities

Okay, it's crunch time! Mmm, perhaps that was a little too cheesy, given that the products in our shop are cookies, but I digress... Anyway, back to reality.

When adding speech capabilities, we can do this in stages; here are the steps we need to follow:

- Add in the markup and styling for our microphone and responses.

- Adjust the markup around the products.

- Adding in the script functionality to make it operational.

- Add in basic styling to make our demo look presentable.

The first stage in our process is to add in the markup that controls the microphone and renders any response on screen – once in, we can test it to confirm our site is receiving speech and will be able to act on it once our product markup and script is in place. Let's dive in and take a look at adding in that markup, so we can start to see our speech capabilities take shape.

Inserting the markup for our microphone

The first part of updating our demo is very straightforward – we first need to add in our markup for both the microphone and various messages or responses and then add in our visual indicators so customers know what to say when using their microphone.

There isn't anything particularly complex in this first part, although there is an interesting use of data tags; we'll explore the reasoning for their use after the demo. Let's first go ahead with updating or adding in the relevant markup to our demo.

ADDING SPEECH PART 1: THE MICROPHONE MARKUP

To add in our markup, follow these steps:

1. All of our changes are in the `index.html` file that came in the shop folder as part of the download – go ahead and open it in your usual text editor.

2. Next, look for the `<div id="sidebar" ....` block, and add in this markup immediately before its closing `</div>` element. We should end up with something like this:

```
<button id="microphone">
  <i class="fa fa-microphone"></i> Click and talk to me!
</button>
<div class="response">
  <span class="output_log"></span>
</div>
<p class="output">You said: <strong class="output_result">
</strong></p>
  <span class="voice">Spoken voice: US English</span>
</div>
```

3. Go ahead and save the file and then minimize it – we will need to revert to it in the next exercise.

4. Next, we need to add in some basic styling for our microphone button and response text. For this, crack open the `styles.css` file, and scroll all the way to the bottom.

5. Once at the bottom, add in the following style rules:

```css
/* SPEECH RECOGNITION --------------------------- */
.speechterm { padding-left: 15px; font-style: italic; }
i.fa.fa-microphone { padding-right: 10px; }
p.output { padding: 10px 0; }
#microphone { margin-top: 20px; }
#microphone:hover { background-color: darkgrey; }
```

6. At this point, save your work, and close the styles.css file – we've added all that we need to for this demo.

7. We can now preview the results of our work – for this, browse to `https://speech/shop/`. If all is well, we should see something akin to the screenshot shown in Figure 9-2.

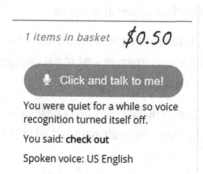

Figure 9-2. The updated shop, with a microphone option added

At this stage, we haven't really made any significant changes – we now have the basis though for a microphone button, along with spaces for various responses from the user or messages back from the API. Rather than explore the code changes at this point, we will do that at the end of the next exercise. So without further ado, let's swiftly move on and explore what needs to be updated to enable each product within the gallery for the API in more detail.

Altering our product markup

With our microphone markup inserted, we can now turn our attention to "enabling" each cookie for use in our speech recognition function.

I say "enable" for want of a better way to express it, but all we're doing is adjusting our markup to make it easier for our code to recognize and add the right cookie into our basket. Trust me – it might not make sense now, but it will all become clear once we complete the exercise! Keeping that in mind, let's make a start on updating the markup.

ADDING SPEECH PART 2: UPDATING PRODUCT MARKUP

To update our product markup, follow these steps:

1. The first stage is to revert back to the `index.html` file we had open from the previous exercise – all of the changes for this part of the demo will be in this file.

2. The first change is to update the Cherry Bakewell cookie – look for the `add_to_cart` <div> element and add in the data tag as indicated:

```
<div class="add_to_cart" data-product="cherry
bakewell">Add to cart</div>
```

3. Next, scroll down a couple of lines and insert this markup immediately below the `<span class="product_price"...` line:

```
<span class="product_price">$0.50</span>
<span class="speechterm"><i class="fa fa-microphone">
</i>"Add a cherry"</span>
```

This will add a microphone and suitable text against the cookie, so our customer has an indication of how to ask for it verbally.

4. We need to repeat steps 2 and 3 for the remaining three products – for the next cookie (Dark Chocolate), add in the data tag as indicated:

```
<div class="add_to_cart" data-product="dark
chocolate">Add to cart</div>
```

5. Immediately below that cookie's `product_price` markup, add in this line of code – this will "enable" the Dark Chocolate cookie for our Speech Recognition function:

```
<span class="speechterm"><i class="fa fa-microphone">
</i>"Add a dark"</span>
```

6. We need to perform a similar change to the Raspberry and White Chocolate cookie too – for this, add in the highlighted code as indicated:

```
<div class="add_to_cart" data-product="raspberry">Add to
cart</div>
```

7. In a similar fashion to previous cookies, we need to add in the microphone markup too – for this, add in the following line immediately below this cookie's product_price line:

```
<span class="speechterm"><i class="fa fa-microphone">
</i>"Add a raspberry"</span>
```

8. Last but by no means least, go ahead and add in the data tag as indicated for the Toffee cookie:

```
<div class="add_to_cart" data-product="toffee">Add to
cart</div>
```

9. There is one more change we need to make for this product – immediately below its product_price markup line, add in this code:

```
<span class="speechterm"><i class="fa fa-microphone">
</i>"Add a toffee"</span>
```

10. Go ahead and save the file – we now preview the results! For this, browse to https://speech/shop; if all is well, we should see all four cookies now have a visual indicator as to what to ask for, when using our microphone (Figure 9-3).

Cherry Bakewell
$0.50
🎤 "Add a cherry"

Figure 9-3. *"We can now speak to one of our cookies..."*

Mmm, just looking at that cookie is making me feel really hungry. *Chuckle!* Leaving thoughts of food aside for the moment, the changes we've added to our code may seem a little unusual, but as promised, there is method in the madness! Before I explain more, let's take a look at the code in more detail.

Dissecting the code

Much of the markup we've used is very similar – the changes we've made fall into two camps: the first is to add in the markup around the microphone button, and the second is to adjust our markup for each product.

The first block adds a standard <button> element into our markup, plus a div element and two spans – the latter are used for displaying responses from the API (such as any errors), responses from the user, and an indication of the voice used by the API. Moving on, we then added in a data-product tag to each cookie, along with a visual indication of what to ask for when using the microphone, in the form of the .speechterm span.

Now, as promised, there is a reason for using data tags. As you will see later in the code, we use a generic .add_to_cart class to trigger the addition of any cookie into the basket. In principle, this seems like a sensible idea, right?

Wrong – if we used this on its own, we would have a problem: it will add in four instances of the same cookie at once! The reason for this is down to how jQuery works – the .add_to_cart class will be applied to all four products, as we use the same class against each product.

To get around it, we add in the data tags so that we have a specific reference to each cookie. The key though is in *how* we trigger the call to add the item – we use the data-tag property which is bound to each add_to_cart div. Referencing this dynamically means we can pass an instance of the add_to_cart div to the event handler:

```
$('[data-product="' + cookieChosen + '"]').trigger("click");
```

Don't worry if it doesn't entirely make sense now – we will revisit this when we go through the code that we add to make our demo work!

Adding the script functionality

Moving on, the next task on our list is to add in the code that we need to operate the speech feature. Much of this you will have seen from previous demos, so it shouldn't be entirely unfamiliar by now; the key to it is in how we turn our speech response into something our code can recognize and use to add in the appropriate cookie. To give you a flavor of how it will look, you can see what will be the completed article in Figure 9-4.

Figure 9-4. A cookie added the basket using our voice

With that in mind, let's turn our attention to setting up our demo.

ADDING SPEECH PART 3: MAKING IT WORK

Let's make a start on adding in the script for our demo:

1. For this exercise, all of the changes we make will be in the `script.js` file, so go ahead and open this in your usual text editor.

2. Scroll all the way down to the bottom, until you see these comments:

```
/* SPEECH RECOGNITION ------------------------------ */
/* Code to be added here */
```

3. This is where we will add in our code – there is a fair chunk to add, so we will go through it block by block.

4. The first block is to add in a number of variable or object declarations and set up values for some of the Speech Recognition API. Go ahead and leave a blank line and then add in the following code below the second comment from the previous step:

```
const log = document.querySelector(".output_log");
const output = document.querySelector(".output_result");

const SpeechRecognition = window.SpeechRecognition ||
window.webkitSpeechRecognition;
const recognition = new SpeechRecognition();

recognition.interimResults = false;
recognition.maxAlternatives = 1;
recognition.continuous = true;
```

5. The first event handler we need to add in takes care of enabling our microphone for use – here we set a couple of properties to configure the instance of the Speech Recognition API. Add in the following code, leaving a blank line after the code from the previous step:

```
document.querySelector("#microphone").addEventListener
("click", () => {
    let recogLang = "en-GB";
    recognition.lang = recogLang.value;
    recognition.start();
});
```

6. The next handler we add in fires when speech has been detected – this includes background noise! For this, add in the following code, leaving a blank line after the code from the previous step:

```
recognition.addEventListener("speechstart", () => {
  log.textContent = "Speech has been detected.";
});
```

7. This next step is where the magic starts to happen – it's here where we detect what has been said, parse the contents, and determine what action to take as a result. It's a fair block of code, so we'll split it into several parts – to set up the basic handler, go ahead and add in this code, leaving a blank line after the code from the previous step:

```
recognition.addEventListener("result", (e) => {
  log.textContent = "Result has been detected.";

  let last = e.results.length - 1;
  let text = e.results[last][0].transcript;

  output.textContent = text;
```

```
// ACTION CODE HERE

log.textContent = "Confidence: " + (e.results[0][0].
confidence * 100).toFixed(2) + "%";
});
```

8. With the basic handler now in place, we can begin to extend it.
    Look for this line of code – `// ACTION CODE HERE` – in the
    previous step, and then replace it with this conditional block:

```
// SR - "Add an X to the basket"
if (text.search(/\badd\b/)) {
  var request = text.split(" ").pop();
console.log(request);
var cookieChosen;

if (request == "cherry") {
  cookieChosen = "cherry bakewell";
}

if (request == "dark") {
  cookieChosen = "dark chocolate";
}

if (request == "raspberry") {
  cookieChosen = "raspberry";
}

if (request == "toffee") {
  cookieChosen = "toffee";
}

$('[data-product="' + cookieChosen + '"]').
trigger("click");
```

9. For the third and final part of this conditional block, go ahead
    and add in the following lines below the data-product
    assignment from the previous step, leaving a blank line in
    between:

```
/* ----------------- */

/* click on checkout */
if (text.indexOf("check") != -1) {
  $("#checkout").trigger("click");
}

/* ----------------- */

/* enter credit card number */
if (text.indexOf("credit card") != -1) {
    $("#cardnumber").val("4111111111111111");
  }

  /* ----------------- */

  /* enter card date   */
  if (text.indexOf("expiry") != -1) {
    $("#cardexpiration").val("10/2022");
  }

  /* ----------------- */
  /* enter CVV number   */
  if (text.indexOf("security") != -1) {
    $("#cardcvc").val("672");
  }

  /* ----------------- */
  /* click on purchase */
  if (text.indexOf("purchase") != -1) {
    $("div.card-form > button > span").trigger("click");
  }
}
```

10. We have three event handlers left, which look simple in comparison to that last event handler! The next one to add in will fire when the API detects no more speech can be heard:

```
recognition.addEventListener("speechend", () => {
  recognition.stop();
});
```

11. This next event handler also fires when no more speech is detected, but there is a subtle difference – this one fires once the API has shut down. Go ahead and add in the following code, leaving a blank line after the previous event handler:

```
recognition.onspeechend = function() {
  log.textContent = 'You were quiet for a while so voice
  recognition turned itself off.';
  console.log("off");
};
```

12. Last but by no means least, we need to implement some basic error handling – for now, we'll just render on screen any errors that are generated by the API. Go ahead and add in the following code:

```
recognition.addEventListener("error", e => {
  if (e.error == "no-speech") {
    output.textContent = "Error: no speech detected";
  } else {
    output.textContent = "Error: " + e.error;
  }
});
```

13. At this point we are done with editing our file. Go ahead and save it and then close the file. We can now preview our results. Browse to `https://speech/shop/`, click the microphone button, and then try saying "Add a cherry" into the microphone. If all is well, we should see something akin to the screenshot shown at the start of this exercise.

We now have a working add to cart process – we should be able to add any of the four cookies into our cart. We've seen it working with the Cherry Bakewell (as indicated in Figure 9-4), but for some there may be a sting in this tale! It's something we've seen happen before (remember the Alexa clone demo?) – before we explore what it is, let's go through the code in more detail, as there are a couple of key changes to what we've used from earlier demos.

Breaking apart our code

Over the course of this chapter, we've covered a good chunk of code, as part of adding in our speech feature – much of it by now should begin to look familiar, particularly as we've used parts from earlier demos in this book. That said, it's still a good idea to go through the code we've added in more detail – there is a key section we need to be aware of, so let's dive in and take a look in more detail.

We kicked off the speech recognition part by defining a couple of constants – we use `.output_log` to display messages from the API and `.output_result` to display transcribed text from the customer. We then create a new instance of the Speech Recognition API; this uses either the native implementation or the vendor-prefixed version, depending on the browser being used. Alongside this, we also set three properties – `interimResults` to false (so we only get the end result), `maxAlternatives` to 1 (we focus on getting the original, detected word and not possible alternatives), and `continuous` to true (so the Speech Recognition API doesn't switch off too quickly).

We then had a series of event handlers. The first allows the customer to enable their microphone from within the browser; this sets the language to use as US English (`"en-US"`), before firing up the recognition service. This is followed by the `speechstart` event handler, which will fire as soon as any spoken text is detected (and not necessarily from the customer!).

The key part of this demo is up next – this is an expanded result event handler. This first detects if spoken text has been recognized by the service, before assigning the contents of the spoken transcript to the text variable. We then split the content of this variable and take the last entry, using the `pop()` method. This is important, as this is stored in the `cookieChosen` variable; we used this to trigger the right add to cart button.

It's worth pausing for a moment, as a glance through the code will show nothing that could be termed as a pure add to cart button handler! We touched on this earlier in the chapter, with good reason – we could create something that assigns a unique ID or class, but getting this right will be tricky. We might end up with a lot of handlers, or a really ugly one-size-fits-all approach.

Instead, we're using a `data-product` tag – we dynamically concatenated the value saved from `cookieChosen` into the event which triggers the click handler that fires the right button. This works, as if you look closely at our markup, you'll see the data-tag is against the `add_to_cart` div, as indicated in Figure 9-5.

```
64        <div class="add_to_cart" data-product="cherry bakewell">Add to cart</div>
65        <span class="product_name">Cherry Bakewell</span>
66        <span class="product_price">$0.50</span>
67        <span class="speechterm"><i class="fa fa-microphone"></i>"Add a cherry"</span>
68    </div>
```

Figure 9-5. *An example of the data-tag used in the markup*

For the remainder of that event handler, we simply used a set of condition checks – if the results of our transcribed text contain certain words such as card, security, or expiry, we enter test values into the appropriate fields. The last step for the event handler adds in a trigger mechanism for submitting payment – we're simulating this in our demo, but it's at this point payment would be made if this were in production use.

You will have noticed the use of fake credit card details in this demo. This is *not* recommended practice; they are there to illustrate a pitfall for this demo. We will go through what this means for us later in the chapter.

The remainder of the code contains event handlers we've used in previous demos – we have the two speechend handlers and one to cover basic error handling in our demo. There is a reason for having two speechend handlers though: the first one (speechend) fires when the service detects that we've stopped speaking (and so shuts itself down); the second (onspeechend) kicks in once this has happened and puts an appropriate message on screen for our customers.

Okay, let's move on. We've constructed a basic shopping cart, which uses a custom checkout process. There is a relatively new API that aims to standardize the checkout form across all browsers. The question is, can we apply the same principles to voice-enable it? In an ideal world, there shouldn't be any difference, except this time we might not be so lucky. To see what I mean, let's take a look at how this change might affect our strategy and whether we might need to reconsider our plans.

An alternative method of checking out

For as long as I can remember (and that's going back just over 20 years!), anyone purchasing goods over the Internet would have no doubt been through a checkout process that was either custom built or developed from one of the commercial offerings such as Actinic. There was nothing wrong with this (at the time), but many are now seen as clunky and difficult to maintain – it's frequently an area where one sees the biggest drop-out during the whole purchasing process!

Over the last few years, the W3C and browser vendors have been developing a standardized API that can be surfaced directly from within the browser – this is now known as the Payment Request API. Although it will look different in each browser, under the covers it offers a standard framework into which payment providers can plug in their own payment handlers, without having to worry about the UI or user experience.

For our next exercise, we're going to make use of this API to produce a simple payment checkout – it won't have all of the bells and whistles that can come with the API, but will at least allow us to run through the checkout process. As a taster, Figure 9-6 illustrates how our demo will look, once we implement the changes needed for the Request Payment API.

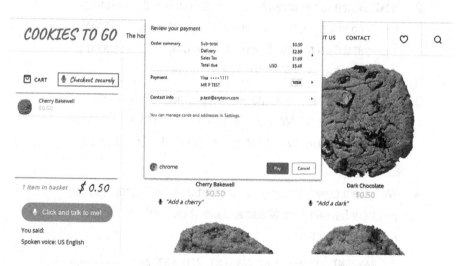

Figure 9-6. *Our alternative method of payment in action*

Now that we've seen what it will look like, let's get stuck into making the changes for our demo.

> ## USING THE PAYMENT REQUEST API
>
> For this demo, I would recommend taking a copy of your completed shop folder
> from the previous demo and then saving it as shop-alternative; we will use
> this as a basis for swapping out the manual checkout for the Payment Request API.
>
> ---
>
> If you get stuck, there is a completed version of this demo in the code download
> that accompanies this book; it's in the shop-alternative – finished version folder.

To complete the swap, go ahead with these steps:

1. The first task is to strip out the payment section in our markup
   file – for this, look for the line starting `<!--- PAYMENT....`,
   and then remove from this down to the closing `</div>` tag just
   before `<div id="header">`.

2. Next, switch to the script.js, so we can remove the modal, as
   this is no longer needed. Look for the line starting `/* MODAL
   ----`, and then remove it and the code down to the closing `});`
   just before the `/* PAYMENT FORM...` line.

3. We also need to remove the original payment block – look
   for and remove the block starting with `/* PAYMENT FORM
   ---...` – remove to just before `/* SPEECH RECOGNITION
   ---....`

4. We have a new block of code to insert as a replacement for our
   payment handler – go ahead and insert this code as the first
   part of our handler:

```
/* PAYMENT FORM USING PAYMENT REQUEST API---------- */
const methodData = [{
  supportedMethods: 'basic-card',
  data: {
```

```
    supportedNetworks: ['visa', 'mastercard', 'amex']
  }
}];
```

5. The real meat of the Payment Request comes in the form of this next event handler – leave a line blank, and then add in the following code below the methodData constant:

```
document.getElementById('checkout').onclick = function (e) {
  if(window.PaymentRequest) {
    let subtotal = Number(countCookies * 0.50);
    let tax = 1.99;
    let shipping = 2.99;

    const details = {
      total: {
        label: 'Total due',
        amount: { currency: 'USD', value: (subtotal + tax
        + shipping).toFixed(2) }
      },
      displayItems: [{
        label: 'Sub-total',
        amount: { currency: 'USD', value: subtotal.toFixed(2) }
      }, {
        label: 'Delivery',
        amount: { currency: 'USD', value: 2.99 }
      }, {
        label: 'Sales Tax',
        amount: { currency: 'USD', value: tax.toFixed(2) }
      }]
    };

  const options = { requestPayerEmail: true };
  const request = new PaymentRequest(methodData, details,
  options);
```

```
    //Show the Native UI
    request
      .show()
      .then(function(result) {
        result.complete('success')
            .then(console.log(JSON.stringify(result)));
      }).catch(function(err) {
        console.error(err.message);
      });
    } else {
      // Fallback to traditional checkout
    }
};
```

6. We're almost done. There is one last block of code to remove. In the Speech Recognition block, look for and remove this code, as it is no longer needed:

```
/* ---------------- */
/* enter credit card number */
if (text.indexOf("credit card") != -1) {
  $("#cardnumber").val("4111111111111111");
}
/* ---------------- */

/* enter card date   */
if (text.indexOf("expiry") != -1) {
  $("#cardexpiration").val("10/2022");
}
/* ---------------- */

/* enter CVV number  */
if (text.indexOf("security") != -1) {
  $("#cardcvc").val("672");
}
```

This might seem a little odd, but there is a good reason for its removal – all will be revealed shortly.

7.   We're done with editing. Go ahead and save both index.html and script.js; they can now be closed.

8.   At this point, we can now preview the results of our changes – fire up your browser, and then navigate to https://speech/ shop-alternative. If all is well, we should see something akin to the view shown in Figure 9-6, where our alternative checkout form is being displayed.

Over the course of this exercise, we've stripped out the original payment form and replaced it with an instance from the Payment Request API. This might seem OK, but notice how we had removed some of the checks done in our original version, as part of step 6? I alluded to this as seeming odd at the time, but there is a good reason for this - for the explanation, and more, let's dive in and take a look at the changes in more detail.

Breaking apart the code

Over the course of this chapter, we've made some radical changes. We kicked off by removing the original payment code from within our markup file, along with the modal. Neither of these was required, as the form would be provided by the Payment Request API from within the browser.

Next up, we did something similar, but in the script.js file – we evicted the entire payment block there, as the original code would be redundant, once we entered in our new Payment Request code.

The real crux of our demo came in the form of the new Payment Request API code; we started by declaring a methodData constant, which defines the accepted payment methods allowed by our browser. We've stuck with basic-card, which is the method that is available out of the box; it's an unsecured method and shouldn't be used in practice, but is okay for testing purposes only.

We then added in an event handler that is fired as soon as the #checkout div is clicked; this can either be by mouse or verbally, as we did in the original version of this demo. This first is a check for window. PaymentRequest, to see if our browser supports it – assuming it does, we define a set of variables for subtotal, tax, and shipping (all others have already been declared elsewhere in the code).

In the next constant (details), we defined an object that contains both the label texts and amounts to display in our form, before initiating an instance of the Payment Request API as request. This is then called as a promise; we first show() the form and then either fire the .complete() method which displays the results in console or throw an error via the catch() trap, to declare that there's been a problem with our payment process.

If you are interested in learning more about the Payment Request API, then you might like to refer to my book, *Checking Out with the Payment Request API*, published by Apress.

Reducing the functionality: A note

Before we finish with this demo, there is something we should consider for a moment – remember how I said we needed to remove a chunk of conditional checks from our code? You can see what I mean in Figure 9-7, where we've removed the original if statements for checking the credit card number, expiry date, and CVV security number.

```
189        ('[data-product="'    cookieChosen    '"]').trigger("click");
190
191        /* -------------------- */
192        /* click on checkout */
193        if (text.indexOf("check")    -1) {
194            ("#checkout").trigger("click");
195        }
196    }
197
198    log.textContent    "Confidence: "    (e.results[0][0].confidence    100).toFixed(2)    "%";
199    });
```

Figure 9-7. *Our updated demo, sans conditional checks*

The reason we can't include these checks is simple – the Payment Request API form is built into the browser and therefore can't be surfaced to allow us to interact with it. It means that while the rest of our basket can be controlled by voice, we can't control the checkout form itself!

In some respects, this can be seen as making the site less accessible – it therefore means that we have to provide a fallback or set it so that the Payment Request API can be enabled over the standard payment checkout process. The great thing is though the API is still in a state of flux; while it is sufficiently stable to use now, things will likely change before it reaches official status, so who knows? Support for the speech API could well be improved!

Let's move on. Our demo is now complete, but it's not the end of the story though! There is unfortunately a bit of a sting in this tale, which will affect our shop. To understand why, let's dive in and take a look at some of the pitfalls we might experience when adding speech capabilities to an e-commerce site, in greater detail.

Exploring the pitfalls of our solution

It's time for a confession. Yes, I hear you. You're probably thinking, *Uh-oh...what's that sting he's referring to, I wonder?* You'd be right to be cautious, but don't worry. It's not all as bad as it might seem! The Speech APIs are still very new and have yet to reach candidate recommendation by the W3C. That doesn't mean we can't use them, but that we need to exercise a certain amount of caution. Let's take a look at some of these pitfalls in more detail:

- The first one is that you might be surprised at some of the visual labels used – notice how none of them give the full name, but something such as "Add a cherry"? There is a good reason for this – had we used the full name, we would have found that not all of the cookies could be added! The cause is down to something we covered back in the Alexa clone demo: the APIs struggle to recognize certain words, particularly if there is little contrast between different syllables. This isn't something that can be fixed as such, but fine-tuned; we need to be careful about which words we choose to select our products, and only testing will identify the best combination to use.

- If you try clicking the microphone button to enable speech and then verbally ask the site to add a product, you may well find that you have to do this twice for the first product. The API takes a few moments to fully activate, so its possible customers will try to add products before the microphone is fully ready. To work around this, we can implement a `Promise()` to make the microphone cues only appear after a certain time – it's a minor change, but definitely worth doing!

- As we've seen with the Payment Request API, we are limited in what we can do – we will be able to display the form using our voice, but from there on in, it's a matter of having to type or click buttons. It does mean that (at least for now) this may be a less attractive option and perhaps enabled only for those who don't want to use voice services. This isn't great, as the Payment Request API is meant to streamline the process; however, as this API is yet to become mainstream, we will have to work with what is available!

- The `recognition.lang` property we've set in our code is something we need to consider carefully – in this multicultural world we live in, not everyone will be able to speak English, let alone US English, which is the default value for the Speech API! While setting a value is easy, setting the *right* value is harder – do we set based on a fixed language for a site or based on what country our customer is from? A lot of this depends on how you operate your site – is it one single site in multiple languages (not good for SEO) or multiple sites, with the same branding but in different languages?

- You will have noticed from the demo that we hard-coded credit card details – in practice, we did this to provide the *process* of submitting the checkout form works and **not** as an excuse to hard-code any values into our solution! We could use the existing API as a basis for recognizing each number entered, but to do this we might have to say "number one," rather than just "one." It's a question of balancing reliability against a desire to not irritate our customers as it takes too long to enter any details!

Hopefully this gives us something to think about. It should not put us off from using the API; we can work around these limitations. It does emphasize the importance though of making sure that we carefully consider the wider implications of using the API and that we factor this into any development work that makes use of these APIs within our solutions.

Okay, let's move on. Now that we've built our basic demo and added speech capabilities to it, it's time to consider how we can expand on our demo. There are a few things that come to mind, to help get you started; let's dive in and take a look at them in greater detail.

Taking things further

If someone were to ask me how we could take our project further, I think my usual answer would be "the world is your oyster" – inasmuch as you can go wherever you want to take it, provided you can get it working! It seems somewhat ironic that this phrase doesn't come from a technical origin, but dates back to Shakespeare's *The Merry Wives of Windsor*, which is over 400 years old! But I digress...

Anyway, back to reality, what can one do? Well, there are a few things that we could look at and implement, over and above adding in the remaining functionality that one would expect to see in a basket and checkout process. Let's take a look at those ideas in more detail:

- One of the obvious ones is better language support – remember how we set recognition.lang to "en-US" in our demo? Well, we could investigate the possibility of implementing a language selector that you often see on web sites, as well as setting the language for the page; it could be used to set a suitable language value at the same time. For example, for sites based in countries such as Estonia, where they speak Finnish, Russian, and English among other languages, you could set values such as `fi-FI`, `ru-RU`, `en-US`, and `et-EE` (for Estonia). This will allow our Speech API to better recognize text based in that country's dialect.

- Staying with the theme of language support, how would we go about localizing our site, to accept requests in other languages? One solution might be to use JSON to provide local language equivalents of each trigger phrase (such as the ones used by each microphone symbol in our demo). We could call each of these instead of hard-coding them into our demo.

- We've used the Speech Recognition API to add products in or to trigger the checkout process – what about using the Speech Synthesis API to give a verbal indication of a completed action? We don't have anything that indicates when each action has taken place (save for seeing it on screen) – it would be helpful to those individuals with sight challenges to have something that tells them when an action has been completed.

- How about avoiding the use of credit cards altogether and implementing a more modern payment method such as Google Pay? There are lots of different companies that offer this support, such as Braintree – you can see an example of how they set up payments using JavaScript at `https://developers.braintreepayments.com/guides/google-pay/client-side/javascript/v3`. The idea here is that if we can implement something (and assuming you have an appropriate account, of course), then it should be easy enough to provide a link to initiating the request to make payment.

This is just a few ideas to get you started – I'm sure you can think of more, but as the lead into this section says, the world really is your oyster!

It's all a matter of thinking where you could use speech capabilities in your site and giving it due consideration as to whether it would really help customers or would just be seen as nothing more than a gimmick that customers would be happy to do without!

Summary

The Web Speech API is a simple tool to implement, but is great for making sites more accessible – despite still being in a state of development! Over the course of this chapter, we've explored how to use it in a basic shopping cart and checkout process; let's review what we have learned.

We kicked off by introducing the chapter and setting the scene. We then went through what would be included in the scope of this chapter, before covering off the tools we would use to architect our final solution. At the same time, we talked briefly about setting expectations, inasmuch as we wouldn't be able to cover every part of the purchase process and would focus on the core element in this chapter.

Next up, we delved into adding the code that would make our speech capability tick; we explored the changes needed to modify our markup, before adding in the script for our demo. We then moved onto exploring an alternative checkout process using the relatively new Payment Request API, to see how this might affect our use of speech in our demo.

We then rounded out the chapter with a look at some of the pitfalls we need to be aware of, when using the Speech APIs in the context of the checkout process, before exploring some of the avenues we could follow to help extend and expand our demo for production use.

Phew! We've come to the end of the book. What a journey! I hope you've enjoyed working through the projects within as much as I have writing this book and that you've now gained a greater understanding of how to use the Speech APIs within your future projects.

APPENDIX

API Reference

API Reference: SpeechRecognition

The SpeechRecognition interface is the controller interface
for the recognition service and takes care of managing the
SpeechRecognitionEvent sent from the recognition service.

Many of the properties in the SpeechRecognition interface are
inherited from its parent interface, EventTarget.

© Alex Libby 2020
A. Libby, *Introducing the HTML5 Web Speech API*,
https://doi.org/10.1007/978-1-4842-5735-7

API Interfaces

A list of interfaces for the Speech Recognition API is displayed in Table A-1.

Table A-1. *A list of interfaces for the SpeechRecognition API*

Interface	Purpose of interface, which represents...
SpeechRecognition	This acts as the controller interface for the recognition service and takes care of the SpeechRecognitionEvent sent from the service.
SpeechRecognitionAlternative	A single word that has been recognized by the speech recognition service.
SpeechRecognitionError	Error messages sent from the recognition service.
SpeechRecognitionEvent	The event object for the result and nomatch events, which contains details and data for interim or final speech recognition results.
SpeechGrammar	The words or patterns of words that we want the recognition service to recognize.
SpeechGrammarList	A list of SpeechGrammar objects. Note: This interface may be removed in subsequent versions of this API, due to confusion around its usage
SpeechRecognitionResult	An instance where the service has recognized one or more SpeechRecognitionAlternative objects.
SpeechRecognitionResultList	One or more SpeechRecognitionResult objects, depending on whether results are being captured in continuous mode.

Constructor

There is only one constructor object for the Speech Recognition API, which is listed in Table A-2.

Table A-2. *Constructor for the SpeechRecognition API*

Constructor	Purpose
SpeechRecognition.SpeechRecognition()	Creates a new SpeechRecognition object.

Properties

The Speech Recognition API has several properties available for us to use, which are detailed in Table A-3.

Table A-3. *Details of the properties available with the Speech Recognition API*

Property	Purpose of property
SpeechRecognition. grammars	Used to manage a collection of SpeechGrammar objects that represent the grammars specified for use in the current instance of the SpeechRecognition interface.
SpeechRecognition. lang	Can return or set the language of the current SpeechRecognition; if this isn't specified, it defaults to either the HTML lang attribute value or the user agent's language setting.
SpeechRecognition. continuous	Determines if Speech Recognition should display results as they are returned or if it should render the final result. The default setting is false, or the final result.
SpeechRecognition. interimResults	Determines if the API should display interim results (true), which have yet to be marked as final (such as the . the isFinal setting being set to false). The default for this value is false.

(continued)

Table A-3. (*continued*)

Property	Purpose of property
SpeechRecognition. maxAlternatives	This sets the maximum number of SpeechRecognitionAlternatives that can be provided for each result – the default value is 1.
SpeechRecognition. serviceURI	Specifies where to host the speech recognition service, used by the instance of the SpeechRecognition API. The default is the user agent's default speech service.

Methods

There are three methods available for us to use with the Speech Recognition API, which are listed in Table A-4.

Table A-4. *Methods available within the Speech Recognition API*

Method	Purpose of method
SpeechRecognition. abort()	Stops the speech recognition service from listening to incoming audio and from returning an instance of the SpeechRecognitionResult interface.
SpeechRecognition. start()	Starts the speech recognition service to listen to incoming audio and sets an intent to recognize grammars associated with that instance of the Speech Recognition API.
SpeechRecognition. stop()	Stops the speech recognition service from listening to incoming audio and returns the results from SpeechRecognitionResult, using the audio captured.

Events

We can listen to any events within the Speech Recognition API, by using
addEventListener() or by assigning an event listener to the oneventname
property of this interface. The events available for us to use in this API are
listed in Table A-5.

Table A-5. Events available in the SpeechRecognition API

Event	Event is fired when...
audiostart/ audioend	The user agent has started, or finished, capturing audio from the microphone.
start/end	The speech recognition service has begun listening to incoming audio within the current instance of the Speech Recognition service; the latter is fired when the service has been disconnected.
error	An error is generated from the Speech Recognition service.
nomatch	The Speech Recognition service returns a final value which is not a clear winner or significant result. It is likely that the result doesn't meet or exceed the desired threshold for confidence.
result	The speech recognition service returns a result which has been positively identified and returned back to the application.
soundstart/ soundend	Any sound, irrespective of whether it is recognizable, has been detected by the service, or has stopped being recognized by the service.
speechstart/ speechend	The service has detected or stopped detecting sound that is recognized by the speech recognition service as speech.

Note   Many of the events in this API Reference are also available via
the on<name> property, such as onstart or onspeechend.

API Reference: SpeechRecognitionEvent

The SpeechRecognitionEvent interface represents the event object and data for the result and nomatch events, which is fired when an interim or final result has been detected.

Many of the properties in the SpeechRecognitionEvent interface are inherited from its parent interface, EventTarget.

Properties

This interface has four read-only properties, which are detailed in Table A-6.

Table A-6. *The properties available for SpeechRecognitionEvent*

Property	Returns...
SpeechRecognitionEvent.interpretation	The semantic meaning of the text result from the user.
SpeechRecognitionEvent.emma	An Extensible MultiModal Annotation (EMMA) markup language or XML-based representation of the result.
SpeechRecognitionEvent.resultIndex	The lowest value result (by index) in the SpeechRecognitionResultList array that has been changed.
SpeechRecognitionEvent.results	A SpeechRecognitionResultList object that represents the speech recognition results for the current session.

API Reference: SpeechRecognitionError

The SpeechRecognitionErrorEvent interface contains information about any errors that occur while processing SpeechSynthesisUtterance objects in the speech service.

Many of the properties in the SpeechRecognitionErrorEvent interface are inherited from its parent interface, EventTarget.

Properties

This interface has two read-only properties, which are detailed in Table A-7.

Table A-7. *Properties for the SpeechRecognitionError interface*

Property	Returns...
SpeechRecognitionError.error	The type of error generated by the interface.
SpeechRecognitionError. message	A message that provides more details about the error.

API Reference: SpeechRecognitionResult

The SpeechRecognitionResult interface represents a single recognition match that may contain multiple SpeechRecognitionAlternative objects.

Properties

This interface has two read-only properties, which are listed in Table A-8.

315

Table A-8. *Properties for the SpeechRecognitionResult interface*

Property	Purpose
SpeechRecognitionResult. isFinal	A Boolean that states whether this result is final (true), and returns the final result, or not (false), and returns interim values. The latter value will be stored with an expectation that this may be updated in the future.
SpeechRecognitionResult. length	Returns the number of SpeechRecognitionAlternative objects contained in the result.
	Note: You may also see this referred to as "n-best alternatives."

Methods

The SpeechRecognitionResult interface has a single method, detailed in Table A-9.

Table A-9. *Methods available in the SpeechRecognitionResult interface*

Method	Purpose
SpeechRecognitionResult. item	Allows the SpeechRecognitionAlternative objects within the result to be accessed via an array syntax.

API Reference: SpeechRecognitionResultList

The SpeechRecognitionResultList interface represents a list of one or more SpeechRecognitionResult objects, depending on whether the results are being captured in continuous mode.

Properties

The SpeechRecognitionResultList interface has just one read-only property, which is listed in Table A-10.

Table A-10.   Available properties for the SpeechRecognitionResultList interface

Property	Purpose
SpeechRecognitionResultList. length	Returns the length of the "array" or number of SpeechRecognitionResult objects in the list.

Methods

The SpeechRecognitionResultList interface has a single read-only method, which is listed in Table A-11.

Table A-11.   Methods available for the SpeechRecognitionResultList interface

Property	Purpose
SpeechRecognitionResultList. item	Allows access to SpeechRecognitionResult objects in the list, using a getter-based array syntax.

API Reference: SpeechRecognitionAlternative

The SpeechRecognitionAlternative interface represents a single word that has been recognized by the Speech Recognition API.

Properties

This API Reference has just one read-only property, which is listed in Table A-12.

Table A-12. *Available properties for SpeechRecognitionAlternative*

Property	Purpose
SpeechRecognitionAlternative. transcript	Returns a string value that represents the transcript of recognized words; this will contain leading or trailing whitespace, if continuous recognition has been enabled.
SpeechRecognitionAlternative. confidence	A numeric estimate of the level of confidence in the accuracy of the recognized content.

API Reference: SpeechSynthesis

The SpeechSynthesis interface manages the speech service and can be used to retrieve information, such as the synthesis voices available on the device, or to start and pause speech.

Many of the properties in the SpeechSynthesis interface are inherited from its parent interface, EventTarget.

API Interfaces

A list of the interfaces available for the Speech Synthesis API is detailed in Table A-13.

Table A-13. *The interfaces available for the SpeechSynthesis API*

Interface	Purpose
SpeechSynthesis	The controller interface that can be used to manage the service or retrieve information such as the synthesis voices available on the device.
SpeechSynthesisErrorEvent	Details any errors that appear while processing SpeechSynthesisUtterance objects.
SpeechSynthesisEvent	Manages the current state of SpeechSynthesisUtterance objects that have been processed in the speech service.
SpeechSynthesisUtterance	Represents a speech request, with information about the content that should be read and how to read it (such as language, pitch, and volume.)
SpeechSynthesisVoice	Represents each voice that the system supports; this contains information such as language, name, and URI.
Window.speechSynthesis	Provides access to the SpeechSynthesis controller and entry point to speech synthesis functionality.

Properties

A list of the Boolean-based properties for the Speech Synthesis API is displayed in Table A-14.

Table A-14. *A list of properties for the SpeechSynthesis API*

Property	Purpose of property
SpeechSynthesis. paused	Determines if the SpeechSynthesis object is in a paused state.
SpeechSynthesis. pending	Determines if the utterance queue contains as-yet-unspoken utterances.
SpeechSynthesis. speaking	Determines if an utterance is currently in the process of being spoken; this includes instances where SpeechSynthesis is in a paused state.

Methods

There are five methods available within the Speech Synthesis API; these are listed in Table A-15.

Table A-15. *Methods available for use in the SpeechSynthesis API*

Method	Purpose of method
SpeechSynthesis. cancel()	Removes all utterances from the utterance queue.
SpeechSynthesis. getVoices()	Returns a list of SpeechSynthesisVoice objects that represent the available voices on the current device.
SpeechSynthesis. pause()	Puts the SpeechSynthesis object into a paused state.
SpeechSynthesis. resume()	Allows the SpeechSynthesis object to resume its previous state.
SpeechSynthesis. speak()	Adds an utterance to the utterance queue, which will be processed when utterances already queued have been spoken.

Events

There is only one event we can use within the Speech Synthesis API – details are listed in Table A-16.

Table A-16. *Events available within the SpeechSynthesis API*

Event	Event is fired when/for...
voiceschanged/ onvoiceschanged	A change has been detected in the list of SpeechSynthesisVoice objects that would be returned by the SpeechSynthesis.getVoices()method.

API Reference: SpeechSynthesisUtterance

The SpeechSynthesisUtterance interface represents a speech request, which can be used to read the content of the speech service or set properties such as volume, pitch, and language.

Many of the properties in the SpeechSynthesisUtterance interface are inherited from its parent interface, EventTarget.

Constructor

There is only one constructor object for the SpeechSynthesisUtterance object, which is listed in Table A-17.

Table A-17. *Constructor for the SpeechSynthesisUtterance interface*

Constructor	Purpose
SpeechSynthesisUtterance. SpeechSynthesisUtterance()	Returns a new instance of the SpeechSynthesisUtterance object.

Properties

The interface for the SpeechSynthesisUtterance object contains several properties we can use – these are detailed in Table A-18.

Table A-18. *Properties available in the SpeechSynthesisUtterance interface*

Property	Purpose – gets and sets...
SpeechSynthesisUtterance.lang	The language of the utterance.
SpeechSynthesisUtterance.pitch/ SpeechSynthesisUtterance.rate/ SpeechSynthesisUtterance.volume	The pitch, rate, or volume of the spoken utterance.
SpeechSynthesisUtterance.text	The text that will be articulated when the utterance is spoken.
SpeechSynthesisUtterance.voice	The voice to be used when speaking the utterance.

Events

There are a handful of events we can use when working with an instance of SpeechSynthesisUtterance – details are listed in Table A-19. These can be triggered using addEventListener() or by assigning an event listener to the oneventname property of this interface.

Table A-19. *Events available within the SpeechSynthesisUtterance interface*

Event name	Fired when...
boundary	The spoken utterance reaches a word or sentence boundary.
end	The utterance has finished being spoken.
error	An error occurs that prevents the utterance from being successfully spoken.
mark	The spoken utterance reaches a named Speech Synthesis Markup Language (SSML) "mark" tag.
pause	The utterance is paused partway through a text.
resume	A paused utterance is resumed.
start	The utterance has begun to be spoken.

API Reference: SpeechSynthesisErrorEvent

The SpeechSynthesisErrorEvent interface contains information about any errors that occur while processing SpeechSynthesisUtterance objects.

Properties

The interface for the SpeechSynthesisErrorEvent object contains just one read-only property, which is listed in Table A-20.

Table A-20. *Properties for the SpeechSynthesisErrorEvent interface*

Property	Purpose of property
SpeechSynthesisErrorEvent. error	Returns an error code that indicates what has gone wrong with a speech synthesis attempt.

Methods

The SpeechSynthesisErrorEvent does not have any methods specific to this interface; all methods are inherited from the SpeechSynthesisEvent interface.

API Reference: SpeechSynthesisEvent

The SpeechSynthesisEvent interface contains information about the current state of SpeechSynthesisUtterance objects that have been processed in the speech service.

Many of the properties in the SpeechSynthesisEvent interface are inherited from its parent interface, EventTarget.

Properties

The interface for the SpeechSynthesisEvent object contains several read-only Boolean properties we can use – these are detailed in Table A-21.

Table A-21. *Properties for the SpeechSynthesisEvent interface*

Property	Returns...
SpeechSynthesisEvent. charIndex	An index position of the character in the SpeechSynthesisUtterance.text that was being spoken, at the time the event was triggered.
SpeechSynthesisEvent. elapsedTime	Returns the elapsed time in milliseconds of the event trigger point, after the SpeechSynthesisUtterance. text started being spoken.
SpeechSynthesisEvent. name	The name associated with certain types of events occurring as the SpeechSynthesisUtterance.text is being spoken: these include the SSML marker reached if relating to a mark event or the type of boundary reached.
SpeechSynthesisEvent. utterance	Returns the SpeechSynthesisUtterance instance that triggered the event.

Methods

The SpeechSynthesisEvent inherits methods from its parent interface, Event, so does not contain any methods specific to this interface.

API Reference: SpeechSynthesisVoice

The SpeechSynthesisVoice interface represents a voice supported by the system, along with details of its own speech service, such as language, name, and URL.

Properties

A complete list of (read-only) Boolean-based properties available for the SpeechSynthesisVoice interface is detailed in Table A-22.

Table A-22. Properties available for the SpeechSynthesisVoice interface

Property	Returns...
SpeechSynthesisVoice.lang/ SpeechSynthesisVoice.name	A BCP47 language tag (and the equivalent human-readable name), indicating the language of the voice.
SpeechSynthesisVoice.default	The voice is the default voice for the current app language (true), or not (false)
SpeechSynthesisVoice. localService	Indicates whether the voice is supplied by a local or remote speech synthesizer service. The default is true, for local speech synthesizer service.
SpeechSynthesisVoice.voiceURI	The type of URI and location of the speech synthesis service for this voice.

API Reference: SpeechGrammar

Future removal of the SpeechGrammar function:

There is an ongoing proposal (https://github.com/w3c/speech-api/pull/58) to deprecate and remove this feature (and SpeechGrammarList) from the Web Speech API specification. Details provided here are purely in the interests of transparency; please refer to comments in Chapter 2 for more details.

The SpeechGrammar interface represents a set of words or patterns of words that we want the recognition service to recognize. A grammar object is defined using the JSpeech Grammar Format (JSGF), although other formats may also be supported in the future.

Constructor

As with many JavaScript-based APIs, there is only one constructor required – details are listed in Table A-23.

Table A-23. *The constructor object for the SpeechGrammar interface*

Constructor	Purpose
SpeechGrammar.SpeechGrammar()	Creates a new SpeechGrammar object.

Properties

There are two properties available within the SpeechGrammar interface – these are detailed in Table A-24.

Table A-24. *A list of properties available within SpeechGrammar*

Property	Sets and returns...
SpeechGrammar.src	A string-based grammar that references the current instance of the SpeechGrammar object.
SpeechGrammar. weight	The weight of the SpeechGrammar object.

API Reference: SpeechGrammarList

We can reference the contents of a SpeechGrammar object using the SpeechGrammarList interface. This represents a list of SpeechGrammar objects containing words or patterns of words that we want the recognition service to recognize; it is normally available in the JSpeech Grammar Format (JSGF).

Constructor

There is a single constructor object available within SpeechGrammarList; this is detailed in Table A-25.

Table A-25.   The Constructor object for SpeechGrammarList

Constructor	Purpose
SpeechGrammarList. SpeechGrammarList()	Creates a new SpeechGrammarList object.

Properties

The SpeechGrammarList interface has one property we can use, which is detailed in Table A-26.

Table A-26.   The sole property available within SpeechGrammarList

Property	Returns...
SpeechGrammarList. length	The number of SpeechGrammar objects contained in a SpeechGrammarList object.

Methods

We can make use of three methods within the `SpeechGrammarList` interface, which are listed in Table A-27.

Table A-27. *Methods available within the SpeechGrammar interface*

Method	Purpose of method
SpeechGrammarList. item()	Allows individual SpeechGrammar objects to be retrieved from the SpeechGrammarList using a getter-based array syntax.
SpeechGrammarList. addFromURI()	Adds a grammar to a SpeechGrammarList as a new SpeechGrammar object, from a specific URL.
SpeechGrammarList. addFromString()	Adds a grammar from a DOMString element (such as a variable) to a SpeechGrammarList as a new SpeechGrammar object.

Index

© Alex Libby 2020
A. Libby, *Introducing the HTML5 Web Speech API*,
https://doi.org/10.1007/978-1-4842-5735-7

Printed in the United States
By Bookmasters